DISCARDED
BY THE
VERMILLION PUBLIC
LIBRARY

VERMILLION PUBLIC LIBRARY
VERMILLION, SD 57069

641.822
U83m
Urvater
Monday to Friday pasta

D0791972

Vermillion Public Library
18 Church Street
Vermillion, SD 57069
(605) 677-7060

DEMCO

MONDAY to FRIDAY

Pasta

MONDAY to FRIDAY

Pasta

MICHELE URVATER

Illustrations by Simms Taback

WORKMAN PUBLISHING · NEW YORK

Copyright © 1995 by Michèle Urvater

All rights reserved. No portion of this book may be reproduced—mechanically,
electronically, or by any other means, including photocopying—without written permission of the publisher.
Published simultaneously in Canada by Thomas Allen & Son Limited.

Library of Congress Cataloging-in-Publication Data
Urvater, Michèle.
Monday-to-Friday pasta / by Michèle Urvater.
p.   cm.
Includes index.
ISBN 1-56305-729-8—ISBN 1-56305-347-0 (pbk.)
1. Cookery (Pasta). 2. Quick and easy cookery. I. Title
TX809.M17U78   1994

641.8'22—dc20   94-22253
CIP

Cover design by Paul Hanson
Book design by Flamur Tonuzi with Barbaralynn Altorfer
Front cover photograph by Michael Harris
Back cover photograph by Walt Chrynwski
Book illustrations by Simms Taback

Workman books are available at special discounts when purchased in bulk
for premium and sales promotions as well as for fund-raising or educational use.
Special editions or book excerpts can also be created to specification.
For details, contact the Special Sales Director at the address below.

Workman Publishing Company, Inc.
708 Broadway
New York, NY 10003
Manufactured in the United States of America

First printing June 1995
10 9 8 7 6 5 4 3 2 1

Dedication

For Barbara Kasman, a most passionate pasta lover and most devoted loyal friend

Acknowledgments

I want to thank everyone at Workman Publishing for helping give birth to *Monday-to-Friday Pasta*, with an especially grateful thank-you to Paul Hanson for his cover concept, a warm thank-you to Suzanne Rafer, the most patient editor in the world, and a loving thank-you to the tireless and ebullient Andrea Glickson in publicity.

As always, I am grateful to my loving husband, Michael, and my wonderful daughter, Alessia, who once again proved to be a perfect pair of enthusiastic yet discriminating tasters.

Contents

Pasta
The Monday-to-Friday-Way

"Another pasta cookbook?" Well, yes— but one with a purpose. Pasta is perfectly suited to today's hectic, health-focused lifestyle. And following my Monday-to-Friday system, it allows the busy cook to put delicious, fresh-tasting, nutritious meals on the table with zero bother.

The *Monday-to-Friday Cookbook*, which was published in 1991, describes a method for getting dinner on the table every night of the week, after a hard day's work and in the face of all sorts of complicated family situations. Not only does it offer easy and quick recipes, it presents a slew of strategies for tackling the everyday obstacles that get in the way of making dinner. The *Monday-to-Friday Cookbook* explains how to build a pantry, how to get organized, how to plan a menu, and how to vary the recipes so they mesh with in-dividual needs. There is a recap of these principles beginning on page 2. Toil-free weekday meals are the focus of *Monday-to-Friday Pasta* too—in this case with pasta as the centerpiece one or two nights of the week.

Why pasta? There cannot be a food that is more universally loved. The fussiest child and the most demanding adult are both easily soothed by a plateful of noodles. What's more, you can prepare an astonishing array of lovely simple dinners with pasta adding just one or two fresh ingredients and a bit of seasoning. Pasta is also a natural choice because it's good for us: Current dietary guidelines exhort us to make grains—cereal, bread, and pasta—the bulk of our diet.

This is not an encyclopedic treatise that will teach you everything you ever wanted to know about pasta, nor is it a reference book that places the recipes within a historical or cultural framework. It doesn't describe the intricacies and technicalities of making fresh pasta. It *does* deal with the many ways you can use pasta to create a meal. The recipes are straightforward, with many possible vari-

ations. You'll discover for instance that one basic recipe can be an Asian dish or a Middle Eastern one, simply by changing the seasoning. There are lean pasta recipes that you can make for yourself and extravagant ones you can share. You'll learn how to make pasta dishes in the form of main-course soups and even desserts. You'll find out how to make a pasta meal out of leftovers in the fridge, and you'll even acquire a repertoire of pasta meals that are suited for those busy nights when members of your family have to eat at different times. You'll find uncomplicated pasta meals that will please the younger set and you'll learn how to exploit the seasons by making pasta dishes with produce at its peak.

THE MONDAY-TO-FRIDAY SYSTEM

Monday-to-Friday cooking means getting a delicious dinner on the table with little effort while coping with the hassled weekdays we all face—whether we are single or married, working outside of the home or tending to a brood of kids. There aren't enough hours in the day to accomplish all we need to do, and who has the patience to prepare an elaborate meal at the end of the day? The Monday-to-Friday system of cooking lets us enjoy flavorful, nutritious meals *and* gain a little time to relax, read a bedtime story, or catch up with friends. All it takes is a little organizing: Stock up on a few ingredients, plan ahead, and take it easy!

THE PANTRY

If you don't have any food in the house, you can't make dinner. And, six or seven o'clock in the evening is not the best time to start thinking about what to cook. Here's where the pantry comes to your rescue. It is the stash of provisions that you should have on hand in the cupboard, as well as in the fridge and in the freezer. Some of these ingredients can become the main course, some the

accompaniments to the main course, and others the seasonings that dress up the main course and its sidekick.

The ideal pantry contains all the fixings even without a single fresh ingredient in the house. But more important, the contents of the pantry stand ready to be combined with fresh ingredients to help you to create from scratch whenever you like.

THE CALENDAR

I suggest that you set up a calendar on which to jot down menu ideas. I keep an erasable monthly calendar on my refrigerator—it's held there with magnets. You can also buy a plain sheet of erasable plastic (the kind you write on with washable ink) and draw your calendar on it. Or create a model calendar on your computer and print out a new version every week or every month. Or, simpler yet, use a sheet of ordinary paper for scribbling your weekly menus.

Jot down the type of meal you'd like to serve each day of the upcoming work-week. It doesn't have to be a precise menu, just the sketch of one. For example, for Monday night I might scribble "pasta and veggie," for Tuesday dinner "chicken and salad," for Wednesday "rice, beans, and vegetable," for Thursday "fish, starch, salad" and for Friday night "clean out the fridge" or maybe treat

the family to "take-out-food."

By jotting down even that much, I know to put on my shopping list at least those main-course ingredients I need in order to cook my planned dinners. This way, I minimize the trips to the supermarket. I might not know yet how I will cook that chicken, but I have to begin by buying some chicken so that I can fix it later. I still have the freedom to decide how to prepare the chicken when the time comes. The recipe I end up using might be dictated by some ingredient in the pantry, or by a vegetable that looks especially fresh at the market, or maybe by a scheduling consideration.

There are a couple of other benefits to having a menu calendar displayed where you can't miss it. If I notice as I am readying dinner that I have planned on fish for dinner the next night, then I'm reminded that I must defrost the fish, if I have purchased it in advance, or pick it up fresh, the following day. I also like having a calendar—a monthly one in particular—because I can see what I cooked the previous week and avoid repeating the meals too soon. So if last week's menus included lasagne, chicken, fish, and rice and beans, then this week's might be made up of a main-course soup, beef stew, a lentil dish, and a pasta salad.

MATCHING MEALS TO SCHEDULES

Before you start on your menu planning, check for any commitments during the upcoming week so that your meals will jibe with everyone's schedule. When I see that my husband will be teaching late one night, for example, I plan a meal that he can reheat quickly. If I see that my daughter will have dinner at a friend's house on another night, I'll pencil in a more sophisticated meal for my husband and me.

If you give absolutely no thought to tonight's dinner at any time before you walk through the door, your dinners won't be as diverse, tasty, or healthful as those you could make with some organization. This planning, supported by a menu calendar and a stocked pantry, is so helpful that I need think about what to make for dinner only when I come home from work. First I glance at the calendar to remind myself of the type of meal I had planned and what our schedules are. Armed with the goodies stashed in my pantry, fridge, and freezer, I can get a good home-cooked dinner on the table within 30 minutes. Really, I mean it!

The Pasta Pantry

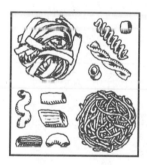

"**P**asta" means a whole slew of things. It is not just a fancy term for spaghetti. An Italian word, "pasta" can mean simply "dough." It can also mean fresh noodles, and it can refer to the dried noodles in boxes on supermarket shelves. "Pasta" can mean the exotic jet-black strands flavored with squid ink as easily as the familiar curved golden tubes we all know as "elbows." In fact, "pasta" describes *all* types of noodles—dry and fresh, Asian and Western.

DRIED PASTA

Dried *pasta* refers to all the types of pasta that are made fresh, then dried and kept without refrigeration. The best type of dried pasta is made from durum-wheat semolina. In my first book I said I preferred DeCecco, an Italian imported brand that holds up after cooking, but I've discovered that DeCecco isn't the only possibility. I taste-tested a variety of American pastas made with a mixture of semolina and finer durum-wheat flour. Then I tested Italian brands made of semolina. Finally I tested Pasta LaBella, an American brand made from pure semolina. I have to say that I found the results fascinating.

The most popular brands of American pastas, even when cooked only until *al dente* ("firm to the bite"), were softer and starchier than I like. They didn't have as firm a texture or as wheaty a flavor as the two Italian brands I tested them against. I also noted that the instructions on the package directed the cook to boil the pasta for too long a time.

Of course, you may not care for the wheaty flavor and firm texture of pure semolina pasta. The domestic part-semolina pastas are certainly good enough, and they absorb more of the sauce than all-semolina varieties. The most popular and widely available domestic brands are also less expensive than both imported pastas and premium domestic brands.

Of the Italian brands, my favorite is still DeCecco, but it is not better than Pasta La-Bella, which is made in the U.S. by the American Italian Pasta Company (AIPC). This company markets their product under names that vary from one part of the country to another. In the East I found it packaged under both "Pasta LaBella" and "Master's Choice," a local supermarket's private label. When shopping for pasta, take a close look at your supermarket's private label. If you find a small red stamp with the initials "AIPC," you have found this excellent manufacturer and you are in for a treat.

When buying colored pasta, make sure the coloring comes from a natural ingredient, such as spinach or mushrooms, not from anything synthetic.

To discourage opened pasta from becoming soggy, reseal the box with heavy tape or transfer the pasta to an airtight glass container. Keep the pasta out of the sun, preferably in a cool, dry place.

FRESH PASTA

In the 1980s the notion took hold that the only good pasta was fresh pasta—and that the only good fresh pasta had to be made at home. We saw dried pasta go out the window as pasta machines and pasta-making attachments to food processors came on the market. I became as enamored of these gadgets as anyone else. But after I struggled to learn how to make it, the fresh pasta I turned out at home was never worth the effort. All my attempts, whether made by hand or with the help of a machine, produced a pasta that tasted sticky and felt like lead in my stomach. And so I decided that, along with millions of Italian housewives, I would leave the making of pasta dough to the professionals. Today I am perfectly satisfied with pasta meals made from the excellent varieties of dried pasta I can buy in my corner grocery store. And on occasion, if the mood strikes me, I buy a good brand of fresh pasta.

Because it isn't easy to make excellent fresh pasta, and especially because of the time it takes to make the dough, Monday-to-Friday cooks shouldn't even consider it. Therefore I'm not including directions for making fresh pasta from scratch.

BUYING AND STORING FRESH PASTA

If you are lucky enough to discover a good source of fresh pasta, or if you know an elderly housewife with thirty years' experience in turning out fresh dough, then do it justice and cook it on the day you buy it. Fresh pasta tastes best when you cook it shortly after it's made. The longer it sits and dries, the less "fresh" it is. Of course it's hard to tell when a batch of commercial fresh pasta was made. One clue is its flexibility: the longer fresh pasta stands around, the more brittle it becomes. If there are shards of dried pasta in the package, chances are that it isn't really fresh at all.

If you can't use the pasta right away, then freeze it. But remember that even in the freezer the ingredients will continue to deteriorate, so try to use it within a couple of weeks. If you have bought a large quantity of fresh pasta, repackage it in smaller portions suited to your needs before freezing it.

SPECIAL PASTAS: OTHER GRAINS, OTHER COLORS, AND WITH FILLINGS

Some pastas are made from flours other than durum wheat. The main thing to remember about these is that they will have a very different texture. Whole-wheat pasta, whether made in Italy or in the U.S., has a slightly softer texture than regular pasta and a flavor three times as intense. Pair this type of noodle with an equally lusty sauce. I usually choose meat sauces, or ones that have a distinctly Mediterranean or Middle Eastern accent, or that include the earthy flavors of wild mushrooms, garlic, or legumes.

Pastas made from grains other than wheat, such as buckwheat pasta, have a powerful grainy flavor. And because they are made from a flour that is gluten-free, buckwheat noodles are flabby, with none of the chewiness people love about wheat pasta. These noodles should also be combined with robust sauces, such as Asian or Eastern European ones, or used in soups.

No doubt you've seen—and maybe tried—some of the elegantly packaged "boutique" pastas displayed in gourmet shops—

pastas flavored with everything from tomato to squid ink. I sampled a number of them for this book, and except for the saffron and squid ink pastas (which are gorgeous to look at), most special boutique pastas were not worth the price. In almost all the ones I sampled, the flavor of the added ingredient did not come through. The only flavors that were easy to recognize were black pepper, garlic, and tomato—and these flavors are better brought into play in the sauce. The one exception to this is the more familiar spinach pasta—it's terrific for dishes where you want the chewiness of durum wheat as well as a color other than the regular tawny pasta hue.

Stuffed pastas, such as ravioli and tortellini, come in a variety of styles: Some are dry, some are fresh, and some are fresh-frozen. The plain ones are stuffed with cheese or ground meat, while other "bou-

tique" varieties are stuffed with unusual ingredients such as Gorgonzola cheese or dried porcini mushrooms.

I stay away from dried stuffed pastas because it seems they must contain a huge quantity of preservatives in order to keep a dough stuffed with perishable meat or cheese from spoiling.

I do, however, like the stuffed pastas that are readily available in the refrigerated case at the supermarket. About once a month I buy a pasta stuffed with pesto, or cheese, or wild mushrooms, either to use right away or to store in the freezer. Stuffed fresh pasta makes a welcome change from the plain dried variety and because the stuffings are rich, a splash of chicken stock or a drizzle of olive oil and a dusting of cheese turns them into a meal.

If you are lucky enough to live in an area that gets imported stuffed pastas, do experiment with the more exotic types, such as tortellini stuffed with Gorgonzola cheese or ravioli stuffed with sweet squash. These are

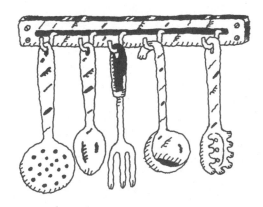

good to serve to guests because they add a festive note without requiring any extra work on your part.

EASTERN NOODLES

Just as Western-style pasta comes in dry and fresh forms, so do Eastern-style noodles. There are many types of dried Asian noodles, but only certain ones are commonly available.

Japanese wheat noodles: Japanese wheat noodles come in a variety of shapes, lengths, and even flavors. *Soba*, perhaps the best known of the Japanese varieties, is a thin flat noodle, made from a mix of wheat and buckwheat flours; it has an earthy flavor with a somewhat brittle texture. *Somen* is a thin, hard wheat noodle, *chuka soba* a wheat noodle that is long and curly, and *udon* a flat, white wheat noodle that comes in various widths. *Ramen*, a Japanese contribution to convenience foods, is actually a pre-cooked skinny soup noodle that rehydrates almost instantly when added to hot liquids. They are quick lunch favorites.

Chinese wheat noodles: Dry and fresh egg noodles are known as *mein*. These noodles are made fresh but are available only in Asian markets. It is a shame they are not more readily available because freshly made Chinese egg noodles are often better than the fresh egg pasta available in supermarkets. Boil them as you do fresh Western noodles; they cook in record time. Linguine and spaghettini make satisfactory substitutes if Chinese noodles are unavailable.

Rice noodles: Rice noodles are made from rice flour. They come in different thicknesses, ranging from thin sticks to broad ribbons. These are wonderful for anyone who is allergic to wheat. But because there is no gluten in rice, the noodles don't hold their shape as do those made from wheat; they are good in soups, where soft noodles are best.

The skinny noodles, also termed "rice sticks" or "rice vermicelli" (*mi-fen* or *mai fun*), can be boiled, or presoaked and then boiled. Skinny rice sticks are wonderful deep-fried and served as a snack.

Substitute capellini or vermicelli for the rice sticks, linguine or fettuccine for the broader rice noodles.

Bean starch noodles: These noodles are made from mung-bean starch (or potato starch or pea starch). They are transparent when cooked, and are slippery and chewy. They are also sold under various names such as "bean threads," "glass noodles," *sai-fun*, *fun si*, or "transparent," "shining," or "cellophane" noodles. These are another variety to

PASTA PORTIONS

3 to 4 ounces = 1 main-course portion
2 to 3 ounces = 1 appetizer portion
1 to 2 ounces = 1 side-dish portion

keep in mind for people who are allergic to wheat, although you should alert diners that they have a somewhat sticky quality. The way to prepare these is to rehydrate them.

PASTAS TO STOCK IN YOUR PANTRY

How do you decide what pastas to have on hand? Three main types of pasta at one time is enough for my family, but to keep things interesting, I change the three types constantly. How much pasta you decide to store in your cupboard, and what shapes and brands of pasta you prefer, can be determined only by your palate, by how avid a pasta fan you are, and by your family's preferences.

I like to stock up on two types of long noodles, a flat "ribbon" noodle such as linguine as well as a round noodle such as spaghettini (I happen to prefer the thinner version of these two shapes). Sometimes I'll alternate with a box of vermicelli, fedelini, or capellini because our daughter likes skinny noodles the best. On occasion, for the sake of variety, I'll buy the fresh, egg-enriched version of linguine or fettuccine.

I keep two types of short shaped pastas on hand. The first is a medium-size shape, either twisted or tubular, which will match well with a chunky pasta sauce. The other might be a smaller shaped pasta like orzo, tubettini, or couscous. These offer a change of pace and are useful in side dishes and soups.

To complete my pasta pantry collection, I buy one pound of something special, such as whole-wheat fettuccine. Or I might buy buckwheat soba, saffron egg noodles, or pesto ravioli.

The following list will give you an idea of the wide variety of Italian pasta shapes available. With so many to choose from, there's no need to ever fall into a pasta rut.

RIBBONS

In Italy flat ribbons of pasta are traditionally coated with buttery or creamy sauces which, so they say, adhere better to wide surfaces. I interchange strand and ribbon pasta with successful results. Many are found in both fresh and dried form.

Name	Description
Taglierini, or Tagliolini	*Extremely thin fresh egg pasta*
Linguine fini	*Little tongues; very thin*
Linguine	*Small tongues; thin*
Fettuccine	*Small ribbons; medium wide*
Mafalda	*1-inch wide, rippled edge*
Margherita, or Margaretta	*Medium-wide, with one straight edge and one rippled edge*
Pizzoccheri	*Medium-wide, made with eggs and some buckwheat flour*
Tagliatelle	*Medium-wide fresh egg pasta*
Pappardelle	*Wide, with crinkled edge*
Lasagne	*Widest ribbon shape, with straight or rippled edges, used in baked dishes*

STRANDS

Strand, or string, pasta goes best with thin sauces that don't have too much texture. The sauce can include minced or finely ground ingredients that almost disappear into the sauce and can be easily captured on the strands as they are wound around the prongs of a fork. The thinner the noodles, the smoother the sauce should be.

Name	Description
Capelli d'angelo, or Capellini	*Angel's hair; very thin strands*
Fedelini, Fidelini	*Thicker than capellini*
Vermicelli	*Thinner than spaghettini*
Fideos	*Coiled strands, about as thick as vermicelli*
Spaghettini	*Thin spaghetti*
Spaghetti	*The basic*
Perciatelli, or Bucatini	*Heavier spaghetti strands with a narrow hole down the middle*
Fusilli lunghi	*Curly long spaghetti*

TUBULAR AND HOLLOW SHORT SHAPES

Tubular and hollow short-shaped pastas include curved and straight varieties as well as medium to large sizes. The name of a shape is sometimes followed by the word *rigati*, which means ridged. These shapes are great for catching chunky sauces. Included here too are the large tubular shapes that are suitable for stuffing or are used in baked dishes.

Name	Description	Name	Description
Ditali	*Thimbles; hollow tubes, usually ¼ to ½ inch wide*	Sedani	*Celery; long macaroni shapes, ridged like celery*
Mezzo ditale	*Medium thimbles; squat tubes, ½ inch long and ⅓ inch wide*	Ziti	*Similar to penne but with straight edges, cut into varying lengths, sometimes curved, used in baked dishes*
Tubetti	*Little tubes; like ditali, although sometimes shorter*		
Maccheroni	*Elbows; medium-size curved tubes (maccheroni refers to other hollow tubes as well)*	Mezzani	*Fat, hollow tubes, wider than ziti, used in baked dishes*
Pipe rigati	*Ridged elbow twists*	Rigatoni	*Very large, ridged, hollow tubes, used in baked dishes*
Cavatappi	*Spiral macaroni; look like two elbow lengths in one piece*	Cannaroni, Zitoni	*Wide tubes*
Penne, or Mostaccioli	*Quills, mustache; 1-inch-long tubes, ¼ inch across, cut on the slant*	Manicotti	*Hollow tubes, 3 inches long, wide enough to stuff*

STUFFED SHAPES

Name	Description
Agnolotti	*Stuffed flat pasta, crescent-shaped, larger than ravioli*
Cappelletti	*Little hats; stuffed flat circular pasta, look like rounded hats*
Ravioli	*Squares stuffed with meat, cheese, or vegetables*
Tortelli	*Rounded shapes stuffed with cheese or vegetables*
Tortellini	*Smaller rounded shapes stuffed with almost anything*
Tortelloni	*Large version of tortellini, usually stuffed with cheese*

TINY SHAPES

These are very small shapes, often the diminutive version of a shape listed in one of the other categories. Use them in soups or as side dishes.

Name	Description
Acini de pepe	*Peppercorns; tiny beads*
Anellini	*Little rings; tiny circles*
Ditalini	*Little thimbles; tiny thimble shapes*
Conchigliette	*Little shells; tiny seashells*
Couscous	*Tiny beads*
Farfallini	*Small bow-ties*
Orzo	*Rice-shaped pasta*
Pastina	*Refers to all the tiny shapes used in soups; the American version is star-shaped and often made with egg*
Perline	*Little pearls; beadlike shapes*
Semi de melone	*Melon seeds; tiny melon-seed shapes*
Stelline	*Little stars; tiny stars*
Tripolini	*Tiny rounded bow-ties*
Tubettini	*Little tubes; tiny tubes*

FANCY SHAPES

Included in this list are all the odd-shaped short pastas that don't fit into other categories. These include twisted shapes, and others with nooks and crevices that make them perfect partners to chunky sauces and to thick creamy sauces.

Name	Description	Name	Description
Conchiglie, or Maruzze	Seashells; medium-size shells, grooved or plain	Orecchiette	Little ears; roundish flat disks
Conghigli	Large seashells; jumbo shells, used for stuffing	Orecchioni	Large ears (bigger than orecchiette)
Farfalle	Butterflies; big, flat bow-ties	Radiatore	Radiators; roundish pasta shapes, corrugated with ridges
Fusilli	Twists, spirals; corkscrew shapes	Rotelle	Wagon wheels, cartwheels; wheel-like shapes; can also refer to corkscrews or spirals
Gemelli	Twins; ½-inch lengths, look like two strands of spaghetti twisted together	Rotini	Corkscrew shapes, larger than fusilli
Gnocchi	Not the potato dumpling gnocchi, these are long, narrow, ripple-edged shapes	Ruote	Wheels; wheel shapes, larger than rotelle

Monday-to-Friday

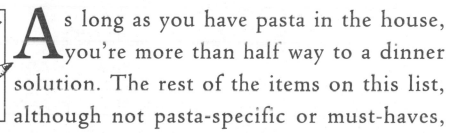

Pantry List

As long as you have pasta in the house, you're more than half way to a dinner solution. The rest of the items on this list, although not pasta-specific or must-haves, will provide you with endless mealtime possibilities. Monday-to-Friday dinners will be that much quicker and easier to prepare—and delicious to boot.

The amounts in this pantry list suit a family of four or five. You may need to make adjustments depending on the number of members in your family.

THE PASTA

1 pound each:
- *Thin or medium-size strand or ribbon pasta such as spaghetti, linguine, or fettuccine*
- *Another strand or ribbon pasta, different from the above, such as perciatelli, capellini, or vermicelli*
- *Short-shaped, medium-size pasta such as elbow macaroni, penne, or fusilli*

Optional:
- *Special pasta such as stuffed shapes, Asian-style noodles, or fresh pasta*
- *Tiny pasta such as tubettini, stelline, orzo, or couscous*

FISH

On the pantry shelves:

2 cans (3½ ounces each) red
  salmon, bones in, preferably packed in water
2 cans (7 ounces each) tuna, preferably packed
  in water, or 1 can (16 ounces) mackerel
1 can (3½ ounces) sardines, smoked or packed in
  water
2 cans (3 to 4 ounces each) smoked fish, such as
  oysters or mussels
1 can (6 ounces) chopped or minced clams

In the freezer:

1 pound fresh fish or shellfish, such as cod, sea
  scallops, or tuna, packed in 4-ounce portions

MEAT

In the freezer:

1 pound ground meat, such as ground round,
  packed in 4-ounce patties
1 pound other meat of your choice, cut into
  strips for stir-frying,
  packed in 4-ounce
  portions
1 package (8 ounces) bacon
  (optional)
1 package (8 to 16 ounces)
  meat sausage (optional)

POULTRY

In the freezer:

1 pound skinless, boneless chicken or turkey
  breasts or cutlets, packed in 4-ounce portions

(cube the poultry or cut it into strips first, if
  you like)
1 pound ground chicken or turkey, packed in
  4-ounce patties

1 pound turkey or chicken sausage (optional,
  instead of meat sausage)
8 ounces turkey bacon (optional)

DAIRY

In the refrigerator:

1 pint plain nonfat yogurt
½ or 1 pint low-fat cottage cheese or 1 pint part-
  skim ricotta cheese
½ pound cheese for grating

On the pantry shelves:

2 cans (12 ounces each) evaporated skim milk

LEGUMES AND GRAINS

On the pantry shelves:

1 or 2 cans (16 to 19 ounces each):
  ■ Black beans
  ■ Chick-peas
  ■ Red or white kidney beans
1 pound dried brown, green, or red lentils

VEGETABLES

In the freezer:

4 packages (10 ounces each):
- *Corn kernels*
- *Petite peas*
- *Two others, your choice*

In the refrigerator:

Fresh seasoning vegetables of choice:
1 to 2 pounds onions
1 head garlic
1 bunch scallions (green onions)
1 bunch carrots
1 bunch celery (optional)
2 bell peppers (optional)
Fresh herbs:
- *1 or 2 bunches fresh parsley, preferably flat-leaf*
- *1 or 2 bunches other, such as basil, dill, or cilantro (optional)*

On the pantry shelves:

2 cans (14½ ounces each) plain "Italian-style," or "pasta-style" tomatoes
2 or 3 cans (14½ or 16 ounces each) crushed tomatoes
1 or 2 jars (6 ounces each) marinated artichoke hearts
1 or 2 jars or cans (about 7 ounces each) eggplant appetizer

1 or 2 jars (about 6½ ounces each) sweet fried peppers with onions

Other Pantry Supplies

OILS

1 bottle (16 to 32 ounces) extra-virgin olive oil
1 bottle (16 to 32 ounces) plain olive oil or vegetable oil for cooking
1 bottle (5 ounces) sesame oil (optional)
1 bottle (8 or 12 ounces) "specialty" oil such as hazelnut, pecan, or walnut (optional)

VINEGARS

1 bottle (12 ounces) red wine vinegar
1 bottle (12 ounces) white vinegar, either wine or tarragon
1 bottle (8 to 12 ounces) "specialty" vinegar, either balsamic, Oriental rice, or Champagne

BROTHS

On the pantry shelf:

4 cans (about 14 ounces each) chicken broth, preferably no- or low-salt
2 bottles (8 ounces each) clam juice

SPIRITS

2 bottles dry white wine or
  1 bottle dry white vermouth

2 bottles dry red wine
1 bottle Cognac or brandy
1 bottle port or Madeira

CONDIMENTS, SEASONINGS, AND ASSORTED GOODIES:

2 cans (2 ounces each) flat anchovies or 1 tube
   (1½ ounces) anchovy paste
1 jar (3 ounces) capers, preferably nonpareil
1 jar (8 ounces) chili paste with garlic or with
   soybean (optional)
1 tube (about 3 ounces) garlic paste (optional)
1 package (1 to 1½ ounces) dried mushrooms:
   porcini, cèpes, or "wild"
1 jar (8 ounces) Dijon mustard
1 can (4 ounces) walnuts or pecans
1 jar (1 ounce) pine nuts (optional)
1 jar (12 or 16 ounces) cured Kalamata black
   olives, Spanish green olives, or 1 jar (3 or 4
   ounces) black olive paste (olivada) or black
   olive sauce

1 jar or tube (4 ounces) pesto sauce or 1 tub
   (4 ounces) frozen pesto sauce
1 or 2 jars (4 ounces) pimientos, roasted red
   peppers, or sweet peppers
1 jar (1 pound) smooth spaghetti sauce
1 jar (1 pound) chunky spaghetti or marinara
   sauce
1 tube (4½ ounces) tomato paste
1 jar (8 ounces) sun-dried tomatoes or 1 tube
   (4½ ounces) sun-dried tomato paste
   (optional)
A selection of your favorite dried spices and
   herbs

Cooking Pasta

Good pasta preparation does not mean complicated cooking; instead, taking some care means more delicious dinners on your table. Following this advice will assure that your pasta ends up as something more than a bland base for sauce.

1. Boiling the water: Bring a large pot of cold tap water to a boil over high heat. Covering the pot will reduce the time this takes.

My rule of thumb is to cook 1 pound of pasta in about 4 quarts of salted water. Some cooks insist that the more water you use, the better the pasta is—probably on the theory that the more water the pasta has to swirl around in, the less it will clump. But my ecological learnings steer me away from waste, and I use the minimum amount of water needed to cook the pasta properly.

While the basic 4:1 water-to-pasta ratio (4 quarts to 1 pound) works in most cases, it doesn't hold true for long-strand or ribbon noodles. For fettuccine and its relatives, you will need 3 quarts of water for half a pound. Just remember that whatever the type of noodles, you need enough water so that the strands can bend and twirl as they cook. If they're crowded, they'll stick together.

There are many old wives' tales about cooking pasta. One is that adding oil to the cooking water prevents the pasta from sticking together. It doesn't seem logical to me that a couple of tablespoons of oil, dispersed in a gallon of water, would keep an entire pound of noodles from clumping. Adding the oil to the cooking water won't hurt, but it won't prevent the noodles from sticking together either. The best antidote to tacky pasta is using a semolina pasta and cooking it in enough water.

2. Adding the salt: I always add salt to the pot of cold water. Some cooks advise you to add it after the water has come to a boil because adding salt to cold water makes it take longer to boil. But I am a forgetful person and I notice that if I don't add salt right away, I often forget to add it before the pasta goes in.

I don't measure the amount of salt I add, but I estimate it is a couple of teaspoonfuls. This step may seem unimportant, but it isn't. If you don't add salt to the cooking water, your finished pasta dish will taste flat and bland. Of course if you are on a sodium-free diet, you have no choice but to omit the salt. To compensate, season whatever sauce you are making with lots of citrus, hot peppers, or fresh herbs.

3. Implements at the ready: While the water is coming to a boil, assemble all the equipment you'll need: Have at the ready a long-handled fork, tongs, or some other im-

SERVING AND EATING PASTA

I serve pasta in shallow plates that are a cross between a flat dinner plate and a deep soup bowl. Look for plates that have sloping edges, which will hold in the heat and will prevent the pasta from slipping around, and that are wide enough to accommodate dishes such as lasagne or manicotti.

It is best to warm the plates so that the food doesn't lose its heat before you have a chance to enjoy it. You can heat them in a low oven, on a shelf above the stove, on a hot tray, or for a few seconds in a microwave. Rinsing them under hot running water will at least keep them from being stone cold.

To eat pasta, all you need is a fork. The American habit of resting the fork on a soup spoon is unnecessary. The trick is to wind just a couple of strands around your fork, which is poised at the edge of the bowl. If you start with only a few strands, you'll end up with a forkful that won't be too big for a proper mouthful.

Italians don't approve of cutting pasta with a fork and knife because that separates the sauce from the noodles, and the whole point of twirling the noodles around the fork is to trap the sauce in the noodles as you go. But they make an exception for little children, and so do I.

plement you can use both to stir the pasta when it starts to cook and to retrieve some later on to test for doneness. (I prefer a wooden fork—it doesn't conduct heat and the prongs help separate the strands as you stir.) Set a colander or strainer in the sink.

Your sauce should be good and hot—either just cooked or reheated. Warm the dishes you will serve the pasta in so that it doesn't cool down before you serve it.

4. Cooking the pasta: When the water is at a full rolling boil, add the pasta. Don't cheat here: You want the water at a rolling boil so that the water will come back to a boil quickly after the pasta is added. Stir the water as you add the noodles so they don't stick together or sink to the bottom.

Cover the pot, keeping the heat up high. Once the water is boiling again, uncover the pot and lower the heat a tad. You want the pasta to cook merrily, but not so violently that the noodles break.

Once the water is boiling nicely, you can relax and just give it a stir every now and again, reaching down to the bottom of the pot and around the sides to dislodge any stray pasta strands that are beginning to adhere to the pot.

5. Timing the pasta: Most people these days know that pasta tastes best when cooked *al dente* ("to the tooth")—that is, until tender but still firm to the bite. How long this takes depends on the type of pasta: what it is made of, its shape, its quality, and even on how old it is (the older it is, the longer it takes to cook).

To guard against overcooking, test a piece about 2 minutes before the time mentioned on the package. The instructions on U.S.-made pasta usually direct the cook to boil the noodles too long. The best test is to bite into the pasta as it is cooking. It is done when it is just tender—still firm but cooked through. Incompletely cooked pasta is chalky inside.

The cooking time begins at the moment the water returns to the boil, *not* the moment you add the pasta to the water. Fresh pasta should be tested after 2 minutes and again each minute after that, because it cooks quickly and will move rapidly from uncooked to overcooked. The average medium-size dry pasta takes 8 to 10 minutes to cook. The timing depends, of course, on the size, shape, and thinness of the pasta. Naturally, filled pastas take longer.

VERMILLION PUBLIC LIBRARY
18 C………
VERMILLION, SD 57069

6. Draining the pasta: When the pasta is cooked, drain it at once. If you are planning to serve it hot, don't rinse it. (Rinsing the noodles just cools them down. It doesn't do anything to wash away excess starch and prevent the noodles from sticking—another myth.)

If you will be serving the pasta chilled, then do rinse it in cold water to stop the cooking process. Drain the noodles again thoroughly.

7. Saucing the pasta: As soon as the pasta is drained, add the sauce. Hot pasta will continue to cook while it sits in the

PASTA REPAIRS

STICKY PASTA

If you choose the right pasta, cook it in enough water, and drain and sauce it properly, it should not stick together. However, things do go awry. Here are some ways to unstick that tangled-up clump of linguine.

If you are going to serve the pasta chilled, or if you want to reheat it later, run cold water over the pasta as you separate it with your fingers. Once the strands are unstuck, you can reheat the pasta by boiling some water, placing the pasta in a strainer, and setting the strainer in the boiling water for 1 to 2 minutes or until the pasta is hot again.

If you need to serve the stuck-together pasta right away, run very hot tap water through it, separating the strands with tongs or two forks. As soon as you've managed to unstick the pasta, make sure it's well drained, then lightly coat the strands with oil or sauce, and serve.

OVERCOOKED PASTA

If you have overcooked the pasta but have to proceed with the meal, you might want to add a bit more sauce than you ordinarily would, or even a drop of Tabasco sauce to help distract the diner from the problem. For contrast, you also could add diced raw bell pepper or cucumber, if you think it would match the sauce you're serving.

But you can make better use of overcooked pasta the next day. Turn it into a salad where other crisp ingredients will camouflage its soft texture, use the pasta in soup, where the soft texture is actually desirable, or turn it into a pasta frittata.

colander, and it will start to clump together if it's not immediately tossed. (If things aren't quite working out as you had hoped and your sauce is not ready, toss the cooked pasta in the pot with about 2 tablespoons of vegetable or olive oil (per pound of pasta)—just enough to coat the pasta and keep it from sticking. Cover the pot until the pasta is ready to be sauced.

There are a couple of ways you can sauce the pasta. The simplest and most informal way is the Italian way: Serve up a portion of pasta in each plate, and ladle the sauce over the center. This way the pasta is served quickly and doesn't get cold, and each person can decide how much sauce is enough. This method is especially handy when you are serving a sauce full of chunky ingredients that are hard to integrate with the pasta. Serve any extra sauce on the side.

The second way is to return the drained pasta to the pot (off the heat) and then add the sauce, tossing the two together with tongs or with a fork. With this method the sauce is more evenly distributed, making it a bit easier for small children to handle.

SPECIAL NOODLES, SPECIAL COOKING

Just about all the rules that apply to cooking durum-wheat pasta apply to cooking Asian and specially flavored pastas as well. Chances are good that the packaging will provide directions and cooking times. However, some of the instructions are confusing, some are poorly translated into English, and some are not even translated. Just in case, here are some cooking tips for specialty pasta.

Asian noodles made with wheat or another grain are cooked just the same way as Italian-style pasta.

Noodles made of rice or mung bean starch need to be presoaked so they do not turn rubbery. The cooking time is short, however, so the two steps don't really add to the total. As with any pasta, begin to test for doneness a couple of minutes before you believe the noodles should be ready.

WHEAT NOODLES

My favorite among Asian wheat noodles are the fresh Chinese egg ones; they are, unfortunately, hard to find. If you have access to a Chinese market, do try them. They are delicious.

FRESH CHINESE EGG NOODLES: *1 to 2 minutes or according to package directions.*

DRIED CHINESE EGG NOODLES (MEIN NOODLES): *6 to 8 minutes or according to package directions.*

DRIED JAPANESE UDON (THICK): *10 minutes or according to package directions.*

DRIED JAPANESE SOMEN (THIN): *4 to 5 minutes or according to package directions.*

DRIED JAPANESE BUCKWHEAT SOBA: *4 to 5 minutes or according to package directions.*

CLEAN-UP

Starch will cling to the colander in which you've drained your pasta. The best way to get rid of it is to scour the colander with a plastic scrubbing pad.

If bits of pasta have stuck to your cooking pot, simply soak the pot in warm soapy water until the pasta is soft; then lift the bits from the pot and wash it out.

RICE NOODLES

These noodles need some soaking first, then a brief cooking (more to give them flavor than to cook them thoroughly). I have tried to use these without cooking, and the texture seemed not right.

The very skinny rice sticks (often called rice vermicelli) are usually reserved for deep-frying, but you can also boil them for 3 minutes after soaking and then use them in salads.

The thicker rice noodles should be soaked in cold water for 20 minutes or in very hot water for about 10 minutes. Then simmer, fry, or boil for 3 to 5 minutes or until done.

MUNG BEAN STARCH NOODLES

These are also known as cellophane, glass, or bean thread noodles. Soak them off the heat in hot water that has just reached simmering temperature for about 20 minutes or until they are transparent and pliable. If they are not done after 20 minutes, soak them in hotter water for longer. (If you add them dry to water that is at its hottest, they clump together and turn into a gelatinous blob.) Then cut them into manageable lengths and stir-fry, simmer, or boil for 2 to 3 minutes or until they have picked up some flavor.

Pasta Sauces

Pasta sauces cover the gamut of flavor and texture, from a fruity olive oil seasoned with minced garlic and parsley to an orchestration of tomatoes, sausage, and broccoli. A sauce can be as light as a basil-flavored vinaigrette or as rich as a pool of Gorgonzola-laced cream.

In Italy, tradition dictates which sauce matches which shapes of pasta, and Italians have firm opinions (with regional variations, naturally) about the "correct" ingredients for a particular dish. They firmly believe that a sauce should just coat the strands of pasta, adding flavor but never upstaging the taste and texture of the pasta.

What do I think? I believe that you should experiment to discover what suits your palate and that you should always cook as you please. The pasta sauces included here are easy to prepare, delicious to eat, and so versatile that you can substitute ingredients to suit your mood, the occasion, your family's preferences, or whatever you happen to have available in your pantry.

The one issue that turns me into a fanatic, however, is the *amount* of sauce. I am as passionate as any Italian cook on this matter. I strongly urge you to just gently dress the pasta with sauce—don't drown it. I detest the way many restaurants serve so much sauce that the pasta itself becomes irrelevant.

MATCHING SAUCES TO PASTA SHAPES

Except in the most general sense, I don't believe it is important to pair particular pasta sauces to specific pasta shapes, as they do in Italy. Some sauces do work better with certain shapes, but if you don't have the pasta that's indicated for the sauce you feel like cooking, go ahead and match the sauce with any pasta you have on hand.

If, however, you haven't yet decided on a sauce, you might let the shape of the pasta inspire you. For example, if there's only fettuccine on the shelf, then plan a sauce that will match it well, one that is smooth enough so that the sauce can be swooped up into the pasta as it is twirled around the fork.

Conversely, if you've decided on a certain sauce, then try to match it with the most appropriate pasta. If you're planning to use that fresh broccoli you picked up at the market, select a short fat pasta, such as penne, to mix with the chunky sauce.

SAUCE PROPORTIONS

The amounts given here are enough for *an individual portion* of pasta.

I outlined the proportions in this manner so that you can multiply them as needed whether you are cooking for one or for eight.

Liquid. Chicken broth, tomato sauce, olive oil, melted butter, crushed tomatoes, yogurt, vinaigrette, cream, puréed vegetables, or some combination thereof are just a sampling of the possibilities.

You'll need anywhere from 2 tablespoons to ½ cup per person, depending upon the texture of the sauce. The thicker and chunkier the sauce, the more liquid it will need because it carries so many other ingredients.

Seasonings. Seasonings give flavor to the liquid that moistens the pasta. They can be as spare as a tangle of caramelized onions or as opulent as a mélange of poultry and vegetables blended with herbs and spices.

GARLIC: *½ to 2 cloves*

ONIONS: *¼ to ½ cup chopped*

DRIED HERBS: *1 to 2 teaspoons, depending upon their strength and the number of other ingredients in the sauce.*

FRESH HERBS: *1 to 2 tablespoons minced, to be tossed in as you ladle the sauce over the pasta so that their freshness is not dissipated by cooking.*

MEAT, POULTRY, BEANS, GRAINS, OR SEAFOOD: *2 to 3 ounces*

VEGETABLES: *⅓ to ½ cup diced*

THIN SAUCES / SKINNY STRANDS

Sauces comprised mostly of broth, melted butter, or olive oil pair best with skinny noodles like capellini, rice vermicelli, or fine egg noodles because their narrow surfaces don't require a sauce with much body or volume.

SMOOTH SAUCES / MEDIUM STRANDS OR RIBBONS

Simple sauces such as plain tomato that have a smooth, silky texture are best matched with pasta shapes that are thick enough to absorb the moisture and flavor of the sauce: hollow long noodles such as perciatelli, medium-thick strands such as spaghetti, and medium-thick ribbon pasta such as linguine.

THICK SMOOTH SAUCES / MEDIUM-WIDE RIBBONS AND SHAPES

Thick-bodied rich sauces, such as a white sauce or one made with cream or melted cheese, call for wide or medium-size ribbon noodles such as fettuccine or tagliatelle, or flat shapes such as bow-ties or orecchiette, which have a broader surface to which the sauce can easily cling.

HOW MUCH SAUCE?

THIN SAUCES: ¼ to ⅓ cup per pound of pasta

SMOOTH SAUCES: ½ to ¾ cup per pound of pasta

THICK SMOOTH SAUCES: ½ to ¾ cup per pound of pasta

PUREED SAUCES: 1 to 1½ cups per pound of pasta

CHUNKY SAUCES: 2 to 4 cups per pound of pasta

PUREED SAUCES / SHORT TUBES AND TWISTS

Short hollow pasta, including elbows, penne, and ziti, or twisted shapes like fusilli, are the choice with such sauces as salsas made with minced raw vegetables because the hollows and the crevices trap the sauce.

CHUNKY SAUCES / MEDIUM TO LARGE TUBES AND TWISTS

Sauces that contain chunks of meat, fish, beans, or vegetables go best with pastas that can hold the ingredients and match their size: rotini, wagon wheels, ziti, and radiatore are examples.

PALATE POINTERS

Use these suggestions as jumping-off points when you feel like creating your own pasta sauce recipe.

AMERICAN FLAVORS

CAJUN
Shrimp, crab, and chicken
Celery, garlic, and scallions
(green onions)
Okra, onions, and bell peppers
Thyme, garlic salt, and cayenne pepper

AMERICAN
Carrots, cabbage, corn, celery, and onions
Peas, parsley, and squash
Allspice, cinnamon, cloves, and nutmeg
Marjoram and sage
Chicken, turkey, bacon, beef, and ham
Clams, salmon, and shrimp
Worcestershire, barbecue, and Tabasco sauces

TEX-MEX
Black beans and corn
Canned and fresh green chiles
Garlic, onions, tomatoes, and cilantro
Chili powder, oregano, cumin, and lime juice

EUROPEAN FLAVORS

FRENCH
Butter, cheese, cream, and apples
Onions, shallots, mushrooms, carrots, and celery
White or red wine
Tarragon, thyme, and parsley
Dijon mustard
Olive oil, black olives, anchovies, and capers
Fennel seeds, garlic, tomatoes, and lemon

GERMAN
Egg noodles
Sauerkraut, cabbage, onions, carrots, and mushrooms
Pork, beef, bacon, and sausages
Mustard, capers, and pickles

HUNGARIAN
Egg noodles
Pork, veal, and sausage
Garlic, onions, bell peppers, caraway, and paprika

ITALIAN
Olive oil
Parmesan, Pecorino, mozzarella, and ricotta
White or red wine
Porcini mushrooms, onions, garlic, and carrots

Tomatoes and fresh fennel
Sage, rosemary, basil, oregano, and
   parsley
Dried red pepper flakes
   and black olives
Sardines, pine nuts,
   anchovies, capers,
   and raisins

MEDITERRANEAN

Olive oil and white wine
Garlic, onions, tomatoes, lemon, and
   eggplant
Oregano, mint, parsley, and dill
Feta cheese and lamb
Raisins, black olives, and pine nuts

SCANDINAVIAN

Dill, beets, onions, apples, red cabbage, and
   turnips
Herring, shrimp, and ham
Dried fruit and horseradish
Sour cream and butter

ASIAN FLAVORS

CHINESE

Black beans, chili paste with garlic, and
   hoisin sauce
Garlic, ginger, scallions (green onions),
   and five-spice powder or anise seed
Sesame oil and dry sherry
Cilantro

SOUTHEAST ASIAN

Pork, beef, shrimp, and crab
Chilies, cayenne, garlic, and scallions
   (green onions)
Cilantro, lime juice, and bean sprouts
Anchovy paste, coconut, tomato paste, and
   peanuts
Rice and mung bean paste noodles

INDIAN

Garlic, fresh ginger, onions, and fresh chiles
Ground coriander, cardamom, and
   cinnamon
Cloves, cumin, turmeric, and cayenne pepper
Yogurt, tomatoes, lentils, and chick-peas

JAPANESE

Buckwheat and rice
   noodles
Seafood and seaweed
Soy sauce, rice vinegar, and sesame oil
Ginger, scallions (green onions), and
   cucumbers

MIDDLE EASTERN

Olive oil
Tomatoes and cucumbers
Lentils, chick-peas, and ground lamb
Raisins, pine nuts, and walnuts
Garlic, onions, lemon, parsley, and mint
Allspice, cinnamon, cloves, and cumin
Yogurt and sesame paste (tahini)

Enraged Tomato Sauce

PASTA: *Thin strands or ribbons, made of semolina or whole-wheat*
MAKES: *About 3 cups, enough for 1 pound of pasta*
TIME: *20 minutes*

This is my version of the classic Italian tomato sauce called *arrabbiata*. It is so fiery hot, it really tastes "enraged," as its name suggests. I have adapted the recipe from a more authentic version, one given to me by my friend Emilio Rossi of Rome.

The tongue-tingling sauce has all sorts of possible variations. Not only is it grand served plain over spaghetti, it is superb as a basic sauce to beef up with a slew of other ingredients. Cheeses that happily accommodate this sauce are Asiago, Romano, aged Provolone, and Parmesan.

4 cloves garlic
1 green bell pepper
¼ cup extra-virgin olive oil
1 can (14 ounces) crushed tomatoes
1 teaspoon dried red pepper flakes
Salt

1. Peel and finely mince the garlic. Core, seed, and finely chop the bell pepper.

2. Heat the oil in a large skillet over medium-high heat. Add the garlic and bell pepper and sauté for a minute, just to start them cooking. Add the crushed tomatoes and red pepper flakes.

3. Cover the skillet, lower the heat, and cook for 10 to 15 minutes or until the sauce is slightly thickened. Season to taste with salt.

VARIATIONS

■ To make the sauce even more nutritious, purée 2 cups freshly cooked chick-peas, or 1 can (16 ounces, drained and rinsed), in a blender or food processor. Add them during the last 5 minutes of cooking.
■ 2 cups diced cooked turkey will turn this into a substantial meal.
■ 1 or 2 cups flaked cooked bluefish or mackerel also works with this strongly seasoned sauce.
■ I like to include 1 to 2 cups diced cooked vegetables, such as carrots or cauliflower, in this sauce.
■ Add 1 cup sliced or chopped pitted green olives without the pimiento.

SAUCE SKETCHES

There is not enough space in one book for all of my pasta sauce ideas, so here are some "sketches" for you to bring to life in your own kitchen. Since these are simply ideas, I leave the measurements up to you.

Almond Chicken Sauce: In butter, sauté a mixture of ground or chopped almonds and ground chicken. Finish with fresh or dried tarragon and lemon juice; serve over ribbon pasta.

Coleslaw Macaroni: Mix cooled cooked elbow macaroni with prepared coleslaw. Add diced smoked ham and chopped fresh bell peppers. Serve chilled.

Corn-Salsa Sauce: Mix spaghetti sauce with lots of tomato salsa and corn kernels; toss over short pasta or spaghetti.

Creamed Spinach Sauce: Combine 1 cup heavy cream with a smashed peeled garlic clove, and bring to a simmer. Add ½ pound chopped washed spinach leaves and simmer until just wilted. Remove the garlic clove and serve over stuffed ravioli or tortellini.

Fresh Oyster Sauce: Bring heavy cream to a simmer and add some shucked fresh oysters. Simmer for a moment, just to warm the oysters, and finish with minced fresh chives. Serve over fresh ribbon pasta.

Cilantro Sauce: Rinse, pat dry, and chop fresh cilantro leaves in olive oil until fragrant. Sauté lots of minced garlic and fresh ginger. At the last minute toss in the cilantro, and finish with a squirt of lime or lemon juice. Season with salt and dried red pepper flakes. Serve over long noodles.

Lamb Arabesque Sauce: In olive oil, cook minced garlic and ground lamb until the meat loses all trace of pink. Finish with raisins and lots of chopped mint leaves. Serve over small or medium-size short pasta.

Middle-Eastern Pasta Sauce: Thin prepared hummus or baba ghanouj with olive oil and lemon juice; use as a dressing for a salad of chilled cooked short pasta.

Salami and Olive Sauce: Sauté diced or sliced hot salami in olive oil. Finish with crushed tomatoes and sliced black olives. Serve over perciatelli.

Real and Red Spaghetti Sauce

PASTA: *Long and short shapes made of semolina or whole-wheat*
MAKES: *2 cups, enough for 1 pound of pasta*
TIME: *20 minutes*

When I say "spaghetti sauce" I mean a chunky tomato sauce, one that is thick with bits of ground meat or vegetables. Delicious on its own, this recipe is also a blueprint that you can alter in countless ways, varying the flavor according to the season, your mood, or whatever is in your pantry. The recipe is also a model for learning how to add flavor to store-bought spaghetti sauce.

What type of pasta do you serve with this? That depends on how finely you cut up the vegetables. If they are minced, the sauce is smooth enough to be served over strand or ribbon pasta. If you keep the vegetables chunky, then the sauce is better with stuffed or short-shaped pasta. Cheeses that go well with this sauce are Parmesan, Pecorino, Asiago, and fresh ricotta.

This sauce is so substantial that the rest of your dinner can be as simple as a salad or a steamed vegetable and a fruit dessert.

In addition to pasta, think of serving this sauce over polenta, cracked wheat, or brown rice.

> 1 onion
> 1 red or green bell pepper
> 2 tablespoons olive oil
> ½ to ¾ pound lean ground beef
> 2 cups Michele's Tomato Sauce (page 245) or a smooth meatless commercial spaghetti sauce
> ¼ teaspoon dried oregano, rosemary, thyme, sage, or marjoram
> Salt and freshly ground black pepper

1. Peel and finely chop the onion. Core, seed, and finely chop the bell pepper.

2. Heat the olive oil in a large skillet over medium-high heat. Reduce the heat to medium, add the onions and bell peppers, and sauté just long enough to coat the vegetables with the oil. Then cover and simmer over low heat until the vegetables are tender, about 10 minutes. Watch them carefully; if they begin to stick to the pan, stir in a tablespoon of water and continue to simmer.

3. Uncover the skillet, crumble the ground beef into the vegetables, and sauté, stirring constantly, until the meat is no longer pink, 2 to 3 minutes. Add the tomato or spaghetti sauce and the herbs. Simmer over low heat until the sauce is hot and the meat is cooked through, about 3 minutes. Season to taste with salt and pepper.

VARIATIONS

Vegetarian Spaghetti Sauce: Omit the meat in step 3. Add the tomato or spaghetti sauce, then add 2 cups cooked drained lentils, chopped beans, or leftover cooked vegetables, or a combination. Simmer until hot, 3 or 4 minutes.

Seafood Spaghetti Sauce: The type of seafoods that work well with a tomato-based chunky sauce are the robustly flavored ones such as monkfish, mackerel, tuna, swordfish, shrimp, crabmeat, and squid. You'll need ¾ pound fresh seafood (flesh only). You could also use canned tuna or salmon.

If you are using fresh fish, cut it into small cubes in step 1. Add the fish in step 3 after you add the tomato sauce. Simmer just until cooked through, about 2 minutes. I happen to like this spaghetti sauce seasoned with some dried red pepper flakes instead of dried herbs.

Spiced Spaghetti Sauce: Use ground lamb instead of the beef. Add 2 minced garlic cloves when you sauté the onions and peppers. And instead of using dried herbs, season the sauce with 1 teaspoon ground cumin, chili powder, dried mint, ground coriander, or some combination thereof. Finish the sauce with 2 tablespoons nonfat plain yogurt, stirred in at the last moment.

ESPECIALLY GOOD FOR CHILDREN

A VEGETABLE CAMOUFLAGE: In a food processor or blender, process ½ cup cooked fresh carrots or thawed frozen carrots with ½ cup spaghetti sauce until smooth. Cook ¼ pound ground beef in 1 tablespoon vegetable or olive oil until no longer pink. Add the tomato-carrot mixture and cook for a few minutes, until hot. If the color betrays the presence of the carrots, camouflage it with more spaghetti sauce or with tomato paste. This should be enough for 2 children's pasta portions.

Mariner's Sauce

PASTA: *Medium-size strands and ribbons*
MAKES: *About 6 cups, enough for 1 pound of pasta*
TIME: *20 minutes*

The inspiration for this sauce is the all-purpose marinara sauce. I had a devil of a time finding any such recipe in an Italian cookbook, so I looked at the ingredients list of commercially prepared marinara sauces. They described nothing more complex than a tomato sauce laced with garlic and, sometimes, anchovies.

What I really had in mind was a delicious seafood sauce, redolent of garlic and tomatoes and the inimitable taste of the sea. Thus my Mariner's Sauce was born, packed with garlic, shrimp, anchovies, and hot pepper.

Create your own versions by using some of the suggestions below. And don't limit yourself to serving this over pasta. It is superb ladled over steamed cauliflower or spooned over crusty sourdough bread.

4 cloves garlic
1 rib celery
1 medium-size carrot, peeled
8 ounces fresh shrimp, peeled and
  deveined
1 can (2 ounces) flat anchovies, drained
¼ cup extra-virgin olive oil
1 can (14½ to 15 ounces) crushed
  tomatoes
1 teaspoon dried red pepper flakes
Salt

1. Peel and mince the garlic. Finely chop the celery and carrot. Finely chop the shrimp and anchovies.

2. Heat the oil in a large skillet over medium-high heat. Add the garlic, celery, and carrots, and sauté over medium-high heat, stirring continuously, until they begin to soften, about 2 minutes.

3. Stir in the anchovies and shrimp, and sauté for just a few seconds, until the shrimp turn pink. Add the tomatoes and red pepper flakes. Cover, lower the heat, and cook until the flavors have come together, about 10 minutes. Season to taste with salt.

VARIATIONS

■ Seafood: Substitute ½ pound sea scallops, trimmed of their tough appendages and finely diced, for the shrimp. Diced fresh tuna or lump crabmeat would also be delicious.

■ Herbs: Add ½ cup finely chopped fresh parsley or dill at the end of the cooking time; these herbs are terrific with seafood.

■ An even shorter cut: Turn this into a pantry sauce (almost). Substitute 1 teaspoon garlic paste for the fresh garlic, 1 tablespoon anchovy paste for the minced anchovies, and 2 cans (4 ounces each) sardines, drained, for the fresh seafood.

Versatile White Sauce

MAKES: *4 cups, enough for about*
2 pounds of pasta
TIME: *15 minutes*

A white sauce is nothing more complex than milk thickened with a cooked butter-and-flour paste. Although not very fashionable these days, white sauce should become a staple in your freezer because it is so handy and versatile. It blends with an infinite number of other ingredients and is a quick and easy way to turn pasta into a complete dinner.

Once the sauce is made and frozen, you simply heat it up, add other ingredients and seasonings, spoon it over the pasta, and dinner is done.

I like to make a sizable batch of this (it's as speedy to make 4 cups of white sauce as it is to make 1 cup) when I have time on a Sunday night. I use part of it to create an old-fashioned macaroni and cheese dish for the evening meal, and I divide the remainder into portions and freeze them for another day. The sauce keeps in the refrigerator for 4 to 5 days and freezes for up to 2 months.

Be sure to make the sauce in a nonreactive saucepan so that it does not turn gray, and stir it with a whisk so that there are no lumps.

3 tablespoons butter, or
2 tablespoons
  vegetable oil
⅓ cup all-purpose flour
4 cups whole or low-fat milk
Salt and freshly ground white pepper

1. Melt the butter in a large nonreactive saucepan over medium heat until it foams.

2. Whisk in the flour and cook for about 1 minute, making sure the whisk reaches all around the bottom of the saucepan so that you gather up all bits of flour into the butter.

3. Slowly add the milk, by tablespoonfuls at first, whisking constantly and vigorously to make sure the flour paste absorbs the milk without creating lumps. When ½ to ¾ cup of milk has been stirred in and you have a smooth mass, you may add the milk at a faster rate, but continue to whisk constantly.

4. When all the milk has been incorporated, increase the heat to high and bring the milk to a boil. Whisk constantly, although not frantically. You want to make sure that the milk does not scorch and that the flour does not sink to the bottom. As the milk reaches the boil, the mass will become harder to whisk. Reduce the heat to low and continue to whisk until the sauce bubbles gently. (This procedure takes about 5 minutes.)

5. Simmer the sauce over low heat until it is thoroughly cooked, 3 to 4 minutes. Season to taste with salt and white pepper. Remove the amount you need for the dish you are preparing, and let the rest cool, covered, to room temperature. (Don't worry about the skin that forms on top as the sauce is cooling; just skim it off or stir it back into the sauce.) Transfer the cooled sauce to containers and freeze until needed.

VARIATIONS

Ivory Sauce for Poultry: For pasta dishes that include poultry, substitute 4 cups chicken broth for the milk. Season as you like. Note that this sauce is thinner than a milk-based one.

Ivory Sauce for Fish: For pasta dishes with seafood, substitute 4 cups fish stock, or 2 cups clam juice mixed with 2 cups chicken broth, for the milk. Season as you like. This sauce also is thinner than a milk-based one.

TURN A WHITE SAUCE INTO A PASTA MEAL

With just a little effort, you can turn a plain white sauce into something so rich and filling that it becomes dinner when combined with the pasta.

Each of the suggestions below is enough for 1 cup of white or ivory sauce, which is just right for 2 portions (½ pound of pasta).

Cheese Sauce: Add ½ teaspoon Worcestershire sauce and a couple of drops of Tabasco sauce to 1 cup plain white sauce and bring to a simmer. Slowly add ¼ to ½ cup grated sharp Cheddar cheese, or a mixture of half Parmesan and half Cheddar. Simmer, whisking constantly, until the cheese has almost completely melted, about 1 minute. Remove the saucepan from the heat and continue to whisk until the cheese has melted entirely. When serving this you may pass additional grated cheese on the side. This cheese sauce blends well with diced cooked poultry or vegetables (1 cup of either one).

Vegetable Sauce: Bring 1 cup plain or seasoned white or ivory sauce to a simmer. Add 1 cup diced steamed or boiled vegetables or 1 package (10 ounces) diced frozen vegetables. Season with 1 tablespoon minced fresh herbs or scallions. Blend in ¼ to ½ cup grated Cheddar, Pecorino, or Parmesan cheese if you wish.

Ham Sauce (or smoked chicken or turkey sauce): Season 1 cup white sauce with 1 sliced scallion, ½ teaspoon Worcestershire sauce, or cayenne pepper to taste. Bring the sauce to a simmer. Then add 6 to 8 ounces diced smoked lean ham, or 2 ounces finely chopped prosciutto, along with 1 cup frozen peas, thawed, or cooked diced carrots. Add 1 tablespoon minced fresh parsley or dill.

Curried Ham Sauce: Stir 1 sliced scallion, ¼ to ½ teaspoon curry powder, 6 to 8 ounces diced baked ham, and 2 tablespoons raisins into 1 cup white sauce. Bring to a simmer and cook until heated through.

Poultry Sauce: Bring 1 cup plain or seasoned white or ivory sauce to a simmer. Whisk in 1 tablespoon white wine,

An Open Letter
ar Valued Customers and Friends

Of you already may have heard, we recently sold our carpet cleaning
ly, we are as surprised as anybody else. The opportunity arose quite
... We hope that it was ...

T & S Nursery

From Hawarden:
South on K-18 to C-12 then left 2 1/2 miles.
20593 C-12 • Hawarden, IA 51023 • 712-552-1917

Hours: Sat. 10 am to 6 pm; Sunday 1 - 5 pm
Weekdays by appointment

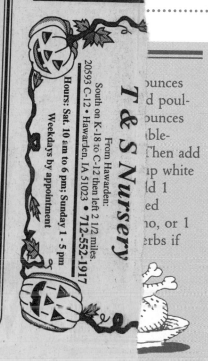

ounces
d poul-
ounces
ble-
Then add
up white
d 1
ed
no, or 1
erbs if

ite sauce
teaspoon
tomato paste, 2 tablespoons minced chives (or ¼ cup finely sliced scallions), and 2 kirby cucumbers (or 1 small regular one), peeled, seeded, and diced. Bring this to a simmer, and add either 6 to 8 ounces diced whitefish fillet, such as sole or orange roughy, or 6 to 8 ounces shellfish, such as peeled and deveined shrimp or lump crabmeat. Simmer until hot, 2 minutes, and season to taste with salt and cayenne pepper.

For a richer seafood sauce, include ¼ cup grated Parmesan and 2 tablespoons cream or 1 tablespoon butter.

Parsleyed Olive Oil Sauce

PASTA: *Thin strands or ribbons, made of semolina or egg dough*
MAKES: *about ¾ cup, enough for 1 pound of pasta*
TIME: *20 minutes*

This recipe is so simple, and you can combine it with so many other ingredients and seasonings, that you'll never be at a loss as to how to dress up a bowl of spaghetti. And because it is made from ingredients that are available in all seasons, you can serve it any time of the year. My favorite side dish—always—is a salad served afterward.

It is important to add the fresh parsley to the hot oil just before tossing the sauce with the pasta so that its vibrant flavor is retained.

If you prefer a milder garlic taste, don't mince the garlic before adding it to the oil. Instead, heat the whole cloves of garlic in the oil, then remove them before serving.

Cheeses that go well with this plain sauce are the hard grating cheeses and such crumbly cheeses as blue cheese and feta. Shreds of smoked cheeses work well, too.

½ cup (packed) fresh parsley leaves
2 cloves garlic
½ cup extra-virgin olive oil
Salt and freshly ground black pepper

1. Rinse, pat dry, and mince the parsley. Peel and mince the garlic.

2. About 5 minutes before the pasta is done, heat the oil with the garlic in a medium-size saucepan over medium heat. When you hear it sizzling, after about 2 minutes, add the parsley and remove the pan from the heat. Season to taste with salt and pepper.

VARIATIONS

▪ The herbs: For the parsley substitute fresh basil, dill, mint, or even cilantro leaves (especially good if you heat the garlic in a combination of sesame and vegetable oil). Sage and rosemary are also delicious with oil and garlic. I use 2 tablespoons minced fresh leaves for this amount of olive oil.

▪ Seasoning additions: Heat the oil and garlic with 1 teaspoon dried red pepper flakes.
   Add 1 to 2 tablespoons anchovy paste, or 2 tablespoons chopped capers, to the oil and garlic just before you add the parsley.
   Add ½ cup seeded chopped fresh tomatoes, ¼ cup lemon juice, or 2 tablespoons black olive paste just before you add the parsley.

After heating the oil and garlic, add either 1 to 2 tablespoons lemon juice or ⅓ cup white wine. Simmer for 30 seconds before adding the parsley.

▪ Low-fat alternative: Substitute ½ cup chicken broth for ¼ cup of the oil; then proceed with the recipe. (You need extra broth in order to get enough moisture into the dish.)

Dijon Butter Sauce

PASTA: *Thin strands or ribbons or stuffed pasta*
MAKES: *About ½ cup, enough for 1 pound of pasta*
TIME: *5 minutes*

The volume of a butter sauce is scant because it is designed to lightly coat the pasta, not blanket it.
   A butter sauce isn't sturdy enough to carry hefty ingredients such as bits of meat, fish, or beans. You can, however, toss in some diced steamed vegetables.
   Serve this sauce with pasta to accompany meat or poultry. If you cannot eat butter or cream, the sauce still works if you substitute vegetable oil for the butter and evaporated skim milk for the heavy cream.

1½ tablespoons Dijon mustard
3 tablespoons light or heavy cream
2 teaspoons dried thyme, rosemary or
    tarragon
3 tablespoons butter, preferably at room
    temperature
Salt and freshly ground black
    pepper

1. In a small mixing bowl, mash the mustard, cream, and herbs together with a wooden spoon. Then stir in the butter (if the butter is chilled, cut it into small bits first).

2. Season to taste with salt and pepper, and toss with freshly cooked hot pasta.

VARIATIONS

Horseradish Butter: Blend together 3 tablespoons unsalted butter, 3 tablespoons cream, 1½ tablespoons prepared horseradish, and ¼ cup minced parsley leaves. In addition to being an unusual pasta sauce, this is especially good with steamed vegetables.

Tomato Butter: Blend together 3 tablespoons vegetable oil, 3 tablespoons butter, and 1½ tablespoons regular tomato paste or sun-dried tomato paste. Add 1 cup finely sliced scallions or ½ cup minced chives. This is especially good with seafood.

Hoisin Butter: Blend 3 tablespoons vegetable oil, 3 tablespoons butter, 1 tablespoon hoisin sauce, ½ cup thinly sliced scallions, and 1 tablespoon soy sauce.

Pesto Sauce

PASTA: *Thin strands or ribbons*
MAKES: *About 2½ cups, enough for 1 pound of pasta*
TIME: *10 minutes*

It is a snap to make fresh pesto in a blender or food processor, so when basil is abundant, make a large batch of this sauce and freeze it in portions to use at a later date (see the instructions below if you are going to freeze it). Pine nuts are delicious but expensive. Less pricy walnuts make a satisfactory substitute.

As you can see by the variations that follow, there are many types of delicious pestos. Don't limit yourself to matching pesto with pasta; pesto is a wonderful partner to many other types of dishes, such as steamed rice. Or add a small amount to mayonnaise and use it to garnish a chicken or turkey sandwich.

When you are making batches of pesto to freeze, omit the Parmesan and the pine nuts. Add the cheese and the chopped nuts after the pesto has thawed, right before you use it in the dish.

2 cups (packed) fresh basil leaves
3 cloves garlic
⅓ cup extra-virgin olive oil
½ cup or more, freshly grated Parmesan
*   cheese, or ¼ cup pregrated*
*   Parmesan cheese*
¼ cup pine nuts (optional)
Salt and freshly ground black
*   pepper*

1. Rinse the basil well and pat dry. Place the leaves in a food processor or blender.

2. Peel and coarsely chop the garlic. Add it to the processor and process with the basil until smooth. While the processor is running, slowly drizzle in the oil. Then add the Parmesan and pine nuts. Process just until all of the ingredients are combined and the nuts are chopped, about 15 seconds. Season to taste with salt and pepper. Add more cheese if you wish. The sauce is now ready to use.

VARIATIONS

Pesto for Dieters: To get a creamy effect without the fat from the oil and nuts, blend the basil and garlic with 2 tablespoons olive oil, 2 tablespoons grated Parmesan, and 1 cup low-fat cottage cheese. For a terrific dish, toss some chopped seeded tomatoes or cucumbers with the pasta and pesto.

Parsley-Mint Pesto: Substitute 1 cup parsley leaves and 1 cup mint leaves for the 2 cups fresh basil. Substitute walnuts for the pine nuts and Asiago cheese for the Parmesan.

Pimiento Pesto: Substitute 4 ounces drained pimientos for the basil and chèvre for the Parmesan.

PESTO POINTERS

If you have gone to the trouble of making your own pesto, then make a double or even triple batch. There is a lot more you can do with pesto than just toss it with pasta:

■ Spread pesto under the skin of chicken or Cornish hens before roasting.
■ Dab freshly cooked fish steaks with a tablespoon of pesto just before serving.
■ Swirl some pesto into a bean soup right before serving.
■ Add a spoonful of pesto to a warm bowlful of plain steamed rice, cracked wheat, barley, or other cooked grain.
■ Finish a simple stir-fry of veal and peppers with a spoonful of pesto.
■ Stir the last of the pesto into a vinaigrette or mayonnaise, and serve the dressing over a vegetable salad.

Fiery Salsa

PASTA: *Ribbons*
MAKES: *About 1½ cups, enough for ¾ pound of pasta*
TIME: *10 minutes*

*S*alsa is the word for "sauce" in Spanish. In this country, however, salsa usually refers to the tomato-packed, spicy condiment served as a dip for corn chips. To me, salsa has come to mean any sort of fiery sauce made with chopped raw vegetables. It might include canned green chiles, or fresh jalapeños, and herbs or chopped fresh tomatoes, cilantro, and cumin. Whatever the mixture, salsa is a terrific sauce and very flattering to pasta.

These uncooked sauces are ideal for summertime, when you have little energy for doing anything beyond boiling water for pasta. The only effort needed is to combine the ingredients in a food processor or blender—and then the machine does the work! Salsas make ideal sauces for people on low-fat diets because they bring lots of fat-free flavor to a recipe.

To turn a bowl of pasta and salsa into a slightly more substantial dinner, add cubes of roast beef, smoked turkey, ham, canned tuna, diced tofu, or steamed vegetables.

1 large ripe tomato
2 or 3 scallions (green onions)
½ cup fresh cilantro leaves
1 clove garlic
1 or 2 jalapeño peppers, fresh or pickled, seeded if fresh
1 teaspoon ground cumin
2 tablespoons lime juice
Salt

1. Cut the tomato in half, and remove the core and seeds. Chop the flesh coarsely and put it in a food processor or blender. Trim the scallions, cut them into pieces, and add to the processor. Rinse the cilantro leaves, pat dry, and add them to the processor along with all the remaining ingredients except the salt.

2. Process until almost smooth, about 5 seconds; leave some texture to the sauce. Season to taste with salt. Covered, this will keep in the refrigerator for up to 4 days.

VARIATIONS

Pimiento Salsa: In a blender or food processor, combine 1 jar (6 to 7 ounces) pimientos or roasted red peppers, drained, 1 seeded fresh jalapeño pepper, 2 cloves garlic, 2 tablespoons olive oil, 2 tablespoons red wine vinegar, and ½ cup fresh parsley leaves. Process until smooth, and season to taste with salt.

Green Salsa: In a blender or food processor, combine 1½ cups (packed) fresh mint, parsley, or cilantro leaves (or a mixture), 2 trimmed scallions, ¼ cup lemon juice, 2 cans (4 ounces each) green chiles, drained, and 1 teaspoon dried red pepper flakes. Process until smooth, and season to taste with salt.

Pantry Salsa: In a blender or food processor, combine ¼ cup olive oil, 1 medium-size dill pickle, 2 tablespoons black olive paste, 2 tablespoons capers, 1 fresh or pickled cherry or jalapeño pepper, 1 can (2 ounces) anchovies, drained, and 1 can (8 ounces) stewed (drained) or crushed tomatoes. Process until almost smooth, and season to taste with salt.

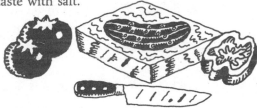

Gazpacho Salsa: In a blender or food processor, combine 2 seeded tomatoes, 1 cored green or red bell pepper, 2 seeded Kirby or 1 medium-size cucumber, 1 clove garlic, 2 tablespoons red wine vinegar, and salt and pepper to taste. Process until almost smooth, and adjust the seasoning. (This salsa is especially delicious over pasta that has been tossed with ½ pound diced water-packed mozzarella cheese.)

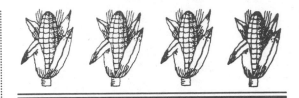

Creamy Corn Salsa Sauce

PASTA: *Medium-size fancy shapes*
MAKES: *About 2½ to 3 cups, enough for 1 pound of pasta*
TIME: *15 minutes*

When puréed, corn kernels make a lovely creamy foundation for a totally nonfat salsa. The taste here is unexpectedly rich, given the lean ingredients.

Diced smoked chicken or ham as well as a diced red bell pepper or two make tasty additions to this sauce.

> 1 package (10 ounces) frozen corn kernels, thawed, or 2 cups fresh kernels, cooked
> 1 cup (packed) fresh cilantro or parsley leaves
> 3 tablespoons red wine vinegar
> 2 jalapeño peppers, fresh or pickled
> 4 scallions (green onions)
> Salt

1. Pat dry the corn kernels and place them in a food processor or blender. Rinse the cilantro or parsley, pat dry, and add it to the

processor along with the vinegar. Seed the jalapeño peppers if you are using fresh ones, and add the peppers to the processor.

2. Process the mixture until it is almost smooth, which will take just a few seconds, and then transfer it to a small mixing bowl. Trim the scallions, slice them thinly, and add them to the salsa. Season to taste with salt. This will keep, covered and refrigerated, for 2 days.

Anchovy, Caper, and Pepper Sauce

PASTA. *Thin strands or ribbons*
MAKES: *About 1½ cups, enough for 1 pound of pasta*
TIME: *15 minutes*

I love this in early summer when I want to eat something light that takes minimal preparation. This bracing, speedy sauce is best served cheeseless over pasta.

> 2 cloves garlic
> 2 cans (2 ounces each) flat anchovies, drained
> 2 tablespoons capers, drained
> 1 red bell pepper
> ¼ cup olive oil
> ¼ cup lemon juice or dry white wine
> Freshly ground black pepper

1. Peel and mince the garlic. Finely chop the anchovies and, if they are large, the capers, too. Core, seed, and cut the bell pepper into ½-inch dice.

2. Heat the oil in a large saucepan over high heat. Add the garlic, anchovies, and capers, and stir until blended. Add the diced peppers and lemon juice. Cover, and simmer over low heat until the peppers are tender, about 5 minutes. Season to taste with fresh pepper.

VARIATION

Add ½ cup crushed red tomatoes to the sauce, or stir in ¼ cup minced fresh parsley.

Emerald Vegetable Sauce

PASTA: *Thin strands or ribbons*
MAKES: *About 2½ cups, enough for 1 pound of pasta*
TIME: *10 minutes*

This is a smart way to get vegetables into your family's diet. The trick to keeping the hue of the sauce gorgeously bright is to purée the vegetables, along with the seasonings, only moments before tossing them with the pasta.

Serve this as a main course with smoked ham or turkey sandwiches to round out the meal.

1 package (10 ounces) frozen petite peas,
thawed or 2 cups steamed diced fresh
vegetables, such as carrots
½ cup (packed) fresh basil or parsley
leaves
4 scallions (green onions)
¼ cup vegetable oil
¼ cup plain nonfat yogurt
Salt and freshly ground black pepper

Pat dry the peas or cooked vegetables and place them in a blender or food processor. Rinse and pat dry the fresh herbs, and add them to the processor. Trim 3 inches off the tops of the scallions, then chop the rest coarsely and add them to the processor. Add the oil and yogurt, and process for a few moments until as smooth as possible. Season the purée to taste with salt and pepper, and transfer it to a bowl. Toss immediately with hot pasta.

VARIATION

Just about any vegetable is appropriate for this recipe, but broccoli, carrots, and lima beans, are especially good. (For 1 pound of pasta, use a head of broccoli or about ¾ pound of carrots or 2 cups (10 ounces) limas.) The vegetables should be cooked thoroughly but not overcooked—just tender enough to be whirled into a smooth purée.

Light Herb Sauce

PASTA: *Thin strands or ribbons, made of*
whole-wheat, rice, or buckwheat
MAKES: *1½ cups, enough for*
1 pound of pasta
TIME: *15 minutes*

This has lots of flavor, few calories, no fat, and is a breeze to prepare. A bowl of pasta tossed with this sauce will be as tasty and filling as any cream-laced recipe.

1 cup chicken, fish, or beef broth
½ cup (packed) fresh herb leaves, such as
parsley, basil, or mint
4 scallions (green onions)
Salt and freshly ground black pepper

1. Bring the broth to a simmer in a medium-size saucepan over medium heat.

2. Rinse, pat dry, and mince the herbs. Trim 3 inches off the tops of the scallions, and thinly slice the remainder.

3. Add the herbs and scallions to the broth and simmer for 30 seconds, just long enough

to release their flavor. Season to taste with salt and pepper, and toss immediately with hot pasta.

VARIATION

Lemon Herbed Sauce: In step 2, grate the zest of a lemon and juice it. In step 3, add the zest and lemon juice to the broth.

Melted Onion Sauce

PASTA: *Ribbons or stuffed shapes, made of semolina or whole-wheat*
MAKES: *2 to 2½ cups, enough for 1 pound of pasta*
TIME: *10 minutes preparation plus 40 minutes no-work cooking time*

Onions cooked long and gently until they melt into a tangle of soft, sweet-tasting strands make a thrifty yet lush sauce. Cooking the onions does take time—but not much effort, so you can go about your chores while the onions cook and the pasta water boils.

Take a look at the variations below for some of the wonderful sauces that can be created from a couple of onions.

1½ pounds (4 large) onions
⅓ cup olive oil
3 tablespoons red wine vinegar
2 tablespoons chili powder
2 tablespoons ground cumin
2 teaspoons curry powder
½ cup dried currants
Salt and freshly ground black pepper

1. Peel the onions and slice them as thinly as you can, either by hand or with the slicing disc of a food processor.

2. Heat the oil in a large skillet over medium-high heat. Add the onions, toss with a slotted spoon, and cook over medium heat until they are well coated with the oil, about 1 minute. Cover the skillet, reduce the heat, and cook for 10 minutes.

3. Stir 1 tablespoon of the vinegar into the onions, cover, and simmer for another 10 minutes over low heat. Add a second table-spoon of vinegar, stir, cover, and continue cooking gently for another 10 minutes. Then add the last tablespoon of vinegar. The onions should be tender and a soft golden hue.

4. Uncover the skillet and cook the onions over high heat, stirring constantly, until the vinegar has evaporated, about 1 minute. Add the spices and currants, and simmer for a couple of minutes longer to cook the spices a bit. Season to taste with salt and pepper. This will keep, covered and refrigerated, for 2 days.

VARIATIONS

■ Crumble leftover cooked hamburger or meat loaf into the cooked sauce. Cover and simmer for a few minutes until the meat is heated through. Serve over penne.

■ Sliced cooked sausages pair well with this onion sauce, as does leftover ham or roast pork. Melted onions without the spices and currants also make a terrific companion to cooked lima beans, spinach, sweet carrots, or parsnips.

■ Omit the spices and currants and toss the cooked onions over pasta; top with 1 cup grated Parmesan or Romano cheese, or crumbled chèvre. Or toss the onions with ¼ cup minced parsley or basil, or with ¼ cup capers and 1 can (2 ounces) anchovies, minced.

Garlicky Mushroom Sauce

PASTA: *Stuffed pastas with cheese, porcini, or pesto filling*
MAKES: *About 2 cups, enough for 1 pound pasta*
TIME: *20 minutes*

This sauce is especially good with stuffed pastas, which tend to be dry. Composed of lots of mushrooms sautéed in bacon drippings, the sauce is awash in natural juices, which moisten and season the pasta.

Serve steamed fresh broccoli or sautéed grated carrots alongside to fill out the meal.

> *4 slices bacon*
> *2 cloves garlic*
> *1 to 1¼ pounds mushrooms*
> *¼ cup dry white wine or chicken broth*
> *Salt and freshly ground black pepper*
> *Grated Parmesan cheese (optional)*

1. Finely chop the bacon. Peel and mince the garlic. Wipe the mushrooms with damp paper towels. Trim the mushroom stems ¼ inch from the bottom; then cut the mushrooms into ¼-inch-thick slices.

2. Heat the bacon in a large saucepan over medium-high heat until it releases some of its fat, about 1 minute. Add the garlic, white wine, and mushrooms. Stir to combine, reduce the heat to medium, and cook until tender, about 7 minutes. Season to taste with salt and pepper. If necessary, keep the mushrooms warm, covered but off the heat, while you finish cooking the pasta. Pass the cheese, if you like, when you serve the pasta and sauce.

VARIATIONS

Creamy Mushroom Sauce: When the mushrooms have finished cooking, add ¼ cup evaporated skim milk and simmer to reduce it and thicken it a bit, about 1 minute.

Lusciously Decadent Mushroom Sauce: Substitute fresh wild mushrooms, such as shiitake, for half the cultivated mushrooms. When the mushrooms are cooked and tender, add ½ cup heavy cream. Simmer until the sauce has thickened slightly, about 2 minutes.

SECOND TIME AROUND

Any remaining stuffed pasta with mushroom sauce can be turned into soup. Heat 2 cups of chicken broth, adding 1 package frozen chopped spinach or petite peas, thawed, and 2 cups leftover pasta with mushroom sauce. Add grated Parmesan cheese to this soup, right before serving. Adjust proportions according to the leftovers you have.

BE PREPARED

The moment you use up a pantry ingredient, write it down on your shopping list. If you don't make a note right away, you may forget to replace it on your next trip to the market.

Peanut Sauce

PASTA: *Thin ribbons, made of semolina or fresh egg dough*
MAKES: *About 1 cup, enough for 1 pound of pasta*
TIME: *10 minutes*

This sauce should appeal to anyone who loves cold noodles with sesame sauce, a Chinese-restaurant favorite. My version is plainer and less spicy than most restaurant recipes and so appeals more readily to kids.

This is a good choice for a night when family members eat at different times because the sauce is delicious over room-temperature or chilled noodles.

> 1 clove garlic
> 2 tablespoons vegetable oil
> 1 tablespoon sesame oil
> 2 tablespoons rice vinegar, or 1 tablespoon white wine vinegar
> 1 tablespoon soy sauce
> ½ cup peanut butter, preferably made from peanuts only
> Salt and freshly ground black pepper

1. Peel and coarsely chop the garlic.

2. In a blender or food processor, combine the garlic, oils, vinegar, soy sauce, and peanut butter. Process until smooth, and then season to taste with salt and pepper.

VARIATION

■ Add thin shards of cold roasted chicken or shreds of cucumber to a dish of cold noodles dressed with Peanut Sauce.

ESPECIALLY GOOD FOR ADULTS

Add a teaspoon of dried red pepper flakes or snippets of a peppery leaf such as watercress or arugula.

Pepper Puttanesca Sauce

PASTA: *Stuffed pasta, with cheese or meat filling, or strands*
MAKES: *4 cups, enough for 1 pound of pasta*
TIME: *20 minutes*

This vibrant chunky sauce is as fantastic for enveloping stuffed pasta as it is for enrobing spaghetti or perciatelli. What dis-tinguishes this version of puttanesca sauce from the classic Italian version is the generous addition of bell peppers.

Keep this sauce in mind, too, when you're searching for a good companion to polenta.

> 2 cloves garlic
> 2 green bell peppers
> ¼ cup extra-virgin olive oil
> ⅓ cup imported black olives, preferably Kalamata
> 1 tablespoon capers, drained
> 1 can (28 ounces) plum tomatoes
> Salt and freshly ground black pepper

1. Peel and mince the garlic. Core, seed, and finely chop the peppers. Heat the oil in a large skillet over medium-high heat. Add the garlic and peppers, cover the skillet, lower the heat, and cook until tender, about 5 minutes.

2. While the peppers are cooking, pit the olives, mince them, and add to the peppers. Add the capers. Pour the tomatoes into a colander or sieve, and while they are draining, break them up with your fingers. Then chop the drained tomatoes and add them to the peppers. Cover, and simmer over low heat for 15 minutes. Season to taste with salt and pepper.

SAUCE FLUIDITY

A sauce composed mostly of puréed ingredients may not be fluid enough to easily coat the strands of pasta. To loosen the sauce, simply add ¼ cup or so of the pasta cooking water to the sauce right before tossing it with the cooked noodles.

Roasted Red Pepper and Walnut Sauce

PASTA: *Strands, ribbons, or medium-size flat or fancy shapes*
MAKES: *About 1½ cups, enough for 1 pound of pasta*
TIME: *10 minutes*

This simple sauce is robust enough to carry the flavor of other ingredients and unusual enough to stand on its own. Although I call for it puréed, you can leave yours a bit chunky, if you prefer.

Served over pasta, the sauce works especially well before a beef, pork, or veal main course. If you add other ingredients to make it your main course, then precede or follow it with a watercress, cucumber, or cabbage salad.

Keep this sauce in mind when you have leftover Thanksgiving turkey. Served cold, it makes a great condiment. The flavor is a welcome and delightful change from the traditional Thanksgiving fare.

1 jar (7 ounces) roasted
   red peppers, drained
1 cup (4 ounces) shelled walnuts
¼ cup olive oil
1 tablespoon lemon juice
Salt and freshly ground black
   pepper

In a food processor or blender, combine the roasted peppers, walnuts, olive oil, and lemon juice; purée until almost smooth. Season to taste with salt and pepper, and transfer to a bowl. The sauce will keep, refrigerated, for 4 days.

VARIATION

■ Leftover strips of roast beef, chicken, or turkey, as well as smoked turkey or fresh mozzarella cheese, are delicious additions to the sauce. Just be sure to remove the ingredients from the refrigerator the minute you begin to make dinner so that they are at room temperature when you mix them with the sauce—otherwise they might cool the pasta too much.

Spaghetti Sauce Orientale

PASTA: *Strands or ribbons, made of semolina, rice, mung bean, or whole-wheat*
MAKES: *About 1½ cups, enough for 1 pound pasta*
TIME: *15 to 20 minutes*

This light sauce is composed of sautéed ginger and garlic mixed with broth and seasoned with Chinese-style spices. It is wonderful over plain spaghetti or over spaghetti topped with a smattering of slivered snow peas, steak strips, tofu, carrots, or bean sprouts, to name just a few companionable ingredients.

2 or 3 cloves garlic
4 quarter-size slices fresh
   ginger
2 tablespoons sesame oil
1 cup chicken broth
2 tablespoons rice vinegar
2 tablespoons light soy sauce
1 teaspoon dried orange peel
½ teaspoon Chinese five-spice powder or
   anise seed
½ teaspoon dried red pepper flakes
Salt

1. Peel and finely mince both the garlic and ginger.

2. Heat the sesame oil in a large skillet over medium-high heat. Add the garlic and ginger, and sauté for a few seconds, until you get a whiff of the garlic aroma. Add the broth, rice vinegar, soy sauce, orange peel, spices, and red pepper flakes. Simmer for 3 to 5 minutes to meld the flavors, then season to taste with salt.

VARIATIONS

■ Combine the sauce with a vegetable such as carrots, bean sprouts, snow peas, and white turnips. Thin strips of steak or lamb, or cubes of tofu make more substantial partners.

■ If you want to pair this sauce with seafood, substitute fish stock or clam juice for the chicken broth.

SAUCE TO TASTE

I like my pasta dishes sauced sparingly. If you like yours more moist, then just double the sauce recipes for each pound of pasta. Do go easy on some of the hotter ingredients. Doubling the amount of chilies or pepper flakes might make the sauce too spicy.

Sun-Dried Tomato Sauce

PASTA: *Strands and ribbons, or stuffed pasta*
MAKES: *About 1½ cups, enough for
1 pound of pasta*
TIME: *20 minutes*

Served as is over spaghetti or cheese ravioli, this sauce is lovely, but it is splendid when asparagus or peas are added. (Choose a stuffed pasta or a small short shape such as tubetti when including the vegetables.)

Cheeses that harmonize well with the sun-dried tomatoes are creamy soft white cheeses like ricotta and fresh chèvre. Grated Parmesan and Asiago are also good.

> 1 onion
> 1 cup sun-dried tomatoes packed in olive
>   oil, drained
> ¼ cup extra-virgin olive oil
> ½ cup Marsala or dry white wine
> Salt and freshly ground black pepper

1. Peel and thinly slice the onion. Cut the sun-dried tomatoes into thin shreds or chop them finely.

2. Heat the oil in a large skillet over medium-high heat. Add the sliced onions and sauté for a minute just to start them cooking. Cover the skillet, reduce the heat, and cook until tender, about 5 minutes. Add the wine and the sun-dried tomatoes. Cover, and simmer until all the ingredients are tender and the flavors have blended, about 10 minutes. Season to taste with salt and pepper.

VARIATIONS

■ When you add the sun-dried tomatoes, include 2 cups shelled fresh peas or 1 package (10 ounces) frozen petite peas, thawed.
■ When you add the sun-dried tomatoes, include 2 cups steamed fresh asparagus tips or steamed fresh asparagus spears cut into 1-inch lengths.

Pasta Soups

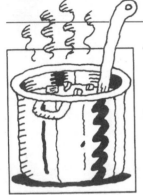

Whenever you want to clear your cupboard shelves of those quarter-filled boxes of dried pasta, then it's time to make some soup. Soup also provides an easy solution to the problem of what to do with odds and ends of roasted meat, steamed vegetables, and cooked legumes.

As in other types of dishes, pasta blends seamlessly with myriad flavors, so you can create an endless variety of soups with different ethnic accents.

The best pasta shapes for soups are the small and medium-size short ones, as well as thin ribbons and strands. These run the gamut from pastina, small bow-ties, tiny shells, stars, and miniature tubes to vermicelli and capellini broken into short lengths. Stuffed pastas are good in some instances, as are Asian pastas like soba, rice sticks, and glass noodles.

Thin, brothlike soups make the most of the narrow strands and small shapes, whereas chunky soups replete with beans, meat, poultry, and vegetables are better suited to thicker and medium-size pasta shapes.

LEFTOVER PASTA SOUP

Pasta soup leftovers should simply be covered, refrigerated, and eaten within a couple of days. Before you reheat the leftovers, however, you'll need to add more broth, water, or vegetable juice because the soup will have thickened. Then go ahead and reheat the soup, either by the portion in a microwave oven or in larger quantities on top of the stove.

When you reheat a thick soup on the stove, be sure to stir frequently so the solids don't sink to the bottom and scorch. Soups that contain melted cheese reheat best in a microwave oven. If this is not possible, reheat the soup in a heavy saucepan over very low heat, stirring constantly so the cheese does not stick to the pan and burn.

To revive the flavor of leftover soup, add a fresh and different ingredient to it, or after reheating, sprinkle the top with chopped fresh herbs.

STORING PASTA SOUPS

Pasta continues to absorb liquid and to soften even when cold, so it is not a good idea to freeze a pasta soup. If you like the idea of making soups ahead of time, cook the soup base to the point where you would add the pasta, and freeze the base. When you're ready to serve the soup, thaw and reheat the base, adding the uncooked pasta once the base comes to a boil.

Comforting Pasta e Fagioli

PASTA: *Medium-size fancy shapes*
MAKES: *4 servings*
TIME: *5 minutes preparation plus 25 minutes no-work cooking time*

Pasta e fagioli simply means "pasta with beans," and it is one of the most comforting dishes I know—easy to prepare, delicious to eat, and incredibly filling.

An authentic Italian *pasta e fagioli* calls for soaking dried beans. However, because this is too time consuming during the week, I've developed a way to make a very good version with canned beans. (Purists can of course substitute dried beans that have been soaked and cooked over the weekend.) I buy the health food store varieties, which are usually less mushy.

During the time it takes to cook the soup, you can prepare another course, such as a salad or a steamed vegetable. Or use the time to work on dessert.

4 cloves garlic
¼ cup olive oil
¾ teaspoon crumbled dried rosemary
4 cups chicken, beef, or vegetable broth
½ pound (2 cups) gnocchi, elbow macaroni or mezzani
2 cans (16 ounces each) small white beans, drained; or 4 cups cooked dried white beans, drained
½ cup grated Parmesan cheese
Salt and freshly ground black pepper

1. Peel and mince the garlic.

2. Heat the olive oil in a large saucepan over medium heat. Stir in the garlic and rosemary, and cook until you can smell the garlic, about 10 seconds. Add the broth and bring

it to a simmer. Then add the pasta, cover the pan, and cook over low heat for 5 minutes.

3. Add the beans, cover, and cook until the pasta is very tender and much of the liquid has evaporated, 20 to 25 minutes. (The soup should be quite thick at the end.) When the soup is done, season it to taste with salt and pepper. Serve it while it is still very hot; pass the cheese on the side.

VARIATIONS

■ With tomatoes: Substitute 1 can (14 ounces) crushed tomatoes for 2 cups of the broth.

■ With vegetables: Finely chop 2 medium-size carrots, 2 celery ribs, or half a fennel bulb. Add the vegetables after you add the garlic. Cover, and simmer over low heat until tender, about 5 minutes. Then add the broth and proceed with the recipe.

■ With herbs: Mince ½ cup (packed) fresh basil or parsley leaves. Add the herbs in step 3 after the pasta and beans have cooked; omit the cheese.

SECOND TIME AROUND

Thin leftovers with tomato or vegetable juice, and add narrow strips of roasted veal, turkey, or ham.

Egg and Parmesan Vermicelli Soup

PASTA: *Thin strands, made of semolina, rice, or mung bean*
MAKES: *4 to 6 servings*
TIME: *20 minutes*

This soup is delicate enough to serve as a starter for an elegant weekend menu, but the luscious combination of eggs, cheese, and noodles also makes a dinner. If you like, serve it with hearty whole-wheat bread and follow it with a vegetable salad.

Kids like this soup a lot (if they like scrambled eggs, that is).

6 cups chicken, beef, or vegetable broth
2 cups (loosely packed) fresh parsley, basil, or mint leaves
¼ pound vermicelli, capellini, or thin rice or cellophane noodles
4 eggs
⅓ to ½ cup grated Parmesan cheese
Salt and freshly ground black pepper

1. Bring the broth to a boil in a large saucepan over high heat.

2. While the broth is heating, rinse, pat dry, and mince the herbs. Break the noodles into 2- to 3-inch lengths. In a bowl, lightly beat the eggs with the Parmesan.

3. When the broth boils, taste it for seasoning. (If you are using frozen saltless broth, add enough salt and pepper to bring out the flavor or your soup will be bland.) Add the noodles, cover, and simmer over medium heat until tender, about 5 minutes.

4. Stir in the herbs. Then, whisking constantly, pour the beaten eggs into the soup. Stir for about 30 seconds or until the eggs have curdled into ribbon-shaped strands. Season to taste with salt and pepper, and serve immediately.

VARIATIONS

Vegetable and Egg Vermicelli Soup: When the broth comes to a boil, add 2 finely chopped carrots or 1 package (10 ounces) frozen petite peas or chopped spinach, thawed. Then add the vermicelli and proceed with the recipe.

Cholesterol-Free Vermicelli Soup: Substitute 8 egg whites for the whole eggs, and omit the cheese.

■ Asian version: Add ¼ cup soy sauce and 1 tablespoon lemon juice to the broth as it is coming to a boil. Substitute 4 thinly sliced scallions for the Parmesan, adding them when you add the herbs in step 3, and use rice or cellophane noodles if possible.

■ Thick and rich version: Double the quantities of vermicelli and Parmesan, and stir in 6 eggs. This thicker soup makes a more substantial meal by itself.

Garlic Vegetable Soup with Orecchiette

PASTA: *Small or medium-size shapes*
MAKES: *4 to 6 servings*
TIME: *35 minutes*

After garlic cooks for a long time, it loses all of its pungency and becomes delicately sweet, smooth, and aromatic. To make it easier to fish out the garlic cloves after cooking, thread them on a bamboo skewer or on a couple of toothpicks.

This soup is wonderful as a main course. It's also a practical soup, one for using up any leftover dried pasta you might have in the house. It accommodates vegetables in season and leftover cooked pasta, as well as bits of leftover meat or poultry. Serve grated cheese with this if you wish; at times I like Parmesan or Romano, other times I opt for shreds of a gooey mozzarella, grated sharp Cheddar, or a crumble of blue.

This is so filling that a simple fruit salad for dessert will round out the meal.

6 to 8 cups chicken, beef, or vegetable
  broth
2 medium-size carrots
2 ribs celery
½ pound mushrooms
10 cloves garlic
¼ teaspoon ground dried sage
¼ teaspoon dried marjoram
¼ teaspoon dried thyme
1 cup small broccoli or cauliflower florets
2 to 3 cups orecchiette, penne, or fusilli,
  or 1 cup pastina
Salt and freshly ground black pepper
1 cup grated cheese of your choice (see
  headnote; optional)

1. Bring the broth to a simmer in a large saucepan over medium heat. While the broth is heating, prepare the vegetables and add them as each is done: Peel and thinly slice the carrots. Finely chop the celery. Trim the mushrooms, wipe them clean with a damp paper towel, and thinly slice them.

2. Peel the garlic, leaving the cloves whole. String them on a bamboo skewer (make sure it fits into your saucepan) or thread them on several toothpicks, and add to the broth. Add the herbs.

3. When the broth is at a full simmer, cover the saucepan and simmer over low heat for 15 minutes.

4. Add the broccoli and pasta, cover the saucepan, and simmer over medium heat until the broccoli is tender and the pasta is cooked, 5 to 6 minutes. Remove the garlic,

season to taste with salt and pepper, and serve while very hot. Pass the grated cheese.

VARIATIONS

■ Substitute 1 cup chopped fennel bulb or diced white turnips, parsnips, or rutabagas for either the carrots or the celery; these vegetables have an affinity for garlic.
■ Omit the broccoli or cauliflower, and after the pasta is cooked, add ½ cup chopped fresh herbs, such as parsley or dill. Or add 2 cups shredded watercress, arugula, or spinach.

**SECOND
TIME
AROUND**

If there are any leftovers, change the character of the soup and thin it at the same time by adding tomato juice or a can of stewed tomatoes, chopped.

Japanese-Style Bean Noodle Soup

PASTA: *Thin strands or ribbons, made of mung beans, semolina, buckwheat, or rice*
MAKES: *4 servings*
TIME: *25 to 30 minutes*

This soup appears to be light but is filling nonetheless. "Glass" noodles have more texture than flavor, but they do swell up as much as wheat noodles, and are great for people who are allergic to wheat.

> 1 package (3½ to 4 ounces) mung bean noodles
> 4 cups water
> 5 or 6 small carrots
> ½ pound mushrooms
> 6 cups chicken broth or water
> ¼ cup soy sauce
> ¼ cup rice vinegar
> ½ pound snow peas
> ½ cup (loosely packed) fresh cilantro leaves
> Salt and freshly ground black pepper

1. Place the mung bean noodles in a large bowl. Bring the water to a boil and pour it over the noodles. Let them stand until they are tender, about 15 minutes.

2. Meanwhile, peel and thinly slice the carrots. Stem the mushrooms and wipe the caps with a damp paper towel; then thinly slice them.

3. Combine the chicken broth, soy sauce, rice vinegar, carrots, and mushrooms in a large saucepan, and bring to a boil over high heat. Cover the saucepan, reduce the heat to medium, and cook until the carrots and mushrooms are tender, about 5 minutes.

4. While that is cooking, snap off the stem ends of the snow peas and pull off the strings; discard any yellow or bruised snow peas. Rinse the cilantro, pat it dry, and mince the leaves. When the noodles are soft, drain

them and cut them into manageable pieces, about 4- to 5-inch lengths.

5. Right before you are ready to eat, add the noodles to the soup and simmer for 1 minute. Add the snow peas and simmer for 1 minute, just to soften them slightly. Add the cilantro and remove the saucepan from the heat. Season to taste with salt and pepper, and serve immediately.

VARIATION

If you are using vermicelli or rice noodles in the soup, cook them separately, then ladle the soup and vegetables over them. This way the pasta will not absorb too much of the liquid and become mushy.

Michèle's Minestrone

PASTA: *Small or medium-size tubes or fancy shapes*
MAKES: *4 to 6 servings*
TIME: *10 minutes preparation plus 25 minutes no-work cooking time*

Plan to make this soup, which comes in as many versions as there are regions in Italy, on a cold night when you know you'll be coming home late and exhausted. The work consists of peeling and dicing the potatoes and the carrots. After that, you just put your feet up while the soup cooks by itself.

This is a filling soup that requires only some slices of crusty bread to round out the meal.

4 carrots
2 medium-size boiling potatoes
8 cups chicken, beef, or vegetable broth or
    water
1 cup canned cannellini beans, drained
    and rinsed
1 package (10 ounces) frozen chopped
    spinach, thawed
1 cup elbow macaroni, small shells, or
    orzo
Salt and freshly ground black pepper
¼ to ⅓ cup grated Parmesan or Romano
    cheese

1. Peel and thinly slice the carrots. Peel the potatoes and cut them into ½-inch dice.

2. Combine the broth, carrots, and potatoes in a large saucepan, and bring to a boil over medium heat. Reduce the heat to low, cover the pan, and simmer until the potatoes are tender, about 10 minutes.

3. Add the beans, spinach, and pasta to the soup. Bring the soup back to a boil and simmer over medium heat, covered, until the pasta is cooked, about 10 minutes. Season to taste with salt and pepper, and remove from the heat. Add the cheese, stirring until it is softened. Serve immediately.

VARIATIONS

■ Substitute ½ pound chopped rinsed fresh spinach for the frozen spinach; add it in batches after the pasta is cooked—not before, because it takes only a couple of minutes to wilt.

■ To give the soup a smoky flavor, add 1 cup diced smoked ham or turkey after the pasta is cooked, and simmer until heated through, about 1 minute.

SECOND TIME AROUND *Cheer up leftovers by adding 1 can crushed or stewed tomatoes, with their juice, and season the soup with some dried oregano or marjoram.*

Hearty Pasta Soup with Herbed Lentils

PASTA: *Tiny shapes*
MAKES: *4 servings*
TIME: *10 minutes preparation plus 30 minutes no-work cooking time*

This uncomplicated-tasting, thick lentil-and-pasta soup provides comfort and warmth on a raw winter's night. The preparation is minimal and the flavor is maximum.

What makes it especially pleasing is the textural balance between the lentils and the *acini de pepe*, a type of pasta often mislabeled "barley." Other small shaped pasta would be equally welcome.

Whenever I am in the mood for such a hearty soup, I am in the mood for nothing else. If this soup meal falls short of your appetite requirements, however, serve either sandwiches or a salad alongside it.

The cheeses that blend well with this flavor are Cheddar, Monterey Jack, Romano, and Parmesan.

*2 slices regular bacon
    or turkey bacon
½ medium-size onion
1 tablespoon vegetable oil
4 cups chicken broth
1 cup water
½ cup lentils
½ teaspoon ground dried sage
½ teaspoon dried oregano
¼ teaspoon ground coriander
1 cup canned crushed tomatoes
½ cup acini de pepe or other tiny pasta
    shapes, such as pastina, anellini or orzo
Salt and freshly ground black pepper
Plain yogurt or grated cheese (optional)*

1. Mince the bacon. Peel and finely chop the onion.

2. Heat the oil in a large saucepan over medium heat. Add the bacon and cook, stirring constantly, until crisp, 3 to 4 minutes. Add the onions and stir to coat them with the oil. Cover, and cook over low heat until the onions are tender, about 5 minutes.

3. Add the chicken broth and water, raise the heat and bring to a boil. Add the lentils, sage, oregano, and coriander. Cover, and simmer over low heat until the lentils are almost tender, about 20 minutes. Stir the soup every now and then to make sure the lentils are not sticking to the bottom of the saucepan.

4. Add the tomatoes and bring the liquid back to a boil. Then add the pasta, cover, and simmer over low heat for 10 minutes. Again, stir it every now and then so the pasta does not stick.

5. When the pasta is tender and the soup is very thick, season to taste with salt and pepper and serve immediately. Pass the yogurt or cheese on the side.

SECOND TIME AROUND

Thin the soup to a desirable consistency with water or vegetable or chicken broth, and bring it to a boil. Add 1 cup diced cooked ham, pork, beef, chicken, or turkey, or 1 package (10 ounces) frozen corn or chopped spinach, thawed. Perk up the flavor even further with a handful of chopped fresh herbs.

Restorative Chicken Noodle Soup

PASTA: *Thin egg noodles or tiny shapes*
MAKES: *4 servings*
TIME: *35 minutes*

A chicken noodle soup recipe is essential to your repertoire, and this one is clean-flavored and uncomplicated.

Although you cannot really taste the lemon juice, it is essential in the soup to balance and sharpen the other flavors. This makes a meal when served with bread, although hearty appetites will perhaps want a salad before the soup or a robust dessert after to complete the meal.

> *6 to 8 carrots*
> *6 cups chicken broth*
> *1 clove garlic*
> *¾ pound boneless, skinless chicken breast*
> *⅓ cup (packed) fresh parsley or dill leaves*
> *2 cups fine egg noodles*
> *2 teaspoons lemon juice*
> *Salt and freshly ground black pepper*

1. Peel and thinly slice the carrots. Combine them with the chicken broth in a large saucepan. Peel the garlic and drop the whole clove into the broth. Cover the saucepan and bring the liquid to a boil over high heat. Then reduce the heat to medium and simmer until the carrots are tender, about 5 minutes.

2. While that is cooking, cut the chicken into ½-inch chunks. Rinse, pat dry, and mince the parsley or dill.

3. Add the chicken and egg noodles to the broth, cover, and cook until the noodles are tender and the chicken is cooked through, about 5 minutes. Stir in the lemon juice and the parsley or dill. Fish out the garlic clove, and season the soup to taste with salt and pepper. Serve immediately.

VARIATION

If you are making this soup with canned broth, which can be salty, use only 3 cups and make up the remaining liquid with 3 cups water. To help pick up the flavor of the canned broth, add a bay leaf or ½ teaspoon thyme or marjoram to the soup.

ESPECIALLY GOOD FOR CHILDREN

Except for the herbs, this soup is a great hit with most kids I know. If your offspring are as fussy as mine about green things floating in their soup, then save the herbs for the adults' portions and leave the fussy eaters' bowls plain.

Spinach Tortellini Soup with Cucumbers

PASTA: *Stuffed pastas*
MAKES: *6 servings*
TIME: *15 to 20 minutes*

This unusual combination of stuffed pasta with cucumbers works beautifully. The colors are lovely together, especially if you use a spinach-stuffed pasta, but try the combination with all sorts of stuffed pasta, including the cheese and meat varieties.

I finish the soup with a sprinkling of Parmesan cheese, just enough to enhance the flavor but not so much as to flavor it with cheese.

Another light course will make a meal with this delicate soup.

> 8 cups chicken broth
> 1 pound stuffed pasta, such as spinach-meat tortellini or mushroom-stuffed cappelletti
> 6 scallions (green onions)
> 2 medium-size cucumbers
> Salt and freshly ground black pepper
> Grated Parmesan cheese

1. Bring the broth to a boil, covered, in a large saucepan over medium-high heat. Add the stuffed pasta and boil gently, uncovered, until they are cooked through and tender, 8 to 10 minutes.

2. Meanwhile, trim 3 inches off the tops of the scallions and thinly slice the remainder. Peel, seed, and chop the cucumber into ¼-inch dice.

3. When the pasta is cooked, add the scallions and cucumbers. Simmer the soup just to warm the cucumbers, less than 1 minute (they should remain crisp). Season to taste with salt and pepper, and serve immediately. Pass the Parmesan separately.

VARIATION

Instead of cucumbers, you could add other quick-cooking vegetables. Two or 3 small carrots, grated, would be a good substitution, as would a 10-ounce package of frozen petite peas, thawed.

ESPECIALLY GOOD FOR CHILDREN *If those cucumber pieces turn your kids off, ladle a portion of the plain soup into their bowls and save the scallions and cucumbers for the adults.*

Tingly Lemon Orzo Soup

PASTA: *Tiny shapes*
MAKES: *4 to 6 servings*
TIME: *20 minutes*

This soup is lemony, zingy, and fresh. You can serve it as a first course if you omit the tofu, or turn it into a plentiful main course by adding a few more vegetables. However you choose to go, you'll find it an easy soup to make and refreshingly simple.

I always serve bread with soup, and the combination is enough to turn this into a meal—but if you're still hungry, vanilla frozen yogurt makes an ideal dessert.

> 1 lemon
> 8 cups chicken, beef, or vegetable broth
> ½ pound mushrooms
> ½ pound firm tofu
> 1 cup (packed) fresh parsley leaves
> 2 scallions (green onions)
> ¾ cup tiny pasta, such as orzo, anellini, farfallini, or stelline
> Salt
> ¼ teaspoon dried red pepper flakes

1. Grate the zest from the whole lemon, and then juice the lemon. Combine the zest, ¼ cup lemon juice, and the broth in a large saucepan. Bring the liquid to a boil over high heat.

2. While that is coming to a boil, trim the mushrooms and wipe them clean with a damp paper towel. Cut the mushrooms into thin slices and add them to the broth. Cut the tofu into small dice and add it to the broth as well. Rinse and mince the parsley. Trim the scallions, cut the white and green parts into thin slices, and set them aside with the parsley.

3. When the liquid is at a full boil, add the pasta and cook until soft, 2 to 3 minutes. Remove the soup from the heat, and add the parsley and scallions. Season to taste with salt and red pepper flakes. Serve the soup immediately.

VARIATIONS

Lemon Parsley Fish Soup: Substitute fish stock or clam juice for the broth, and 8 ounces of diced fresh fish for the tofu. Add the fish at the same time you add the pasta.

Lemon Parsley Chicken Soup: Use chicken broth, and substitute ½ pound boneless, skinless chicken breast for the tofu. Cut the chicken into thin long shreds, and add them when you add the pasta.

SECOND TIME AROUND

Vary the broth on the second pass in a dramatic fashion: Spoon a few teaspoons of miso paste into the leftovers and voilà—an instant Japanese-style soup.

Toasted Noodle Soup

PASTA: *Thin strands*
MAKES: *4 servings*
TIME: *30 to 35 minutes*

This incredible soup will soothe you on a cold winter's evening, not only because of its satisfying flavor but also because of the minimal effort required to cook it.

Toasting the skinny noodles gives their flavor an intriguing taste, and simmering the soup uncovered makes it thick and appealing. This is popular with children.

With the soup serve crusty whole-wheat bread and a green or cabbage salad.

> 1 onion
> 6 ounces vermicelli, capellini, or very fine egg noodles
> ⅓ cup olive oil
> 6 cups chicken, beef, or vegetable broth
> 1 cup canned crushed tomatoes
> ½ teaspoon dried oregano
> ¼ teaspoon ground cumin
> ¼ teaspoon Tabasco sauce (optional)
> Salt
>
> GARNISHES (OPTIONAL):
> Sour cream or plain yogurt
> Chopped green olives
> Sliced pimientos

1. Peel and finely chop the onion. Break the noodles into 1-inch pieces.

2. Heat the olive oil in a large saucepan, over medium-high heat. Add the broken noodles and sauté them, stirring constantly, until they are golden brown, about 2 minutes. (Don't worry if they do not all brown or if they do not brown evenly.) Using a slotted spoon, transfer the golden noodles to a bowl and reserve them for later.

3. Add the onions to the remaining oil in the saucepan, and sauté for a minute or so. Then cover the pan and simmer the onions over low heat until they are tender and golden, about 5 minutes.

4. Add the broth, tomatoes, oregano, cumin, Tabasco, and sautéed noodles. Season with salt (you'll need 2 teaspoons at least). Bring to a simmer over medium heat and cook, uncovered, until the noodles are very soft and the soup is quite thick, 15 to 20 minutes. Adjust the seasoning, and serve with the optional garnishes.

VARIATION

Add some zip by garnishing each portion with a spoonful of plain yogurt or sour cream, topped with chopped green olives and sliced pimientos.

Rich and Creamy Pasta Dishes

In this chapter I have gathered recipes that combine pasta with milk, cream, cheese, and/or eggs. Although recipes in other sections of this book also call for dairy products, the selection here contains an abundance of these ingredients and takes its character from them.

CHEESE WITH PASTA

As we know from macaroni and cheese, Parmesan-topped spaghetti, and ricotta-rich lasagne, the match between noodles and cheese is magical and enduring. It is one of the great food marriages, and few combinations taste quite as natural, or as good and as right.

And yet here we are, cooks of the 1990s, torn between craving the rich good taste of cheese and knowing better. Too much cheese doesn't lead to heart healthiness.

What's the solution? I am unwilling to live completely without cheese. I continue to eat cheese with pasta, so that I don't miss out on the wonderful taste, but I'm more conservative in how often I serve fettuccine with cream and Parmesan.

CHEESES FOR GRATING OVER PASTA

Hard tangy cheeses are the ones to grate over pasta. Their sharp bite goes a long way in flavoring noodles.

Pass the cheese grater at the table. That way, each person can add just the amount he or she wants.

Parmesan: This cheese is thought of as the "generic" pasta cheese. Most of us tend to add grated Parmesan (a hard cow's-milk cheese) to our pasta dishes. And why not? It is truly wonderful, and its sharp nutty flavor is superb with noodles.

The best Parmesan, imported from Parma, Italy, is known as Parmigiano-Reggiano and is quite expensive. Its flavor is exquisite, and the cheese is moist enough for eating straight as well as grating. There are, however, less expensive grating cheeses from Italy, labeled Grana.

If you can't get these cheeses in chunk form, then look for their freshly grated versions, which will be stored in the refrigerator case. Failing that, consider "Parmesan" cheese imported from Argentina. This does not have the same flavor as the real Italian stuff, but it is much cheaper. It is also somewhat more readily available, and it is definitely superior to any type of dry grated Parmesan "topping." Stay away from the boxed stuff—it's better to substitute any other fresh hard cheese you can get your hands on. Even sharp Cheddar is better than the boxed Parmesan.

As good as Parmesan is, though, it is not the only hard cheese that is delicious over pasta.

Asiago: Another sharp, nutty cow's-milk cheese, aged Asiago is quite wonderful grated over pasta dishes. It is saltier than Parmesan, and I like it with pasta dishes that have an American flavor, such as ones with hot peppers, corn, chiles, tomatoes, and ground beef. I often use domestic Asiago (it's made in Michigan and Wisconsin) because it is delicious and is less expensive than the imported kind.

Aged Gouda: Gouda (also a cow's-milk cheese) is a favorite of mine because it is such a fine eating cheese. I've discovered that aged Gouda is hard enough for grating (at least with a rotary grater) and is a welcome addition to a dish of plain noodles or a vegetable-and-pasta combination.

Aged Monterey Jack: The cheese most people know in its popular semisoft form also has a drier aged version. A cow's-milk cheese that comes from California, aged Monterey Jack is especially good over pasta dishes with Southwestern accents such as green chiles, tomato sauce, chili powder, and cumin.

Aged Mountain Gorgonzola: I love this salty, aromatic cheese grated over plain linguine or spaghetti. For a slightly more elaborate dish, I'll add it to pasta coated with a tomato sauce. Aged Gorgonzola is also wonderful on its own, maybe with sliced tomatoes or with ripe pears, plums, or figs. It tastes quite different from the soft young Gorgonzola, which is delectable as an ingredient in pasta dishes.

Aged provolone: Like any other cheese, when aged long enough, provolone becomes hard enough to grate. Even though I find it rather bland, I buy provolone occasionally to serve to children, who enjoy its mild flavor.

Pecorino Romano: This is a sharp, salty, pungent grating cheese made from sheep's milk. It is good with plain noodles, with pasta and greens, and with pasta dishes that have a Middle Eastern or Indian flavor.

CHEESES FOR CRUMBLING OVER PASTA

Easy-to-crumble cheeses taste best in pasta dishes when they are sprinkled over the top.

Blue cheeses: Stilton from England, Gorgonzola from Italy, and American Maytag blue are delicious when crumbled over pasta dishes. I like these blue cheeses in dishes that are simple enough to let their flavor shine through: vegetables with pasta, grain and bean pasta dishes, and plain pasta.

STORING AGED CHEESE

If you are lucky enough to find an excellent grating cheese such as Parmigiano-Reggiano, you'll want to get the most out of your purchase. Wrap the cheese tightly in several layers of freezer wrap or aluminum foil, and store it in the refrigerator. Each time you use some, be sure to rewrap the cheese completely.

Goat's-milk cheeses: Mild semifirm goat cheeses, domestic and imported, work well with plain pasta dishes as well as those flavored with chopped fresh tomatoes or lots of herbs. I also happen to love a dry chèvre crumbled over a chicken and pasta dish.

Sharper goat's- and sheep's-milk cheeses: These include Brindza (U.S.), feta (Greece), Kashkaval (from the Balkans), and ricotta salata and Pecorino Romano (Italy). They are a lot saltier and tangier than the soft chèvres, but they, too, are wonderful with an array of noodle dishes. Feta is the most commonly available of these, and I think it's especially lovely in cold pasta salads that are packed with vegetables such as peppers, zucchini, spinach, and tomatoes. I also enjoy bits of these sharp cheeses in warm pasta dishes that contain vegetables, lamb, or beef.

CHEESES TO LEND CREAMINESS

These are the cheeses that give pasta a certain richness, and that make good stuffings for baked dishes such as lasagne. Often bland by themselves, they are a pleasure when flavored with fresh herbs, scallions, and garlic. Many are available in low-fat versions; these are especially good to have on hand if you are on a diet because they add a deliciously creamy texture without adding the unwanted calories and fat.

Cottage or pot cheese: I always have cottage cheese (also called pot cheese) in the house because I enjoy eating it with fruit. It is also a great alternative to ricotta, which is slightly richer. If you have purchased cottage cheese and you find the texture too dry to mix into pasta, just add a few tablespoons of milk, chicken broth, or plain yogurt.

Farmer's cheese: This moist cheese is firmer than cottage cheese, which is why I use it in baked pasta puddings and sweet noodle dishes.

Ricotta cheese: More than cottage cheese, ricotta brings a real creaminess to pasta dishes, especially baked ones. Although I find part-skim ricotta an acceptable substitute for the whole-milk variety, the low-fat all-skim version is just too watery for my taste.

Fresh goat's-milk cheese: Fresh chèvre has a soft texture and a milder flavor than aged goat's-milk cheeses. I use it less often than I do cottage or ricotta cheese because of its assertive taste and its higher fat content.

CHEESES FOR MELTING OVER PASTA

Fontina: This satiny smooth cheese has a nutty flavor and a wonderful texture for melting. Just cut the thinnest of slices, arrange them on top of a pasta dish, and cook until the cheese melts.

Emmental, Gruyère, and Jarlsberg: These well-known cheeses are commonly known as "Swiss cheese." Emmental is the real "Swiss" cheese because it comes from Switzerland; Gruyère, with its nuttier and sharper taste, comes from France; and Jarlsberg, the silkiest and mildest of them all, comes from Norway. All of these are good when diced or shredded over pasta dishes, or when used in baked pasta recipes, because they melt quite nicely. I also like these cheeses cubed and added to vegetable-and-pasta salads.

Mozzarella: This is perhaps the ideal melting cheese; its long strings are the "goo" in "gooey" cheese. You can still find real water buffalo mozzarella, but the usual fresh type now (including Italian mozzarella) is made from cow's milk. Fresh mozzarella, packed in water, is a wonderful eating cheese and excellent in pasta salads, but is not a good choice for baked pasta dishes because it doesn't melt as well as ordinary supermarket mozzarella.

OTHER TYPES OF CHEESES TO SERVE WITH PASTA

Caerphilly: This is a crumbly, gently tangy white cheese originally from Wales and now made in Somerset, England. I love its flavor and I find it as great for crumbling over pasta as for eating. I especially like it in pasta salads or with pasta dishes that contain vegetables or ham.

Cheddar: A good sharp Vermont Cheddar is perfect with noodle dishes that include peas, ham, smoked turkey, and/or tomatoes.

Smoked cheeses: A smoked fontina or mozzarella, finely diced, is delicious in pasta salads that contain tomatoes, cucumbers, and other summer or early fall vegetables.

EGGS WITH PASTA

Even if I don't eat eggs on a daily basis, I can't imagine a Monday-to-Friday kitchen without a dozen on hand. Eggs offer the perfect way to get a quick and nutritious dinner on the table.

Eggs and pasta make a great match. Most often, I make a savory omelet out of leftover noodles scrambled with eggs and seasoned with onions and peppers. Sometimes I toss some freshly boiled noodles with eggs and heat them gently over very low heat until the eggs barely curdle. Or I create a baked noodle dish, either sweet or savory, by mixing cooked pasta with eggs and a variety of seasonings.

Here are some tips for buying, storing, and using eggs.

■ The best eggs are graded AA. All eggs should be kept refrigerated; they deteriorate rapidly when stored at room temperature.
■ If you have some eggs in the fridge and can't remember when you bought them, here's how you can tell if they're fresh: Crack an egg open onto a plate. If the white hugs the yolk and the yolk is round and plump, it is fresh. If the white spreads out over the plate and the yolk looks flat, it isn't.
■ Make sure the eggs you use in a dish are well cooked. Heat destroys any salmonella bacteria, a cause of food poisoning.

American Spaghetti Carbonara

PASTA: *Thin strands or ribbons*
MAKES: *4 servings*
TIME: *30 minutes*

True-blue spaghetti carbonara is made with pancetta, Italian unsmoked bacon. Pancetta is delicious, but unfortunately it's not readily available in the U.S., so I substitute good old American bacon.

I have, however, kept the other authentic aspect of this Italian dish: the technique of warming the eggs in the heat of the cooked pasta so they form an unctuous coating for the spaghetti.

I realize that some cooks are wary of not cooking eggs enough, so I've included other ways of making this dish. Note, however, that when you cook the eggs through, they will curdle, and the dish won't look nearly as glamorous.

Since this has all the elements of a hearty breakfast, keep it in mind for a late Sunday morning brunch. It's also a favorite with the younger set at any time of the day.

Salt
¼ pound bacon or pancetta, thinly sliced
2 cloves garlic
4 large eggs
½ cup grated Parmesan cheese, or half Romano, half Parmesan
Freshly ground black pepper
1 pound spaghettini, linguine fine, or spaghetti
1 tablespoon vegetable oil

1. Bring a large pot of salted water to a boil for the pasta.

2. While the water is heating, cut the bacon crosswise into ¼-inch pieces. Peel and mince the garlic. Beat the eggs and Parmesan together, and season with salt and pepper.

3. Add the pasta to the water and cook until it is tender but still firm to the bite, 8 to 10 minutes.

4. While the pasta is cooking, heat the oil in a medium-size skillet over high heat. Add the bacon and sauté, stirring occasionally, until it has rendered its fat and is beginning to turn crisp, about 5 minutes. Add the garlic and sauté for a few seconds, until you get a whiff of its aroma. Remove the skillet from the heat, cover it, and set it aside, until the pasta is done.

5. Drain the pasta well and return it to the pot, off the heat. Thoroughly stir in the bacon and garlic with the oil and bacon fat. Stirring the pasta continuously, preferably with a long wooden pasta fork, slowly pour in the egg mixture. Toss well again, taste for seasoning, and serve immediately.

VARIATION

Cautious Carbonara: Divide the carbonara among four dinner plates, and then zap each plateful in the microwave for 1 minute; this will cook the eggs thoroughly.

Or, in step 5, return the pot to low heat, then add the eggs. As you stir, you will see soft curds forming around the noodles, a sign that the eggs are cooked through.

Middle Eastern Pasta Pancake

PASTA: *Ribbons or strands*
MAKES: *4 servings*
TIME: *20 to 25 minutes*

This is the perfect way to turn leftover cooked pasta into a nutritious and intriguing meal. Simply cook the noodles with lots of spices and some eggs over low, low heat until the mixture shapes itself into a crispy pancake. Serve it with plain yogurt, and dinner is done!

I like to season the eggs with this combination of Middle Eastern spices, but let your imagination lead you to other possibilities.

If you want to add some cheese to the mix, cook the pancake in a nonstick skillet; the cheese will cause the pancake to stick.

This is another dish to remember when you are wondering what to serve for a Sunday brunch.

4 large eggs
1 teaspoon ground cardamom
½ teaspoon anise seeds or caraway seeds
1 teaspoon ground coriander
¼ teaspoon ground cumin
½ teaspoon sugar
4 cups cooked tagliatelle, fettuccine,
    spaghettini, or linguine
Salt and freshly ground black
    pepper
3 tablespoons butter or vegetable oil
1 cup plain yogurt or sour cream
    (optional)

1. In a mixing bowl, whisk together the eggs, spices, and sugar. Add the cooked pasta and combine thoroughly. Season with salt and pepper.

2. Heat the butter or oil in a large skillet over medium-high heat. When the butter begins to turn golden or the oil simmers, add the pasta mixture and immediately reduce the heat to the lowest setting. Cover the skillet and cook the mixture very gently until the bottom is crisp, 15 minutes. To serve the pancake, invert the skillet over a platter. Cut the pancake into wedges, and pass the yogurt or sour cream alongside.

ESPECIALLY GOOD FOR CHILDREN

Reduce the amount of spices if you are going to serve this to kids. A tiny bit of cinnamon or allspice will please most younger children.

Creamy Chèvre and Basil Tagliatelle

PASTA: *Thin ribbons or strands, or fresh egg noodles*
MAKES: *4 servings*
TIME: *30 to 35 minutes*

Sensational ingredients come together so harmoniously in this pasta dish that it's hard to identify the individual flavors of goat cheese, basil, onion, garlic, and peppers.

If you are cooking for two, you'll have time to wash some spinach or arugula for a salad. But if you are cooking for more and don't have time to wash a pound of gritty greens, serve a cucumber salad as a starter.

Keep this recipe in mind for leisurely weekend entertaining. It's also a wonderful side dish to serve with roast leg of lamb.

Salt
1 onion
1 red bell pepper
2 cloves garlic
¼ cup olive oil
Freshly ground black pepper
½ cup (packed) basil leaves
¼ pound (½ cup crumbled) creamy mild
    chèvre
1 tablespoon olivada (black olive paste;
    optional)
¾ pound fresh tagliatelle or fettuccine, or
    dry linguine fine or fedelini

1. Bring a large pot of salted water to a boil for the pasta.

2. Peel and quarter the onion. Core, seed, and quarter the red pepper. Peel the garlic cloves. Finely chop all the vegetables together in a food processor (or, of course, by hand).

3. Heat the oil in a large skillet over high heat. Add the chopped vegetables and sauté for a few seconds, until you smell a whiff of the garlic. Cover the skillet, reduce the heat, and cook until the vegetables are very tender, about 5 minutes. Season to taste with salt and pepper.

4. While the vegetables are cooking, wipe out the bowl of the food processor, and add the chèvre and basil (and olivada if you're using it), and purée until smooth. Transfer the purée to a bowl and set it aside.

5. Add the pasta to the boiling water and cook until it is tender but still firm to the bite, 4 to 8 minutes depending on the pasta you are using. Drain the pasta and return it to the pot, off the heat. Add the chèvre purée and the cooked vegetables, and toss thoroughly. Adjust the seasoning and serve immediately.

VARIATIONS

■ Feta cheese version: Substitute ¼ cup crumbled feta cheese and ¼ cup sour cream for the chèvre.

■ Sun-dried tomato version: Add ¼ cup finely chopped sun-dried tomatoes (packed in oil and drained) to the chèvre and basil purée.

Fettuccine with Cream and Parmesan

PASTA: *Ribbons or fresh egg noodles*
MAKES: *4 to 6 servings*
TIME: *20 to 25 minutes*

Here is my take on Fettuccine Alfredo. Although still incredibly rich, this version is a lot lighter and fresher tasting than the "Alfredos" you may have sampled in restaurants. The cream makes a special occasion out of a midweek meal. The parsley adds pretty flecks of color, and its fresh taste helps balance the richness.

If you serve this as a main course, precede it with a salad of slightly bitter escarole and tomatoes or even with gazpacho. Any light fruit dessert would be fitting after this rich dish.

Salt
1 clove garlic
½ cup fresh parsley leaves
1 pound fettuccine or medium-wide egg
*   noodles*
½ cup chicken broth
½ cup heavy cream
½ to ¾ cup grated Parmesan cheese
2 tablespoons butter
Freshly ground black pepper

1. Bring a large pot of salted water to a boil for the pasta.

2. Meanwhile, smash the garlic clove with the broad side of a chef's knife and peel it, leaving it whole. Rinse, pat dry, and mince the parsley.

3. Add the pasta to the boiling water and cook until it is tender but still firm to the bite, 8 to 10 minutes for dried pasta, or 2 to 3 minutes for fresh.

4. About 5 minutes before the pasta is done, combine the broth, cream, and garlic clove in a large skillet over medium-low heat. Simmer until slightly thickened, 1 or 2 minutes.

5. Drain the pasta and return it to the cooking pot, off the heat.

6. Remove the garlic clove from the cream mixture, and stir in the cheese. Remove the sauce from the heat. Stir in the parsley and butter, and season to taste with salt and pepper. Pour the sauce over the pasta, toss well to combine, and serve immediately.

VARIATION

Instead of flavoring the cream sauce with garlic, mince a small bunch of fresh chives and add it to the sauce with the parsley.

SECOND TIME AROUND

Add a fresh dose of herbs the second time around to perk up the flavor. Reheat the leftovers in a microwave oven or a double boiler, or spoon them into a baking dish, top with bread crumbs, and bake at 350°F until hot, about 20 minutes.

Linguine with Herbed Ricotta

PASTA: *Thin ribbons or strands*
MAKES: *4 servings*
TIME: *25 minutes*

An old stand-by, this recipe is richer than its first incarnation, Capellini with Herbed Cottage Cheese, which appeared in the *Monday-to-Friday Cookbook*—and the variations are even richer. Capellini (angel-hair pasta) is really too delicate for such a thick sauce; a slightly thicker strand holds up better.

This works as a first course any time of the year. And it makes an especially welcome main course during the summer because there is no cooking to do other than boiling the pasta. I usually serve a salad of some sort either with the pasta or before it.

Salt
¾ pound linguine fine, spaghettini, or fedelini
2 shallots or 4 scallions (green onions)
¼ cup fresh parsley leaves
8 tablespoons (1 stick) butter, at room temperature
1 tablespoon dried tarragon
¾ teaspoon grated lemon zest
2 tablespoons lemon juice
½ cup ricotta cheese
Freshly ground black pepper

1. Bring a large pot of salted water to a boil. Add the pasta and cook until it is tender but still firm to the bite, 7 to 10 minutes.

2. While the pasta is cooking, peel and halve the shallots (or trim the scallions and cut them into 2-inch pieces) and drop them into a food processor. Rinse and pat dry the parsley, and add it to the shallots along with the butter, tarragon, lemon zest, lemon juice, and ricotta. Purée the mixture until smooth. Season to taste with salt and pepper.

3. Drain the pasta, reserving ¼ cup of the cooking water, and return it to the pot, off the heat. Add the cheese mixture and the reserved cooking water, and toss thoroughly. Serve immediately.

VARIATIONS

- Cottage cheese version: In place of the butter, use 1 cup cottage cheese mixed with ¼ cup olive oil.
- Decadent ricotta version: Add ¼ cup heavy cream or mascarpone to the mixture before puréeing.
- Goat cheese version: Substitute ½ cup crumbled chèvre for the ricotta.

Instant Lasagne

PASTA: *"Instant" lasagne sheets or cooked noodles*
MAKES: *4 to 6 servings*
TIME: *15 minutes preparation plus 30 minutes no-work cooking time*

Lasagne made from scratch doesn't cut it, Monday-to-Friday. It isn't that the work is so onerous, it's that the total preparation and cooking time runs close to 2 hours.

You can make lasagne during the week in about 45 minutes, however, if you can find the new Italian precooked lasagne squares or if you have enough leftover noodles (of any variety).

The "instant" lasagne sheets don't look anything like traditional lasagne noodles. They are very thin squares of dried pasta that look like corrugated cardboard. Although the package directions say to use a 9-inch-square baking pan, I recommend using an 8-inch pan.

At first I was skeptical about the taste and texture of this pasta. I anticipated a soft, gluey texture. To my delight these sheets, made from 100% semolina, are not at all rubbery or gummy. Take care, however, to cover the noodles *completely* with moist ingredients—cheese or sauce—or they'll remain brittle and uncooked.

If you are going to make lasagne with leftover noodles, make sure they have been boiled but not sauced. If they are clumped together, just chop them and layer them between the ricotta and the spaghetti sauce.

For a traditional lasagne recipe—along with some ideas on ways to vary the flavor and what to serve with it—turn to Sunday's-Best Lasagne (see Index).

5 or 6 "instant" lasagne sheets (Delverde brand), or 4 cups cooked noodles
½ pound ground lean beef
2 jars (14 ounces each) spaghetti sauce
Salt and freshly ground black pepper
1 container (15 ounces) part-skim ricotta cheese
1 cup grated Parmesan cheese

1. Preheat the oven to 400°F. If you are using instant lasagne sheets, soak them in a bowl of hot water. As they soften, remove them from the bowl and pat them dry (if you leave them in the water for too long, they will stick to each other).

2. In a medium-size skillet over medium heat, sauté the beef, breaking up the clumps with a spoon. Sauté until there are no more traces of pink in the meat, about 5 minutes.

3. Pour the spaghetti sauce into a bowl, and mix in the meat and its juices. Season to taste with salt and pepper.

4. Spoon ½ cup of the meat sauce in the bottom of an 8-inch-square baking pan, and top with a sheet of "instant" lasagne or 2 cups of cooked noodles. Spread the pasta with dabs of ricotta and some of the sauce. Be sure to spread the cheese and sauce all over the sheet of lasagne or noodles. Sprinkle with some Parmesan cheese. Repeat the layering until you have used all the ingredients, ending with a sheet of lasagne, completely covered with the sauce (even the corners). If using cooked noodles, make only 2 layers of noodles. Bake, covered, for 30 minutes. Then uncover and bake for 5

minutes. Remove the pan from the oven and let the lasagne set for 5 minutes before slicing and serving.

VARIATIONS

Tex-Mex Instant Lasagne: In step 2, season the sautéed meat with 1 teaspoon each of ground cumin, oregano, and chili powder. Then, in step 3, add ¼ cup salsa and 1 can (4 ounces) green chiles, chopped, to the spaghetti sauce. Arrange the layers as described, substituting grated sharp Cheddar or Monterey Jack for the Parmesan cheese.

Vegetarian Instant Lasagne: Omit the meat. Instead, chop up 1 can (16 or 19 ounces) chick-peas, drained, and mix them into the spaghetti sauce. Proceed with the recipe.

Spaghetti à la Lasagne

PASTA: *Strands*
MAKES: *4 servings*
TIME: *25 minutes*

I included a slightly different version of this recipe in the *Monday-to-Friday Cookbook,* and it proved to be a great hit—with chil-

dren because of the taste and with adults because of the ease of preparation.

I appreciate a good lasagne but hate the work and time involved—precooking the noodles, layering the dish, and baking it for an hour. So I came up with this uncomplicated spaghetti recipe which combines all the elements of a good lasagne without the trouble. Adults with more sophisticated tastes should take a look at some of the variations below.

Salt
2 cups tomato or spaghetti sauce, homemade (see page 245) or commercially prepared
¾ to 1 pound spaghetti, spaghettini, perciatelli, or bucatini
¼ cup olive oil
½ pound (1 cup) ricotta cheese (whole or part-skim)
¼ cup grated Parmesan cheese
Freshly ground black pepper

1. Bring a large pot of salted water to a boil for the pasta. Heat the tomato sauce in a small saucepan. (Or do this at the last minute in a microwave for 1 minute.)

2. Add the pasta to the boiling water and cook until it is tender but still firm to the bite, 8 to 10 minutes.

3. Meanwhile, combine the olive oil, ricotta, and Parmesan in a small mixing bowl and season to taste with salt and pepper.

4. When the pasta is done, drain it and return it to the pot, off the heat. Add the spaghetti sauce and toss well.

5. Ladle the pasta and sauce into deep bowls, and top each portion with a dollop of the ricotta mixture.

VARIATIONS

Spaghetti à la Lasagne with Meat: Crumble ½ pound ground veal or beef in a large skillet and cook, stirring constantly, over medium heat until the meat is no longer pink. Stir into the spaghetti sauce, bring the sauce to a simmer, and proceed as directed.

Spaghetti à la Lasagne with Beans: Heat 1 can (16 ounces) red, black, or white beans, drained, in the sauce in step 1 and proceed as directed.

ESPECIALLY GOOD FOR ADULTS

In step 3, once you have combined the cheeses and olive oil, add:
- *¼ cup chopped fresh parsley or basil, 1 tablespoon minced fresh tarragon or sage, or 1½ teaspoons crumbled dried tarragon, marjoram, sage, or rosemary.*
- *Or 2 tablespoons of a more aromatic cheese, such as Maytag blue.*
- *Or 1 tablespoon olive paste, anchovy or sun-dried tomato paste, tapenade, or pesto.*

Pasta with Four Cheeses

PASTA: *Thin strands, ribbons, or small shapes*
MAKES: *2 servings*
TIME: *10 to 15 minutes*

While working on this book, I often ended the week with bits and pieces of leftover cheese in the refrigerator—so I decided to find a way to use them up in a quick pasta sauce.

Because I was using what I had on hand that day, the sauce, although scrumptious, turned out stringier than I would have liked because it contained too much mozzarella. You can use mozzarella, of course, but you'll have a smoother sauce if you don't. And the sauce will be creamier if you include at least one soft cheese such as ricotta, cottage, or a mild chèvre.

Salt
1 cup mixed cheeses, such as Gruyére, mozzarella, ricotta, and chèvre
1 tablespoon dry white wine
2 cups fine egg noodles, vermicelli, or small pasta shapes
Freshly ground black pepper

1. Bring a medium-size pot of salted water to a boil for the pasta.

2. Dice the Gruyère and mozzarella into ¼-inch cubes. Combine the cheeses with the white wine in the top of a double boiler, or in a microwave-proof dish that's large enough to accommodate the cooked pasta. Cover the microwaveable dish and set it aside. If you are using a double boiler, melt the cheese in the top pot over simmering water while the noodles are cooking.

3. Add the pasta to the boiling water, and cook until it is tender but still firm to the bite, 3 to 8 minutes (depending on the pasta you are using).

4. When the pasta is done, toss it with the melted cheese. Or if you are using a microwave oven, heat the cheese for 1 minute. Whisk it vigorously and return it to the microwave for 20 seconds. Add the drained pasta to the melted cheese, right in the microwave dish, and toss. Season with lots of freshly ground pepper.

VARIATIONS

■ Other cheese combinations to try: Cottage cheese with Cheddar; ricotta with Parmesan; Gorgonzola with cottage or ricotta; Brie with cottage or ricotta; Parmesan, Gruyère, and cottage; feta with ricotta.
■ Other ingredients to add while you are tossing the melted cheese and pasta: 1 small tomato, diced, and/or ¼ cup minced fresh herbs, such as parsley or basil.

Linguine with Gorgonzola and Walnuts

PASTA: *Thin ribbons*
MAKES: *4 to 6 servings*
TIME: *25 minutes*

Emilio Rossi, a friend from Assisi, is a wonderful pasta cook, and this recipe is based on one he prepares often. Emilio's recipe calls for heating half a pound of sweet Gorgonzola, along with some whole garlic cloves, in the top of a double boiler and serving it over short pasta. That's it. Nothing could be easier or more delicious—ideal when you have weekday dinner guests!

Unfortunately not everyone can get sweet (dolce) Gorgonzola, and the type generally available in this country is too salty to be used plain. To soften and sweeten the regular Gorgonzola, I add cream, broth, and sometimes Madeira or butter. The addition of a liquid makes the sauce thinner than Emilio's version, so I serve it over long pasta instead of short shapes.

To complete the meal, follow this with a salad, which might include a few leaves of sharp-flavored greens such as escarole or watercress. The linguine is wonderful as an appetizer before veal roast, sautéed chicken breasts, or poached salmon.

This sauce looks especially pretty over spinach or beet noodles. But don't go out of your way to hunt them down—they contribute to the color but not to the flavor of the dish.

Salt
1 pound linguine fine, or spinach or beet
   fettuccine
½ pound Gorgonzola, Roquefort, or
   another good-quality blue cheese
½ cup chicken broth
½ cup heavy cream
1 clove garlic, peeled
1 cup shelled walnuts
Freshly ground black pepper

1. Bring a large pot of salted water to a boil. Add the pasta and cook until it is tender but still firm to the bite, 8 to 10 minutes.

2. Meanwhile, crumble the cheese in the top of a double boiler. Add the broth, heavy cream, and garlic clove. Set the double boiler over medium-high heat, cover, and cook, until the cheese has melted, 3 to 4 minutes. Keep the sauce warm in the double boiler over low heat. While the sauce is heating and the pasta is boiling, chop the walnuts.

3. Drain the pasta and return it to the cooking pot. Discard the clove of garlic, and toss the Gorgonzola sauce with the pasta. Season

to taste with lots of black pepper. Sprinkle walnuts over each portion and serve immediately.

VARIATIONS

There are so many ways you can vary this recipe that just listing a few should point you in the right direction toward creating your own.

Rossi Porcini: Emilio softens dried porcini mushrooms (see Variations, page 83), then chops them and adds them to the double boiler as the cheese is melting.

Melted Gorgonzola with Currants: Add ¼ cup currants to the cheese in the double boiler.

Melted Gorgonzola with Spirits: Substitute ½ cup Madeira for the broth, or use ¼ cup each of broth, Madeira, cream, and butter.

Melted Gorgonzola with Herbs: In step 3, toss the pasta and sauce with ¼ cup minced parsley or snipped chives.

SECOND TIME AROUND

Reheat the pasta and sauce in the top of a double boiler over simmering water. Or if you have enough leftovers, place them in a baking dish, sprinkle the top with bread crumbs, ground pecans, or ground walnuts, and bake, uncovered, until heated through, about 30 minutes.

MICROWAVE SAUCE

If you don't own a double boiler and don't want to go to the trouble of creating a makeshift one, you certainly can make the Gorgonzola sauce (preceding recipe) in the microwave. Prepare it just before the pasta will be done.

Combine the chicken broth and cream (omit the garlic) in a 10-inch glass or ceramic dish (preferably round). Heat at 100% power, uncovered, for 1 minute.

 Crumble the cheese over the top, cover, and heat for 1 minute more. Using a whisk, beat the cheese into the liquid.

New-Fashioned Macaroni and Cheese

PASTA: *Small or medium-size tubes and fancy shapes*
MAKES: *4 servings*
TIME: *25 minutes*

This is a repeat of a recipe I included in the *Monday-to-Friday Cookbook*. If I don't have a batch of frozen white sauce on hand when I crave macaroni and cheese dur-

ing the week, I make it this way. Melting cheese into a cornstarch-thickened milk mixture cuts the preparation time in half. Choose the larger amount of cheese if you prefer a heady cheese flavor over a subtle one.

For a more authentic old-fashioned macaroni and cheese, turn to Super Deluxe Macaroni and Cheese (see Index). Kids love both versions.

> Salt
> ½ pound elbow macaroni, penne, gemelli, or gnocchi pasta
> ¼ to ½ pound sharp Cheddar cheese, or half Cheddar and half Parmesan
> 2 cups milk, preferably low-fat
> 2 tablespoons cornstarch
> 2 teaspoons Worcestershire sauce
> Cayenne pepper

1. Bring a large pot of salted water to a boil. Add the pasta and cook until it is tender but still firm to the bite, 7 to 8 minutes.

2. While the water is coming to a boil, grate the cheese, or cut it into ¼-inch cubes.

3. Add the pasta to the boiling water, and then begin the sauce: Whisk the milk and cornstarch together in a nonreactive medium-size saucepan. Slowly bring the mixture to a simmer, whisking constantly, over medium heat. As the milk comes to a simmer, it will thicken.

4. Stir three-quarters of the cheese into the sauce and reduce the heat to low. Cook, stir-

ring constantly, until the cheese melts, about 1 minute. Add the remaining cheese, remove the pan from the heat, and let that cheese melt by the heat of the sauce. Add the Worcestershire sauce, and season to taste with salt and cayenne pepper.

5. Drain the pasta and return it to the pot, off the heat. Toss the pasta with the sauce and serve immediately.

VARIATIONS

Quick Macaroni and Cheese with Ham: In step 4, fold 1 cup diced lean ham into the macaroni and sauce.

Peas and Macaroni and Cheese: In step 3, add 1 package (10 ounces) frozen petite peas, thawed, to the thickened milk and simmer for a minute just to heat through.

Perciatelli with Curried Yogurt Sauce

PASTA: *Strands or stuffed pasta*
MAKES: *4 to 6 servings*
TIME: *25 minutes*

Here's a delightfully different sauce to pair with pasta. As with all of the recipes in this book, it is a blueprint for myriad variations. Take a look below to see how this sauce also accommodates vegetables and ground meat.

For a dessert after a pasta dish with an exotic sauce like this one, try a combination of mango, banana, and pineapple slices topped with chopped fresh mint.

Salt
1 pound perciatelli,
*   spaghettini, or*
*   meat-filled ravioli*
2 cloves garlic
1 onion
1 quarter-size slice fresh ginger
1 teaspoon ground cumin
1 teaspoon ground coriander
1 teaspoon curry powder or ground
*   turmeric*
½ teaspoon ground cinnamon
½ teaspoon ground cardamom
2 tablespoons vegetable oil
1 cup canned crushed tomatoes
1 cup plain yogurt, preferably
*   nonfat*
Freshly ground black pepper

1. Bring a large pot of salted water to a boil. Add the pasta and cook until it is tender but still firm to the bite, about 10 minutes. (If you are using fresh ravioli, wait until after the sauce is done because fresh ravioli takes only 3 or 4 minutes to cook.)

2. Meanwhile peel the garlic, onion, and ginger, and then finely chop them in a food processor. Measure out the spices and combine them in a little cup.

3. Heat the oil in a medium-size skillet over medium heat. Add the onions, garlic, and ginger and sauté until slightly tender, about 3 minutes.

4. Stir the mixed spices into the onions. Add the tomatoes, cover, and simmer over low heat until the onions are very soft, 5 to 10 minutes. Add the yogurt and simmer, uncovered, over low heat just until it has warmed. Do not let it boil or the yogurt will separate and curdle (don't worry if it does, the sauce will still taste good). Season to taste with salt and pepper. Remove the skillet from the heat and keep warm, covered, off the heat.

5. Drain the pasta and portion it out. Ladle some sauce over each portion and serve immediately.

VARIATIONS

■ With meat: In step 4, right after you add the spices, stir in ½ pound ground beef or lamb; cook until the meat is no longer pink. Then add the tomatoes and proceed with the recipe.

■ With vegetables: In step 4, after you have simmered the onions with the tomatoes, add

1 package (10 ounces) frozen petite peas or lima beans, thawed, or chopped fresh spinach. Simmer, covered, just until heated through, 3 or 4 minutes, then add the yogurt.

■ With herbs: In step 4, after you have added the yogurt, stir in ½ cup chopped fresh cilantro or mint.

Pesto Tortellini with Four Cheeses

PASTA: *Stuffed pasta*
MAKES: *4 to 6 servings*
TIME: *20 to 25 minutes*

I f you are among the lucky few who don't count calories, then go ahead and make this any day of the week. The rest of us will indulge in this luxurious pasta only on special nights. It is great to serve to guests during the workweek because the flavor is grand but the work is undemanding.

With this opulent dish, the only other course you might serve would be a green salad tossed with strips of fresh fennel or a plate of steamed vegetables. If you think you'll have room for dessert, make sure it is light and fruit-based.

Salt
1 pound stuffed pasta, such
   as tortellini or ravioli filled
   with pesto, meat, or porcini
   mushrooms
2 ounces Gorgonzola dolce, Roquefort,
   or other blue cheese
2 ounces fresh soft chèvre or feta
   cheese
2 ounces fontina or Gouda cheese
1 cup heavy cream
½ cup grated Parmesan or Asiago
   cheese
Freshly ground black pepper

1. Bring a large pot of salted water to a boil. Add the pasta and cook until it is tender but still firm to the bite, about 5 minutes.

2. While the water is coming to a boil, crumble the Gorgonzola and chèvre (you'll have about ⅓ cup of each) and dice the fontina into tiny bits.

3. About 5 minutes before the pasta is done, bring the cream to a simmer in a large skillet over medium-low heat. When it is bubbling, add the fontina, Gorgonzola, and chèvre. Whisk continuously over low heat until the cheeses are melted, about 2 minutes. Add the Parmesan and simmer until it has melted into the cream, about 30 seconds. Season to taste with fresh pepper.

4. Drain the pasta and portion it out. Spoon some cheese sauce over each portion and serve immediately.

VARIATIONS

■ Lighter version: Substitute low-fat mozzarella for the fontina and nonfat ricotta for the chèvre. Use only 1 ounce of Gorgonzola and omit the Parmesan. Simmer the cheese in 1 cup chicken broth or evaporated skimmed milk instead of the heavy cream, and stir in 1 cup thinly sliced scallions.

■ With herbs: In step 3, when all the cheese has melted into the cream, add ¼ cup minced fresh basil, chives, or Italian parsley, or 1 tablespoon minced fresh sage. Or you could simmer the heavy cream with ½ teaspoon crumbled dried rosemary or thyme.

■ With mushrooms: Soften ½ ounce dried mushrooms in ¼ cup of hot water, and then chop them. In step 3, before adding the cheeses, simmer the mushrooms in the heavy cream for 3 minutes. Or sauté ½ pound sliced fresh mushrooms in 1 tablespoon butter until soft, add them to the heavy cream, and continue.

SECOND TIME AROUND

Reheat leftovers in a microwave oven or in a double boiler. Or top the leftovers with bread crumbs and bake them at 300°F until hot, about 20 minutes.

Puffed Creamy Pasta

PASTA: *Small tubes or cut ribbons*
MAKES: *4 servings*
TIME: *20 minutes preparation, plus 20 minutes no-work cooking time*

During the week, it makes sense to serve this for dinner if you already have cooked pasta on hand. It is also a good bet on a night when you have more time than usual to prepare dinner or when guests are coming over. The dish looks special, yet many of the steps can be prepared the day ahead. If you are going to serve this to guests, use a colorful mix of pasta like "tricolor" fusilli. Also keep it in mind for a night when you are eating "seriatimly" because it tastes as good at room temperature as it does hot from the oven.

Serve this with a salad on the side and follow it with a luscious dessert. If you are entertaining, you might want to start with a vegetable soup to stretch the number of courses.

4 cups cooked medium-size pasta, such as elbow macaroni, or cut-up noodles, such as fettuccine
¼ cup grated Parmesan or Romano cheese
2½ tablespoons butter or margarine
2 tablespoons all-purpose flour
1 cup milk (whole or skim)
Salt and freshly ground black pepper
2 ounces thinly sliced prosciutto or smoked ham
4 large eggs, separated

1. Preheat the oven to 375°F.

2. Place the cooked pasta in a large mixing bowl. Add the cheese and stir to combine. Set aside. Use ½ tablespoon of the butter to lightly butter a shallow glass or ceramic baking dish that will hold a generous quart.

3. Melt the remaining 2 tablespoons butter in a small saucepan over medium heat. When the butter has melted, whisk in the flour and cook just until the two are well combined. Add the milk in fourths, beating vigorously after each addition to create a smooth paste and avoid lumps. When all the milk is in, bring the sauce to a simmer, whisking constantly, and simmer to cook out the raw taste of the flour, 1 minute. Season to taste with salt and pepper, and let the sauce cool while you move on to the next step.

4. Cut the prosciutto into thin shreds and mix them into the milk sauce. Whisk the egg yolks, one at a time, into the sauce and beat thoroughly after each addition. Work fast so

that the eggs don't have a chance to curdle from the heat of the sauce. Mix the sauce into the pasta and cheese.

5. Beat the egg whites until they are stiff but not dry. With a rubber spatula, fold them quickly into the pasta mixture. Turn it into the prepared baking dish and bake until the eggs have set, 20 to 25 minutes. Serve immediately or at room temperature.

VARIATIONS

■ The luxurious version: In step 3, add to the sauce ⅓ cup heavy cream and ¼ pound wild mushrooms that have been cooked in 2 tablespoons butter.

■ The low-fat version: Use a vegetable cooking spray to grease the baking dish. In step 2, make the sauce with oil instead of butter and with chicken broth instead of milk. In step 3, substitute sautéed turkey bacon for the prosciutto and omit the egg yolks. Beat 6 egg whites instead of 4 whole eggs.

■ With vegetables: In 2 tablespoons butter sauté either 1 cup sliced mushroom caps or 1 bell pepper (cored, seeded, and sliced) until soft. Add to the sauce in step 3.

SECOND TIME AROUND

Cut up leftovers and toss them with spaghetti sauce. Reheat them in a microwave or a toaster oven.

Spanish Eggs and Pasta

PASTA: *Small tubes or cut strands or ribbons*
MAKES: *4 servings*
TIME: *30 minutes*

This creamy scrambled egg and macaroni mélange convinced my daughter that eggs were not "yucky."

Onions and peppers, the flavors in a Spanish omelet, camouflage the eggy taste—as do the tomato sauce and chili powder, which also give the dish its yellow-orange hue.

A light broth would be a good choice for a first course, if you really need one, but this is filling enough to serve as dinner.

1 onion
1 green or red bell pepper
¼ cup olive oil
4 or 5 large eggs
¼ cup spaghetti or tomato sauce
1 teaspoon chili powder
1½ to 2 cups cooked elbow macaroni or cut-up strands, such as fettuccine
Salt and freshly ground black pepper

1. Peel and finely chop the onion. Core, seed, and finely chop the pepper.

2. Heat the oil in a large skillet, preferably nonstick, over medium-high heat. Add the

onions and peppers, and stir to coat them with the oil. Cover, and cook over low heat until tender, about 4 minutes. Meanwhile, in a small bowl, beat the eggs with the spaghetti sauce and chili powder.

3. When the onions and peppers are tender, stir the pasta into them and mix well. Add the beaten egg mixture. Using a wooden spoon, stir the mixture until the eggs are evenly distributed throughout the other ingredients. Cover, and cook over low heat until the eggs have completely set, 5 to 8 minutes. Stir the eggs every now and then so they don't stick to the bottom of the pan and scorch. Season to taste with salt and pepper, and serve immediately.

VARIATIONS

■ Instead of cooking the onions with peppers, combine them with 2 chopped carrots or ½ cup chopped celery, fresh fennel, or leftover cooked vegetables.

■ Stir ¼ cup grated cheese, such as Parmesan or Cheddar, into the eggs during the last minute of cooking. Heat the mixture just enough to melt the cheese.

■ After the eggs have set, layer very thin slices of mozzarella over them, cover the skillet, and continue to cook just until the cheese has melted.

OLD MOTHER HUBBARD PASTA

When you have absolutely nothing in the house except a package of pasta and a jar of salad dressing, you still have the makings of dinner if you turn that dressing into your pasta sauce.

Dress the hot, drained, cooked pasta with the salad dressing; the heat of the pasta will release the flavor of the dressing, and you'll have a ready-made tangy sauce.

Pasta with Poultry

Perhaps even more than meat or seafood, poultry blends with a wide variety of pasta recipes. The neutral flavor of chicken adapts well to almost any sort of pasta, sauce, or seasoning, while the stronger flavor and firmer texture of turkey call for

hearty tomato-based sauces. Both are superb in stir-fries tossed with cooked pasta.

The best cuts of poultry for these recipes are the ones that require the least amount of preparation; they can be cooked and sauced in no more time than it takes to boil the pasta. These include boneless, skinless poultry breasts; ground poultry; poultry sausages; and turkey bacon.

Chicken breasts: It is more economical to buy whole boneless chicken breasts or boneless "tenders" than the precut cubes or strips. (A "tender," or "tenderloin," is the little strip of chicken found underneath the larger half chicken breast.) I prefer the whole breast because many packages of precut strips or cubes are made with meat cut from different parts of the bird, which cook at different rates.

I always have at least a pound or two of skinless, boneless chicken breasts in the freezer. Some of them I store as cutlets to use in sautés, some I cut into small thin strips, and some into chunks. I wrap them in individual 4-ounce portions so that I can defrost just the quantity I need. The strips and chunks are ready to be used in a pasta sauce, but they are also perfect for soups, stews, and salads.

Turkey breasts: When it comes to turkey breast, matters are a little different. A turkey breast is a very big piece of meat, and my family doesn't eat enough of it to make it worth our while to buy the entire breast. In this case I find it more economical to buy boneless cubes or strips of turkey breast, which I then use the way I would boneless pieces of chicken breast. Sometimes I'll divide the pound into smaller 4-ounce packages for freezing so they will fit our needs.

The supermarket packages indicate whether the strips or chunks are taken from a mixture of light and dark meat or from the white breast meat only. Dark and light poultry meats cook at different rates. Be sure to use either all-light or all-dark turkey so it cooks evenly. I also recommend that instead of the turkey packaged by the supermarket, you buy cuts of turkey packaged by a reputable company, with a brand name you know and like. I avoid the supermarket's own packaged turkey because I'm not sure

about the quality. But if you've tried it and have always had satisfactory results, then go ahead and use it.

Ground poultry: These days ground turkey, fashioned from the breast of turkey or from a mix of breast and dark meat, is as readily available as ground chicken. With its more pronounced flavor, it is a lovely change from ground chicken, and in fact, I prefer it. If the ground turkey includes both light and dark meat, it will have more flavor and texture than if it is taken from the breast alone. If you don't mind the additional fat, choose the mixed turkey to substitute for ground beef in spaghetti sauces, meatballs, chilis, and so on. If, however, you are on a very strict fat-free diet, then stick with ground turkey that is made purely from the breast.

Ground turkey is extremely perishable and should be used on the day of purchase. If you can't use it right away, freeze it, packaged in 4-ounce portions; it will keep for up to a month.

Because turkey tends to stay clumpy as it cooks, when sautéing it, you'll have to keep breaking it up with a spoon until it is cooked through.

Smoked poultry breasts, poultry sausage, and turkey bacon: The smoked version of both chicken and turkey breasts are available at the deli counter in your supermarket. You can purchase a smoked chicken breast whole and turkey breast by the pound. The smoking adds an entirely different flavor to a dish and with no extra work on your part.

If you love sausages and bacon but stay away from them because of their high fat content, you should experiment with the wonderful lean poultry sausages and turkey bacon now commonly available in supermarkets. They are ideal in pasta dishes, where they add a spicy bite without the usual fat.

There are several varieties of chicken and turkey sausages on the market, from sage-imbued breakfast links to fiery hot Italian-style sausages. Try different ones to discover those you prefer. I happen to love the hot Italian-style sausages because they are so peppery. All of these are great sliced and sautéed, and then tossed over pasta with a ready-made spaghetti sauce—a delicious and filling meal that you can assemble at a moment's notice.

MATCHING POULTRY CUTS TO PASTA SHAPES

In general, pasta sauces made with ground or minced poultry should be paired with ribbons or strands, such as spaghetti.

Pasta dishes with larger chunks of chicken or turkey are best matched with short tubes or fancy shaped pasta, such as penne or rotelle. The larger the piece of poultry, the larger the pasta shape.

The only exception I would make is when you are cooking chicken cutlets to serve with pasta. In this case select a soft ribbon noodle, like fresh linguine, as a pasta bed for the cutlets, or choose a small pasta like orzo and serve it on the side.

LEFTOVER POULTRY FOR PASTA DISHES

There are few easier ways of recycling leftover poultry than including them in a freshly made pasta dish.

If you have leftover roasted chicken, game hens, or turkey, remove all the skin and fat, and then cut the leftover meat into cubes or strips. Toss the pieces in a dressing and you have the makings of a pasta salad.

Or you can reheat the poultry in a homemade white sauce (see Index) or a commercial spaghetti sauce and toss the sauce over the pasta.

You can also toss the cubes of leftover poultry with a spoonful or so of a pesto or salsa, reheat it, and mix it with cooked pasta.

Compose a soup with chicken broth, thawed frozen vegetables, diced leftover poultry, and some tiny shaped pasta or broken pieces of thin vermicelli.

Stir-fry some fresh vegetables in olive oil, add the strips or cubes of leftover poultry to reheat them, toss in some fresh herbs, and serve that over pasta.

Caribbean Chicken with Tender Noodles

PASTA: *Fresh ribbons or egg noodles*
MAKES: *4 to 6 servings*
TIME: *25 to 30 minutes*

My preference for the exotic clearly comes through here. This is a recipe for those who like the contrast of sweet and fiery hot. The smoked chicken breast called for is a lovely alternative to plain chicken and can be found at supermarket deli counters, in gourmet stores, and in butcher shops.

Salt
8 cloves garlic
½ to ¾ pound smoked chicken breast
  (1 whole breast)
2 tablespoons vegetable oil
1 can (14½ ounces) stewed
  tomatoes
2 tablespoons lime juice
1 teaspoon dried oregano
1 teaspoon dried red pepper flakes
½ cup golden raisins
¾ pound fresh linguine or fettuccine
Freshly ground black pepper

1. Bring a large pot of salted water to a boil for the pasta.

2. While the water is heating, peel and mince the garlic. Remove the skin and fat from the smoked chicken, and cut it into ½-inch cubes.

3. Heat the oil in a large skillet over medium-high heat. Add the garlic and sauté until you get a whiff of its aroma, about 10 seconds. Add the tomatoes, lime juice, oregano, dried pepper flakes, raisins, and chicken. Cover and simmer until all the ingredients are hot, about 5 minutes.

4. While the sauce is simmering, add the pasta to the boiling water and cook until it is tender but still firm to the bite, 3 to 4 minutes.

5. Drain the pasta and arrange some on each plate. Season the sauce with salt and pepper, and ladle some over each portion. Serve immediately.

Curried Turkey Casserole

PASTA: *Ribbons or egg noodles*
MAKES: *4 to 6 servings*
TIME: *20 minutes preparation plus 20 minutes no-work cooking time*

To be sure, there is no dearth of recipes for using up Thanksgiving leftovers. But it couldn't hurt to add a quick and easy one to the repertoire. After all that work, it's

...other meal with...
...casserole,

...gg

...eas,

powder
...black pepper
...lmonds

...oven to 350°F.

2. Bring a large pot of salted water to a boil. Add the noodles and cook until they are tender but still firm to the bite, about 6 minutes.

3. Meanwhile, combine the peas, turkey, and vegetable oil in a large mixing bowl. In a small bowl, whisk the evaporated milk and curry powder together; then add this to the peas and turkey.

4. Drain the noodles and add them to the ingredients in the mixing bowl. Toss well to combine, and season to taste with salt and pepper. Turn the mixture into a 9-inch square baking dish, and top it with the sliced almonds. Bake until the casserole is very hot and the top is somewhat crusty, about 20 minutes. Serve immediately.

VARIATIONS

Green Chili Turkey Casserole: Substitute 1 can (14½ ounces) stewed tomatoes, drained and chopped, for the evaporated milk. Instead of the peas, mix in 1 package (10 ounces) frozen corn kernels, thawed, and 1 can (4 ounces) green chiles, chopped. Omit the curry and season with 1 teaspoon chili powder. Stir in ½ cup shredded sharp Cheddar cheese, and top with bread crumbs instead of almonds.

Four-Cheese Turkey Casserole: Omit the curry powder and sliced almonds. Toss the noodles, peas, and turkey with the evaporated milk and ¼ cup each of four chopped, grated, or shredded cheeses, such as blue, mozzarella, Parmesan, and ricotta. Top with bread crumbs, and bake until the cheeses have melted and are bubbling.

Tomato and Olive Turkey Casserole: Omit the curry powder, evaporated milk, and sliced almonds. Toss the noodles, peas, and turkey with 1 can (16 ounces) crushed tomatoes, ½ cup sliced black or green olives, and 2 tablespoons drained capers. Top with bread crumbs mixed with grated Parmesan cheese.

Feisty Chicken and Black Beans over Gnocchi

PASTA: *Medium-size fancy shapes*
MAKES: *4 to 6 servings*
TIME: *25 to 30 minutes*

I love this earthy pasta dish—especially with a side of fresh greens or hot corn on the cob.

Salt
¾ pound gnocchi pasta or
    medium-size shells
⅓ cup olive oil
2 lemons
2 cups freshly cooked or 1 can (16 ounces)
    black beans
¾ pound smoked chicken breast
    (1 whole breast)
2 medium-size tomatoes
2 jalapeño peppers (fresh or pickled)
Freshly ground black pepper

1. Bring a large pot of salted water to a boil. Add the pasta and cook until it is tender but still firm to the bite, 8 to 10 minutes.

2. Meanwhile, pour the olive oil into a large mixing bowl. Grate the zest of the lemons directly into the mixing bowl. Squeeze enough juice to make ¼ cup and add it to the bowl. Drain and rinse the black beans and add them. Remove the skin of the smoked chicken and cut off any fat. Cut the chicken into ½-inch cubes and add them to the mixing bowl. Quarter the tomatoes and remove their seeds with a spoon. Chop the tomatoes and add them to the bowl. Mince the jalapeño peppers and add them. Toss all the ingredients together, and season to taste with salt and pepper.

3. Drain the pasta and rinse it under cold water. Drain it again and add it to the other ingredients. Toss and serve at room temperature, or cover and chill until later.

SECOND TIME AROUND

Make a sharp dressing by combining mayonnaise or plain yogurt, fresh lemon juice, and chopped fresh cilantro or parsley. Toss the leftovers with enough dressing to moisten them.

Herbed Turkey and Walnuts over Margherita Noodles

PASTA: *Fancy strands*
MAKES: *4 servings*
TIME: *25 to 30 minutes*

W ith its not-too-assertive but delicious flavor, this is a dish that ought to appeal to a range of people. Paprika adds a gentle kick, but more important, it masks the grayish hue of the turkey.

This is light enough to need a second course, so I serve either grated carrots with the pasta dish or a beet salad afterward.

Salt
¾ pound Margherita pasta or fusilli lunghi
1 small onion
1 cup fresh parsley leaves
1 cup shelled walnuts
¼ cup vegetable oil
¾ pound ground turkey
1 tablespoon paprika
¼ cup plain nonfat yogurt
Freshly ground black pepper

1. Bring a large pot of salted water to a boil. Add the pasta and cook until it is tender but still firm to the bite, about 8 minutes.

2. Meanwhile, peel and finely chop the onion. Rinse, pat dry, and mince the parsley. Finely chop the walnuts.

3. Heat the oil in a large skillet over medium-high heat. Add the onions and cook, stirring occasionally, until they begin to soften, about 2 minutes. Stir in the turkey, breaking up the clumps with a spoon. Cook, stirring continuously, until the meat turns white-gray and is well crumbled, about 2 minutes.

4. Stir in the paprika, walnuts, and parsley, and cook until heated through, about 1 minute. Remove the skillet from the heat and stir in the yogurt. Season to taste with salt and pepper. Keep warm, covered, off the heat, until the pasta is done.

5. Drain the pasta and divide it among four plates. Spoon some turkey sauce over each portion and serve immediately.

VARIATION

In step 4, stir in 2 tablespoons drained capers and 2 tablespoons minced sun-dried tomatoes (packed in oil); omit the yogurt.

Pesto Chicken with Second-Time-Around Pasta

PASTA: *Ribbons or strands*
MAKES: *1 serving*
TIME: *10 to 15 minutes*

Here's an absolutely delicious way to make a meal out of leftover cooked pasta. The recipe is for one portion, so just multiply the proportions as needed, depending upon the number of people you are serving and the amount of pasta you have.

1 cup cooked ribbon or strand pasta
3 to 4 ounces skinless, boneless chicken breast, turkey breast, or chicken "tenders"
1 tablespoon olive oil
1 tablespoon prepared pesto
Few drops lemon juice, or to taste
Salt and freshly ground black pepper

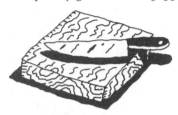

1. Chop the pasta into 1-inch lengths. Cut the chicken into ¼-inch cubes.

2. Heat the oil in a medium-size skillet over medium-high heat. Add the chicken and cook, stirring occasionally, until the pieces turn white and are almost cooked through, about 3 minutes.

3. Add the pasta, stir in the pesto, and reduce the heat. Cover, and simmer over low heat until all the ingredients are heated through, about 2 minutes. Squeeze a few drops of lemon juice into the mixture, toss, and season to taste with salt and pepper.

ESPECIALLY GOOD FOR CHILDREN

Young children might prefer either 2 tablespoons prepared spaghetti sauce or 1 tablespoon barbecue sauce to the pesto.

Rosemary Chicken and Mushrooms over Linguine

PASTA: *Ribbons or egg noodles, preferably fresh*
MAKES: *4 servings*
TIME: *25 to 30 minutes*

I love the firm texture of the chicken and carrots against the tender fresh linguine. If it is hard for you to find fresh pasta, then substitute dry egg noodles.

Think of this as a blueprint recipe—a model for countless variations on ways to combine chicken breasts and pasta.

Salt
¾ pound skinless, boneless chicken breast, turkey breast, or chicken "tenders"
3 cloves garlic
2 medium-size carrots
½ pound fresh mushrooms
⅓ cup olive oil
¼ cup dry white wine
1 teaspoon dried rosemary
Freshly ground black pepper
¾ pound fresh linguine or medium-size ribbon egg noodles
¼ to ½ cup grated Romano or Parmesan cheese (optional)

1. Bring a large pot of salted water to a boil for the pasta.

2. While the water is heating, cut the chicken into thin strips about 2 inches long and ¼ inch wide. Peel and mince the garlic. Peel the carrots and cut them into thin rounds. Stem the mushrooms and cut the caps into thin slices (reserve the stems to use in soup).

3. Heat the oil in a large skillet over medium-high heat. Add the carrots and cook, stirring continuously with a slotted spoon, for about 1 minute. Add the chicken strips and sauté in the same manner until most of the strips have turned white, about 1 minute. Add the mushrooms and garlic and cook, stirring continuously, for another minute. Add the white wine and rosemary, and cook over medium-high heat until the chicken is cooked through, 1 or 2 minutes. Season to taste with salt and pepper, and remove from the heat. Keep warm, covered, off the heat, until the pasta is done.

5. Add the pasta to the boiling water and cook until it is tender but still firm to the bite, about 4 minutes.

6. Drain the pasta and divide it among four plates. Immediately top each portion with some of the chicken, vegetables, and juices. Sprinkle with the cheese if desired, and serve.

VARIATION

■ Vegetables: For the carrots and mushrooms substitute 6 carrots, peeled and cut into thin rounds; or 1 fennel bulb, cored and cut into matchstick strips; or ¼ head of cabbage, cored and shredded; or 2 bell peppers (red or green), cored, seeded, and thinly sliced.

GIVING ROSEMARY CHICKEN A DIFFERENT CHARACTER

■**Asian flavor:** For the olive oil, substitute part sesame oil and part mild vegetable oil or peanut oil. Use fresh shiitake mushrooms, and/or ¼ pound snow peas. Substitute soy sauce and rice vinegar for the chicken broth, and omit the rosemary and cheese. Finish the dish with chopped fresh cilantro.

■**Tex-Mex flavor:** Substitute corn oil for the olive oil. For the mushrooms substitute 1 pack frozen corn kernels, thawed, and one 4-ounce can chopped green chiles. Substitute oregano for the rosemary and sharp Cheddar for the Romano. Season well with dried red pepper flakes or chili powder, and finish the dish with chopped fresh cilantro.

■**Indian flavor:** Substitute vegetable oil for the olive oil. Forget the white wine and rosemary; instead sauté 1 teaspoon each of ground cumin, coriander, cinnamon, ginger, and turmeric after you have added the chicken. Add ½ cup crushed tomatoes instead of the white wine. Omit the cheese; serve with plain yogurt, if you wish.

Saffron Pasta with Poultry Sausages

PASTA: *Medium-size or large tubes*
MAKES: *4 to 6 servings*
TIME: *30 to 35 minutes*

Although you can make this recipe by sautéing the sausages, as described, it is even better when they are grilled, making this a good choice for summertime.

If you have prepared a fire in the grill, then go ahead and create an even more delicious meal by adding grilled bell peppers, eggplant, or onions to the pasta instead of the pimientos.

Salt
4 small tomatoes
1 jar (7 ounces) pimientos or roasted red
    peppers
½ pound ziti, mezzani, or rigatoni
¾ pound spicy chicken or turkey sausages
2 tablespoons olive oil
⅛ teaspoon powdered saffron
2 tablespoons balsamic or sherry vinegar
Freshly ground black pepper

1. Bring a large pot of salted water to a boil for the pasta.

2. While the water is heating, halve the tomatoes, remove the seeds with a spoon, and cut the tomatoes into ½-inch dice. Set the diced tomatoes in a mixing bowl. Slice the pimientos or roasted peppers and add them to the tomatoes.

3. Add the pasta to the boiling water and cook until it is tender but still firm to the bite, about 10 minutes.

4. Meanwhile, thinly slice the sausages. Heat the olive oil in a medium-size skillet over medium heat. Add the sausages and sauté until they are cooked through, about 5 minutes. Add the saffron and stir until well combined. Add the vinegar and cook until some of it has evaporated, about 5 seconds.

5. When the sausages are done, add them and their juices to the mixing bowl.

6. Drain the pasta and add it to the other ingredients. Toss well and season to taste with salt and pepper.

VARIATIONS

■ If you use grilled sausage and vegetables in this recipe, omit step 2 and the sautéing instructions in step 5. Stir the saffron and vinegar together in the mixing bowl in step 5, before adding the grilled ingredients.
■ Chorizo, the hard spicy Spanish sausage, would be an excellent substitution in the sautéed version, as would ¼ pound of smoked mussels.

Smoked Cajun Chicken and Mezzani

PASTA: *Medium-size or large tubes*
MAKES: *4 to 6 servings*
TIME: *30 to 35 minutes*

This fabulous mouth-lashing recipe is as easy to make as it is superb to eat. Timid palates will enjoy it just as much if they go easy on the Tabasco.

A simple vegetable salad would be a fine contrast here, as would a plateful of steamed vegetables drizzled with lemon juice. If dessert is in the cards, then serve something with a coffee, nut, or chocolate flavor.

Salt
1 onion
4 cloves garlic
¼ cup vegetable oil
½ to ¾ pound smoked chicken breast
    (1 whole breast)
1 teaspoon ground cumin
1 teaspoon dried thyme
2 tablespoons Worcestershire
    sauce
1 teaspoon Tabasco sauce
1 jar (14 ounces) spaghetti
    sauce, or 2 cups Michèle's
    Tomato Sauce (page 245)
¾ pound mezzani or ziti

1. Bring a large pot of salted water to a boil for the pasta.

2. While the water is heating, peel and finely chop the onion. Peel and mince the garlic.

3. Heat the oil in a large skillet over medium-high heat. Stir in the onions and garlic, then reduce the heat, cover, and cook until tender and golden, 5 to 7 minutes. While the onions are cooking, remove the skin of the smoked chicken, remove any fat, and cut the meat into ½-inch cubes.

4. When the onions are soft, stir the cumin and thyme into the skillet. Then add the Worcestershire, Tabasco, spaghetti sauce, and the diced chicken. Cover, and simmer over low heat until the sauce and chicken are hot, about 10 minutes.

5. Meanwhile, add the pasta to the boiling water and cook until it is tender but firm to the bite, 8 to 10 minutes.

6. Drain the pasta and return it to the pot, off the heat. Season the sauce to taste with salt and more Tabasco if you wish, and add it to the pasta. Mix the ingredients thoroughly, and serve immediately.

SECOND TIME AROUND   *Add grated Parmesan cheese and sour cream to the leftovers. Transfer them to a buttered baking dish, top with very finely chopped walnuts, almonds, or pecans, and bake at 350°F until heated through, about 30 minutes.*

Smoked Turkey and Sweet Turnips with Rotelle

PASTA: *Medium-size fancy shapes*
MAKES: *4 servings*
TIME: *30 to 35 minutes*

Be bold—try this unusual recipe. The interplay of sweet turnips, smoked turkey, and sharp Romano cheese is quite remarkable. What's just as remarkable is how incredibly easy it is to make!

I like to serve dark pumpernickel bread and a watercress salad alongside. The only variation that would not break the harmony of the ingredients would be to substitute a high-quality smoked ham for the turkey.

> *Salt*
> *1 can (14½ ounces) stewed tomatoes*
> *1 pound (4 medium-size) white turnips*
> *¼ cup olive oil*
> *½ pound smoked turkey in a single slice*
> *½ pound rotelle (wagon wheels),*
>   *radiatore, or orecchiette*
> *1 cup grated Pecorino Romano cheese*
> *Freshly ground black pepper*

1. Bring a large pot of salted water to a boil for the pasta.

2. While the water is heating, empty the can of stewed tomatoes into a large saucepan and mash the tomatoes against the sides of the pan with a wooden spoon. Peel and cut the turnips into ½-inch dice, and add them to the tomatoes along with the olive oil. Simmer the tomatoes and turnips, covered, over low heat until the turnips are tender, 10 to 15 minutes.

3. While the turnips are simmering, cut the turkey into ½-inch dice. Add the pasta to the boiling water and cook until it is tender but still firm to the bite, about 10 minutes.

4. Drain the pasta and return it to the pot, off the heat. Add the turkey, turnips and tomatoes, and half the cheese. Toss to combine, and season to taste with salt and pepper. Serve immediately, and pass the remaining cheese on the side.

Tarragon Chicken with Bow-Ties

PASTA: *Medium-size fancy shapes, egg noodles, or fresh ribbons*
MAKES: *4 servings*
TIME: *30 to 35 minutes*

This has a divine flavor, illustrating how a few carefully chosen ingredients can harmonize to create a fine-tasting dish.

This is not a very "sauce-y" dish because the natural juices from the chicken provide plenty of moisture for the noodles. Precede or follow it with a light vegetable, such as steamed asparagus or summer squash, or a salad of cold vegetables.

Salt
½ pound bow-ties (farfalle), broad egg noodles, or fresh fettuccine
4 small skinless, boneless chicken breast halves, or ¾ pound chicken "tenders" or turkey pieces
2 cloves garlic
½ small red bell pepper (optional)
2 tablespoons vegetable oil
1 teaspoon dried tarragon
½ cup dry white wine
Freshly ground black pepper
1 to 2 tablespoons butter, cut into small pieces
¼ cup grated Gruyère or Parmesan cheese (optional)

1. Bring a large pot of salted water to a boil. Add the pasta and cook until it is tender but still firm to the bite, about 10 minutes (if you are using fresh pasta, it should only take 2 to 3 minutes).

2. Meanwhile, cut the chicken into thin strips, about 1 inch long and ¼ inch wide.

Peel and mince the garlic. Core, seed, and finely chop the bell pepper.

3. Heat the oil in a large skillet over medium-high heat. Add the chicken and stir to coat it with the oil. Add the garlic and cook, stirring frequently, until the chicken looks white but is still tender inside, 2 to 3 minutes.

4. Add the tarragon and white wine, and cook until the wine has evaporated somewhat, about 30 seconds. Cover, and cook over low heat until the chicken is cooked through, about 5 minutes. Season to taste with salt and pepper. Keep the chicken warm, covered, off the heat, until the pasta is done.

5. Drain the pasta and add it, along with the butter, to the chicken in the skillet. Toss with a slotted spoon until the ingredients are well mixed. Serve immediately, topped with the diced bell pepper. Pass the grated cheese separately.

VARIATION

Rosemary Chicken with Bow-Ties: Omit the butter, and substitute ¼ cup fruity olive oil for the vegetable oil. Substitute  ground sage or rosemary for the tarragon and serve with Parmesan cheese instead of Gruyère.

ESPECIALLY GOOD FOR DIETERS

In step 3, cook the chicken in 1 tablespoon oil in a nonstick skillet. In step 4, add ¼ cup chicken broth to the skillet as the chicken is cooking. And in step 5, omit the butter and cheese.

DUST OR FLAVOR?

The quality and age of the dried herbs and spices in a dish have a profound effect on its flavor. Be sure to take a sniff of any herbs and spices before you begin to cook—if they have no aroma, they won't have any flavor. Store dried herbs and spices away from the light, in a cool place where the temperature is constant.

Turkey Meatballs with Spaghetti

PASTA: *Medium-size or wide strands*
MAKES: *4 servings*
TIME: *30 to 35 minutes*

Meatballs made with ground turkey or veal are lighter than those made with beef or pork. But of course you can substitute beef here if that pleases your palate.

You'll notice that the meatballs are pretty small in diameter. Their petite size, plus the fact that they are made of turkey, means that they will cook quickly—always the goal in Monday-to-Friday cooking.

A watercress salad, with or without sliced oranges, would be a wonderful way to start the meal or to complete it.

Salt
1 scallion (green onion)
1 small clove garlic
1 egg
¾ cup fresh bread crumbs
2 tablespoons grated Parmesan cheese, plus additional for serving (optional)
1 pound ground turkey, veal, or beef
Freshly ground black pepper
5 tablespoons olive oil
2 cups tomato or spaghetti sauce
1 pound spaghetti or perciatelli

1. Bring a large pot of salted water to a boil for the pasta.

2. Thinly slice the scallion. Peel and mince the garlic.

3. In a mixing bowl, whisk the egg, scallion, and garlic together until well combined. Stir in the bread crumbs, Parmesan cheese, and ground turkey. Using your hands, squeeze the ingredients together until they are evenly mixed; season to taste with salt and pepper.

4. Shape the mixture into small meatballs, about 1 tablespoon per meatball, and set them on a plate.

5. Heat 3 tablespoons of the olive oil in a large skillet over high heat. Add the meatballs in a single layer (do it carefully, the hot oil may splatter) and let them cook, undisturbed, until one side is a deep brown, 1½ to 2 minutes. With a slotted spoon, turn each meatball over and cook, undisturbed again, until the other side is a deep brown, about 2 minutes. Loosen the meatballs from the bottom of the skillet with your slotted spoon, to make sure they are not sticking, and stir in the tomato sauce. Cover, and simmer for 10 to 15 minutes.

6. While the meatballs are cooking, add the pasta to the boiling water and cook until it is tender but still firm to the bite, about 10 minutes.

7. Drain the pasta, return it to the pot, and toss it with the remaining 2 tablespoons olive oil. Dish a portion of pasta onto each plate, and spoon some meatballs and sauce in the center. Serve immediately, and pass additional grated cheese if you wish.

ESPECIALLY GOOD FOR DIETERS

In step 3, substitute ¼ cup minced parsley for the Parmesan cheese. In step 5, use 1 tablespoon olive oil and cook the meatballs in a nonstick skillet.

COOKING TIP

These two secrets will ensure that your meatballs don't fall apart while they cook: First, make sure the oil you cook them in is very hot. Second, once you add the meatballs to the hot oil in the skillet, let a crust form on one side before you even touch the meatballs. I know it is tempting to push, shove, pat, and poke them the minute they go into the pan, but resist or your meatballs will crumble into pieces.

Turkey Tetrazzini with Butterfly Pasta

PASTA: *Medium-size fancy shapes or tubes*
MAKES: *4 to 6 servings*
TIME: *30 to 35 minutes*

I don't know the origins of this old-fashioned recipe but I do know that this dish is terrific for using up leftover Thanksgiving turkey. Here I have combined the traditional elements of turkey tetrazzini—poultry, pasta, mushrooms, and a cream sauce. Because this version sticks with the classic flavors, it will appeal to the entire family.

Ample enough to count as dinner, this recipe is so rich in taste and substance that I'm not sure you'll have room for dessert. If you do, though, fresh fruit would be best.

Salt
¾ pound bow-ties (farfalle), orecchiette,
*   penne, or fusilli*
½ onion
1 red bell pepper
½ pound fresh mushrooms
2 tablespoons vegetable oil
1 cup chicken broth
½ to ¾ pound roasted or smoked turkey, in
*   a single slice*
2 tablespoons all-purpose flour
1 cup evaporated skim milk or heavy
*   cream*
Freshly ground black pepper

1. Bring a large pot of salted water to a boil. Add the pasta and cook until it is tender but still firm to the bite, about 10 minutes.

2. Meanwhile, peel and finely chop the onion. Core, seed, and finely chop the bell pepper. Stem, rinse, and thinly slice the mushroom caps (reserve the stems to use in another recipe).

3. Heat the oil in a large skillet over medium-high heat. Stir in the onion, peppers, and mushrooms. Reduce the heat, cover, and simmer until tender, 5 to 7 minutes. If the vegetables start to stick to the bottom of the skillet, add some of the chicken broth. While this is cooking, cut the turkey into ½-inch dice.

4. When the mushrooms are soft, stir the flour into the skillet. Then add the remaining chicken broth and the evaporated milk. Using a whisk, stir the ingredients together. Bring the liquid to a simmer, stirring constantly so the sauce does not lump. When the liquid is simmering, add the turkey cubes. Continue to cook gently, uncovered, until the turkey cubes are hot, about 5 minutes. Season to taste with salt and pepper.

5. Drain the pasta and return it to the pot, off the heat. Add the turkey sauce and mix the ingredients thoroughly. Serve immediately.

VARIATIONS

Ham and Pasta Tetrazzini: Substitute smoked or baked ham for the turkey.

■ When you add the turkey cubes, add 1 package (10 ounces) frozen petite peas, thawed.

SECOND TIME AROUND

Add grated cheese to the leftovers, turn them into a buttered baking dish, and top with bread crumbs. Bake at 350°F until heated through, about 20 minutes.

Sweet and Tangy Chicken Livers with Fettuccine

PASTA: *Medium-size strands or ribbons*
MAKES: *4 servings*
TIME: *30 to 35 minutes*

The combination of smoky bacon, sweet dried fruit, and wine creates a perfect foil for chicken livers. I prefer to set off the fairly dull-looking sauce with a brightly colored pasta such as spinach fettuccine, saffron linguine, or tricolor fusilli. Pairing a chunky sauce with fettuccine is not in keeping with proper pasta etiquette, but not many short pasta shapes come in interesting hues.

Salt
½ onion
2 strips bacon, preferably turkey bacon
½ to ¾ pound chicken livers
¾ pound spaghetti, spinach fettuccine, or linguine
2 tablespoons vegetable oil
¼ cup dry white wine
½ teaspoon dried thyme
½ cup chicken broth
⅓ cup diced currants or dried cherries
Freshly ground black pepper

1. Bring a large pot of salted water to a boil for the pasta.

2. While the water is heating, peel and finely chop the onion. Finely chop the bacon. Trim and discard any green spots from the chicken livers. Cut the livers into ½-inch chunks.

3. Add the pasta to the boiling water and cook until it is tender but still firm to the bite, about 10 minutes.

4. Meanwhile, heat the oil in a large skillet over medium-high heat. Add the bacon and cook until crisp, about 2 minutes. Reduce the heat, add the onions, and sauté until tender, about 2 to 3 minutes. Add the chicken livers and cook over high heat, stirring constantly, until browned, about 2 minutes.

5. Reduce the heat to medium, add the wine and thyme, and cook until the wine has reduced somewhat and the alcohol has evaporated, about 2 minutes. Add the chicken broth and currants. Simmer, uncovered, until the chicken livers are cooked through, about 2 minutes. Season to taste with salt and pepper.

6. Drain the pasta and divide it among four shallow bowls. Spoon the chicken livers and sauce over each portion, and serve immediately.

VARIATIONS

You can vary the flavor by changing the spirits and the fruit: Instead of white wine, use hard apple cider with raisins or chopped dried apples or pears. Or substitute Madeira or port and combine that with a small dice of pitted prunes.

Pasta with Seafood

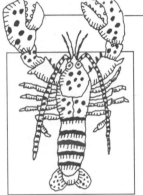

Seafood and pasta are particularly complementary to each other. Seafood is lean, delicious, quickly cooked, and a natural Monday-to-Friday choice. Pasta, with its sedate flavor, marries beautifully with the delicate taste of all fish and shellfish.

In theory, any type of seafood is a possible player in a pasta dish. Some types are better than others because of their texture or because of their flavor, and some are also better with certain varieties of pasta sauces than with others. The match of seafood and pasta depends on the type of pasta you are cooking, the flavor of the fish, and the taste of the sauce you'll be serving.

Lean fish, such as sole or cod, pairs well with strand or ribbon noodles and a rich sauce. You can cook the fish separately and just pose it on a bed of ribbon noodles, or flake it into tiny shaped pasta such as couscous or orzo. You could also cook it right in the sauce, where its flesh will break up and become an integral part of the sauce.

The sauces designed to accommodate lean fish should be delicate enough to let the taste of the fish shine through; a velvety white sauce or a smooth butter sauce are good examples.

Firm-textured and strongly flavored seafood calls for short pasta shapes. Chunks or dice of shrimp or tuna will just sink to the bottom of a bowl of linguine whereas they can be captured by the nooks and crannies of fusilli or rotelle.

Headier-flavored seafood, such as swordfish, tuna, scallops, clams, and shrimp, blend well with robust pasta sauces.

Don't forget to stock up on canned clams, tuna, and salmon as well as sardines or smoked fish. In a moment's notice you can make a meal out of a couple of cans of tuna fish or smoked clams tossed over spaghetti and olive oil.

BUYING AND STORING FRESH SEAFOOD

In the best of all possible worlds, all the ingredients you cook with would be the freshest possible and at their peak. Then there is reality. You can't always count on finding fresh-caught fish and shellfish. Seafood, though, is the one ingredient that never forgives if it is less than perfectly fresh, so if you live in an area where it is really difficult to get fresh fish, you'll do better to buy fish that has been frozen correctly or to substitute a preserved seafood such as smoked clams or oysters.

Whether you have access to a wide array of seafood or the selection is limited in your neck of the woods, you need to be an informed consumer. There are ways of telling whether "fresh" seafood is really fresh and whether frozen seafood has been properly frozen, packed, and stored.

■ Fresh fish and shellfish smell sweet, don't have an unpleasant odor, look shiny, and are springy to the touch.

■ When possible, buy fish and shellfish from a reputable fish market. They will always be fresher than the seafood in a supermarket.

■ If you have no alternative to prepackaged seafood in a supermarket, make sure the fish looks shiny and moist and doesn't have gaping gashes throughout its flesh, which would indicate that it is deteriorating.

■ When buying frozen fish, look for flesh that is solidly frozen and glossy looking, without marks of discoloration, which indicate freezer burn. The wrapping should be in direct contact with the fish. Avoid packages of frozen fish that contain "snow," which is a sure sign that the fish has thawed and refrozen.

■ Eat the fish the same day you buy it, or if that is not possible, freeze it for another day. To freeze seafood, place the unwrapped fish or shellfish, in individual portions, in a baking pan or on a cookie sheet and freeze until it is solid. Then wrap each portion, prefer-

ably in freezer wrap, label it, and store it in the freezer. Lean fish, such as sole or salmon, will keep for 3 to 4 months if well packaged; oily species, like bluefish, will keep for only 2 months.

LEFTOVER SEAFOOD WITH PASTA

There aren't as many ways you can recycle the remains of a fish-and-pasta dish as there are ways you can a poultry- or meat-and-pasta recipe. For starters, seafood is really fragile, and after cooking it just won't keep for more than a day. There is also the delicacy of the fish itself: the flesh may dry out or fall apart. However, you don't always have to throw out your leftovers because there are a couple of satisfactory ways you can recycle them—but you must do so within a day.

The first way is to create a soup: Simply reheat the remains of a pasta-seafood dish in fish broth or in a soup base created from stewed tomatoes and clam juice. Be sure to apply a gentle hand to the reheating process (no rolling boils, thank you). Sprinkle a generous dose of minced fresh herbs or sliced scallions on top, and you are ready with a second-time-around dinner.

Another way to use up those pasta-and-seafood leftovers is to bring to a simmer either a white sauce or a ready-to-eat spaghetti sauce (whichever would match the leftovers most successfully), add the leftovers, and simmer just until they are hot.

When the leftover dish is not too heavily sauced and doesn't include butter (which congeals when served cold), you can create a salad the following night: Toss the leftovers with a tangy dressing—such as Anchovy Mayonnaise (see Index) or a lime vinaigrette—and a healthy portion of diced fresh raw or lightly steamed vegetables, or minced fresh herbs. Crunchy bell peppers, strips of raw cabbage, and florets of steamed broccoli are excellent choices for the vegetables, and a generous sprinkling of fresh herbs will go a long way in reviving the dish and making it look more attractive.

Curried Crab with Fusilli

PASTA: *Medium-size fancy shapes or tubes*
MAKES: *4 servings*
TIME: *30 minutes*

If you taste this sauce by itself, you might find the curry flavor overpowering. But once the sauce is tossed with the pasta, the amount of seasoning will seem just right.

To round out the meal, follow the pasta with a substantial dessert such as a berry tart.

Salt
4 scallions (green onions)
2 medium-size ripe tomatoes
¾ pound lump crabmeat or firm skinless
fish fillets, such as monkfish or fresh
tuna
¾ pound (about 4 cups) fusilli or penne
1½ tablespoons vegetable oil
1½ tablespoons all-purpose flour mixed
with 1 tablespoon curry powder
1½ cups milk (whole or skim)
3 or 4 drops Tabasco sauce, or more to
taste

1. Bring a large pot of salted water to a boil for the pasta.

2. Trim the scallions and cut them into thin rounds. Core and halve the tomatoes, and using a spoon, remove the seeds. Cut the tomatoes into small dice, place them in a large mixing bowl, and set them aside. Pick over the crabmeat carefully for any cartilage and shells. If you are using fish, cut it into ½-inch cubes.

3. Add the pasta to the boiling water and cook until it is tender but still firm to the bite, 8 to 10 minutes.

4. While the pasta is cooking, prepare the sauce: Heat the oil in a medium-size saucepan over medium heat. Add the curry and flour mixture, and cook until it is bub-

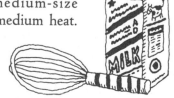

bling, about 15 seconds. Then add ½ cup milk, about ¼ cup at a time, whisking until the sauce is smooth and thickened. Add the remaining milk. Stir in the sliced scallions and simmer for 2 minutes. Add the crabmeat or diced fish, and simmer until the seafood is just cooked through, about 2 minutes. Season to taste with salt and Tabasco, and remove from the heat. Keep warm, covered, off the heat until the pasta is done.

5. Drain the pasta and add it to the tomatoes. Pour in the sauce and toss all the ingredients together. Adjust the seasoning. Ladle a portion of pasta into each bowl, and serve immediately.

VARIATIONS

Curried Tofu with Fusilli: Substitute ½ pound tofu, cut into ¼-inch cubes, for the seafood.

Curried Crab with Sugar Snap Peas: To make the pasta dish more substantial, add 2 cups sugar snap peas or frozen petite peas, thawed. In step 3, cook the snap peas for 2 minutes in the boiling water that you will use to cook the pasta. Remove them with a sieve or slotted spoon, bring the water back to a boil, and then cook the pasta. Add the drained snap peas to the tomatoes, and proceed with the recipe.

If you are using thawed petite peas, place them in a sieve and hold the sieve in the boiling water for 15 seconds; then cook the pasta.

Warm Crab and Pasta Slaw

PASTA: *Medium-size flat shapes*
MAKES: *4 to 6 servings*
TIME: *25 to 30 minutes*

I like this best in later September, when the warm summer days are almost over and there is a newborn coolness in the air. The only cooking you have to do is to boil the pasta, which is tossed while still hot with the cool crab, cabbage, and dressing.

The tender pasta and crabmeat contrast beautifully with the firm celery and crisp cabbage.

Salt
1 pound bow-ties (farfalle) or orecchiette
¾ cup mayonnaise
¼ cup lime or lemon juice
¼ small red onion
¼ head green cabbage
2 ribs celery
1 pound lump crabmeat or peeled cooked shrimp
Dried red pepper flakes or freshly ground black pepper

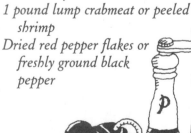

1. Bring a large pot of salted water to a boil. Add the pasta and cook until it is tender but still firm to the bite, about 10 minutes.

2. Meanwhile, in a blender or food processor, combine the mayonnaise, lime juice, and red onion. Process until the onion is puréed into the mayonnaise. Transfer the dressing to a large mixing bowl.

3. Cut the cabbage into fine shreds and add them to the mixing bowl. Trim the celery ribs, cut them into ¼-inch dice, and add them to the mixing bowl. Pick over the crabmeat carefully for any cartilage and shells, and add it to the mixing bowl. Toss all the ingredients together, and season to taste with salt and red or black pepper.

4. Drain the pasta thoroughly, add it to the mixing bowl, and toss until the ingredients are well mixed. Adjust the seasoning and serve immediately, while the pasta is still warm.

VARIATIONS

■ For extra zip, add 1 teaspoon of Dijon mustard to the mayonnaise, and some chopped bell pepper instead of or in addition to the celery.

Chilled Crab and Pasta Slaw: If you prefer to serve this as a cold salad, boil the pasta, drain it, and rinse it under cold water. Drain the pasta thoroughly and add it to the mixing bowl. Toss the ingredients together, cover the bowl, and chill the salad for 2 hours.

Scallops Casino with Bow-Ties

PASTA: *Medium-size flat or fancy shapes*
MAKES: *4 servings*
TIME: *30 to 35 minutes*

Smoky bacon, sweet scallops, and crisp celery and green peppers come together in this classic American combination. The mix of bacon and scallops pleases most people, even those who are not usually fond of fish.

Salt
½ pound bow-ties (farfelle) or orecchiette
8 slices (¼ pound) bacon
2 ribs celery
2 scallions (green onions)
1 green bell pepper
2 cloves garlic
*1 pound sea or bay scallops, or firm-
    fleshed skinless fish fillets such as
    monkfish or tilefish*
2 tablespoons vegetable oil
Freshly ground black pepper

1. Bring a large pot of salted water to a boil.

2. Meanwhile, finely chop the bacon. Cut the celery ribs into ¼-inch dice. Trim 3 inches off the scallion tops, and then slice the remainder into thin rounds. Core, seed, and finely chop the bell pepper. Peel and mince the garlic. Remove the tough, rubbery appendage from each sea scallop, and slice them horizontally into ¼-inch-thick rounds. (Or cut the fish into 1-inch pieces.)

3. Add the pasta to the boiling water and cook until it is tender but still firm to the bite, about 10 minutes.

4. While the pasta is cooking, heat the oil in a large saucepan or large deep skillet over medium-high heat. Add the bacon, cover, and cook until it is crisp and the fat is rendered, about 5 minutes. Add the celery, green pepper, scallions, and garlic, and sauté for a moment until the ingredients are combined. Cover and cook until tender, about 5 minutes. Remove the cover, add the scallops or fish, and sauté until they turn milky white, 2 to 3 minutes. Season to taste with salt and pepper.

5. Drain the pasta and return it to the pot, off the heat. Add all of the ingredients and juices from the skillet, and toss well to combine. Adjust the seasoning and serve immediately.

Scallops and Penne Rigati in a Saffron Broth

PASTA: *Medium-size tubes or fancy shapes*
MAKES: *4 to 6 servings*
TIME: *30 to 35 minutes*

Saffron gives this dish a distinctive golden color and a luxurious flavor, but if it is too dear or too difficult to find, omit it and you'll still have a yummy dinner.

I like to make this for company as well as for the family because the initial cooking can be done a day or more ahead.

Salt
3 cups penne rigati, regular penne, fusilli,
   or rotelle (wagon wheels)
2 cloves garlic
4 medium-size carrots
2 tablespoons olive oil
¼ cup dry white wine
1 cup fish stock or clam juice
1 can (14 ounces) crushed tomatoes
¼ teaspoon crumbled saffron
¼ teaspoon dried orange peel
1 cup (2 to 3 ounces) snow peas, or
   1 cup frozen petite peas
¾ pound sea or bay scallops, peeled and
   deveined shrimp, or lump crabmeat
Freshly ground black pepper
2 tablespoons butter, at room temperature
   (optional)

1. Bring a large pot of salted water to a boil. Add the pasta and cook until it is tender but still firm to the bite, about 10 minutes.

2. Meanwhile, peel and mince the garlic. Peel and thinly slice the carrots.

3. Heat the olive oil in a large saucepan or large deep skillet over medium-high heat. Add the garlic and sauté it until you can smell its aroma, about 10 seconds. Add the white wine, fish stock, crushed tomatoes, carrots, saffron, and dried orange peel. Cover and simmer until the carrots are quite tender, about 6 to 7 minutes.

4. If you are using snow peas, snap off the stem ends and pull off the strings. If you are using sea scallops, remove the tough appendage from each scallop and slice the scallops horizontally into thin rounds. If you are using crabmeat, pick it over carefully for any cartilage and shells.

5. When the carrots are tender, add the scallops (or other seafood) to the sauce. Cover and simmer over medium-high heat until they are cooked through, 2 to 3 minutes. Add the snow peas or petite peas and cook, uncovered, until they are just tender, about 2 minutes. Season to taste with salt and pep-

per. Right before serving, add the butter to the sauce, if desired, and stir just until it has melted.

6. Drain the pasta and dish out each portion. Ladle the scallops and sauce over the pasta, and serve immediately.

VARIATIONS

Chicken and Penne in Saffron Broth: Substitute ¾ pound skinless boneless chicken or turkey breasts for the scallops, and chicken broth for the fish stock. In step 2, cut the chicken into ½-inch dice.

Vegetarian Penne in Saffron Broth: Instead of the seafood, use 1 can (16 or 19 ounces) red kidney beans or chick-peas, drained, or 2 cups cooked lentils; substitute chicken broth for the fish stock. Add the beans or lentils in step 5 when the carrots are tender, and simmer until they are heated through, 3 to 4 minutes. Then add the snow peas.

ESPECIALLY GOOD FOR COMPANY

You can prepare and cook the base in advance up to and including step 3. Cool, cover, and refrigerate until the next day or freeze (up to a week) until you need it.

To finish: Thaw the base if it's frozen. After you add the pasta to the boiling water, bring the base to a full boil, then reduce the heat. Add the scallops, cover, and proceed with the recipe from step 5 on.

Shrimp Piquante with Fusilli

PASTA: *Small or medium-size fancy shapes or tubes*
MAKES: *4 servings*
TIME: *30 minutes*

This dish is arrestingly beautiful *and* delicious. Children like it (without the cayenne pepper) as much as adults do.

When it's in season, serve sweet corn on the cob either before or after. A plum dessert—a tart, stewed, or simply fresh and ripe—would make a fine close to this delectable meal.

Salt
¾ pound (about 4 cups) fusilli, medium-size shells, or elbow macaroni
1 or 2 cloves garlic
2 medium-size green or red bell peppers
12 jumbo shrimp, peeled and deveined, or ¾ pound firm skinless fish fillets, such as monkfish, mako, or swordfish, or ¾ pound lump crabmeat
1 can (4 ounces) smoked oysters, drained
2 tablespoons vegetable or olive oil
1 teaspoon paprika
1 scant teaspoon dried thyme
¼ teaspoon cayenne pepper
¼ cup dry white wine or white vermouth
½ cup chicken broth
2 tablespoons butter (optional)

1. Bring a large pot of salted water to a boil. Add the pasta and cook until it is tender but still firm to the bite, about 8 minutes.

2. Meanwhile, peel and mince the garlic. Core, seed, and cut the bell peppers into ¼-inch dice. Dice the shrimp or fish into ¼- to ½-inch chunks. Chop the oysters.

3. Heat the oil in a large skillet over medium heat. Add the garlic, paprika, thyme, cayenne, and chopped bell peppers (in that order) and sauté for 1 minute. Then add the white wine, cover, and simmer over low heat until the peppers are almost tender, about 3 minutes. Add the shrimp (or other seafood) and oysters, cover, and simmer until the shrimp are cooked through, another 2 minutes.

4. Uncover the skillet, add the chicken broth, and cook until the broth has reduced slightly, about 1 minute. Remove the skillet from the heat, swirl in the butter if desired, and season to taste with salt.

5. Drain the pasta and return it to the pot, off the heat. Add the shrimp mixture and toss well with the pasta. Ladle a portion into each pasta bowl and serve immediately.

SECOND TIME AROUND

Serve any leftovers the following night mixed with a basic vinaigrette and chopped fresh parsley or watercress leaves.

Thai-Style Shrimp with Rice Noodles

PASTA: *Thin strands or ribbons*
MAKES: *4 servings*
TIME: *30 to 35 minutes*

How wonderful to have great taste without guilt. This scrumptious mix of noodles, shrimp, and carrots bathed in peppery fish broth is a treat for gourmets and dieters alike.

For dessert, combine chunks of fresh pineapple with sliced bananas and drizzle them with port or serve them over frozen yogurt.

Salt
3 cloves garlic
2 cups fish stock or clam juice
2 cups water
2 nickel-size slices fresh ginger
1 teaspoon dried red pepper flakes
6 carrots
2 limes or lemons
¾ pound peeled and deveined shrimp, or sea scallops or lump crabmeat
½ cup (packed) fresh cilantro, mint, or parsley leaves
1 pound medium-size rice noodles, spaghettini, or linguine fine

1. Bring a large pot of salted water to a boil for the noodles.

2. Peel the garlic and thread the cloves on a toothpick (so you can easily retrieve them from the broth later on). In a large saucepan, combine the fish stock, water, ginger, red pepper flakes, and threaded garlic. Bring the liquid to a simmer over medium heat.

3. While the stock is heating, peel the carrots, cut them into ¼-inch dice, and add them to the stock. Grate the lime zest directly into the stock. When the stock comes to a simmer, cover the pan and cook over low heat until the carrots are very tender, 5 to 7 minutes.

4. Meanwhile, juice the limes and set the juice aside. Cut the shrimp into ¼ inch dice. Rinse, pat dry, and mince the cilantro.

5. When the carrots are tender and the water is boiling for the noodles, add the shrimp to the stock and add the noodles to the water. Simmer the shrimp gently for 5 minutes. Cook the noodles until they are tender but still firm to the bite, about 5 minutes.

6. When the shrimp is cooked, add the lime juice and cilantro and immediately remove the stock from the heat. Season to taste with salt. Discard the garlic.

7. Drain the noodles and divide them among four deep soup bowls. Ladle broth, carrots, and shrimp over each portion and serve immediately.

VARIATIONS

■ Substitute 2 cups carrot juice for the water. You could also substitute 2 cups freshly made carrot and fennel, carrot and celery, or carrot and spinach juice.

■ Substitute chicken broth for the fish stock and a small dice of fresh poultry breast for the shrimp.

SECOND TIME AROUND

Mix leftovers with more broth and serve as a soup. You can perk up the flavor by adding freshly minced herbs or fresh spinach leaves, rinsed and cut into fine shreds.

HOW TO ZEST LEMONS AND LIMES

Nothing adds a more distinctive citrus flavor than the grated peel of lemons or limes. Also known as zest, grated peel is produced by rubbing the skin of the fruit against the small holes of a four-sided hand-held grater or against a metal zester. As you are rubbing the fruit against the tool, watch that you grate only the colored part of the skin; the white pith is bitter.

Confetti Monkfish with Spinach Fettuccine

PASTA: *Ribbons or medium-size or small tubes*
MAKES: *4 to 6 servings*
TIME: *25 minutes*

The brightly colored vegetables and herbs make a flavorful textured sauce that is gorgeous to look at *and* wonderful to eat. It is especially attractive when served over spinach fettuccine, but the taste is divine even with plain elbow macaroni.

As a first course, I like to serve soup or salad, and for dessert, a bowlful of fresh strawberries.

Salt
¾ pound spinach fettuccine (fresh or dry),
 penne, or elbow macaroni
1 red bell pepper
6 cloves garlic, peeled
1 package (10 ounces) frozen corn
 kernels, thawed
¾ to 1 pound skinless monkfish fillet
½ cup (packed) fresh parsley leaves, rinsed
 and patted dry
¼ cup vegetable oil
¼ cup dry white wine or
 vermouth
Freshly ground black
 pepper

1. Bring a large pot of salted water to a boil. Add the pasta and cook until it is tender but still firm to the bite, 6 to 8 minutes (less if it's fresh).

2. Meanwhile, core and seed the bell pepper. Combine it with the garlic and corn in a food processor, and chop medium fine. Transfer this mixture to a plate, and coarsely chop the monkfish and the parsley in the processor.

3. Heat the oil in a medium-size skillet over medium-high heat. Add the corn mixture and sauté until you get a whiff of the garlic, about 1 minute. Add the chopped fish and parsley, and the white wine, and continue to sauté, breaking up the fish with the side of a spoon and tossing it in the skillet as it cooks. Continue to cook until all of the fish has turned into little opaque beads, about 3 minutes. Season to taste with salt and pepper, remove the skillet from the heat, and cover.

4. Drain the pasta, return it to the pot, off the heat, and add the monkfish sauce. Toss the two together and serve immediately.

SECOND TIME AROUND

Turn the leftovers into soup by adding just enough tomato juice, fish stock, or clam juice to make the mixture soupy.

Spiced Monkfish Couscous

PASTA: *Tiny shapes*
MAKES: *4 to 6 servings*
TIME: *25 to 30 minutes*

The subtle sweetness of carrots and raisins combines with pepper and saffron to flavor a seafood version of North African couscous. You might not think that these ingredients would complement the taste of the fish but they do—try it!

This is a deeply satisfying dish in itself, and you'll need no accompaniment to round out the meal. If you have room for dessert, then serve a lemon sherbet, or fresh strawberries with cream.

1 onion
2 green bell peppers
4 carrots
¼ cup vegetable oil
1 can (14½ ounces) plum tomatoes
½ teaspoon ground cumin
¼ teaspoon crumbled saffron (optional)
½ teaspoon dried red pepper flakes
1 pound skinless monkfish fillet
⅓ cup raisins
1 can (16 or 19 ounces) chick-peas, drained
2 cups fish stock or clam juice
2 cups (one 10-ounce box) couscous
Salt and freshly ground black pepper

1. Peel and finely chop the onion. Core, seed, and finely chop the bell peppers. (You may chop these together in a food processor.) Peel and cut the carrots into ¼-inch-thick rounds.

2. Heat the oil in a large saucepan over medium-high heat. Add the onions and peppers, and sauté until the onions begin to sizzle, about 1 minute. Cover, and simmer over low heat until the onions are tender, about 5 minutes.

3. Add the tomatoes, with their juices, to the saucepan. Using a spoon, break up the tomatoes by mashing them against the bottom and sides of the saucepan. Add the cumin, saffron, and red pepper flakes. Cover, and simmer until the carrots are tender but not mushy, about 5 minutes.

4. While the tomatoes are cooking, cut the fish into 1-inch chunks. When the carrots are tender, add the raisins, chick-peas, and fish. Cover and simmer until the fish is cooked through, about 10 minutes.

5. While the monkfish is cooking, bring the fish stock to a boil in a small saucepan over high heat. Stir in the couscous, and immedi-

ately cover the pan and remove it from the heat. Let the couscous steep until it has swelled up, about 5 minutes. Season to taste with salt and pepper. (I don't usually cook couscous this way because the texture is a bit gummy, but that's unimportant in this soupy fish sauce.) Ladle some couscous into each bowl, top it with the monkfish "stew," and serve immediately.

SECOND TIME AROUND

This dish is so liquid that you can easily turn the leftovers into soup by adding some fish stock, clam juice, or tomato juice. Sprinkle some chopped fresh cilantro or parsley on top.

WASHING HERBS

If your herbs are particularly sandy, as dill can be at times, here's an easy way to clean them: Soak the herbs in cold water for 5 minutes. Then swish them around a couple of times, and *lift* them out of the water, leaving the grit and sand behind.

Tomato-Braised Orange Roughy with Spaghetti Twists

PASTA: *Medium-size fancy strands*
MAKES: *4 servings*
TIME: *25 minutes*

Sweet orange roughy is available in parts of the U.S. where it is usually hard to find fresh fish. Its delicate texture (like sole) makes it suitable for this quick yet gentle way of cooking, and the unfussy tomato base should appeal to a variety of palates.

When you toss the pasta with the sauce, the fish will break apart into small pieces, making it easier to eat. If you'd like a salad before your pasta, try cucumber.

Salt
¾ pound double twists (gemelli), or fedelini or vermicelli broken into 2-inch lengths
1 pound skinless orange roughy or sole fillets
1 small onion
2 carrots
¼ cup olive oil
1 can (14 ounces) stewed tomatoes
1 teaspoon dried oregano
Freshly ground black pepper

1. Bring a large pot of salted water to a boil. Add the pasta and cook until it is tender but still firm to the bite, 8 to 10 minutes.

2. Meanwhile, remove any stray bones from the fish with tweezers. Then cut the fish into thin strips, about ½ inch wide and 2 to 3 inches long. Peel and finely chop the onion. Peel the carrots and cut them into ¼-inch-thick rounds.

3. Heat the oil in a medium-size skillet over high heat. Add the onions and carrots, and sauté for a few seconds just to coat them with the oil. Cover, lower the heat, and cook until the vegetables are tender, about 5 minutes.

4. Add the stewed tomatoes and oregano, and using a spoon, break up the tomatoes by mashing them against the bottom and sides of the skillet. Bring the mixture to a simmer, add the fish, and cover the skillet. Simmer over low heat just until the pieces of fish turn opaque, 2 to 3 minutes. Season to taste with salt and pepper.

5. Drain the pasta and divide it among four shallow bowls. Ladle the fish sauce over each portion, and serve immediately.

Swedish-Style Dilled Salmon with Penne

PASTA: *Medium-size or small tubes*
MAKES: *4 to 6 servings*
TIME: *25 minutes*

This recipe is a play on Swedish gravlax, the delicious dill-cured salmon that's often served with a sweet mustard sauce. I've changed the flavor slightly by adding yogurt, and the apple contributes a whiff of not-too-sweet fruitiness. Cucumber salad would be the natural choice for a side dish.

Keep this in mind as a "second time around" solution for leftover cooked salmon, trout, or perch.

Salt
¾ pound (4 cups) penne or elbow
   macaroni
1 can (15 ounces) salmon, or
   2 cups cooked salmon fillet
1 small Granny Smith apple (optional)
½ cup fresh dill leaves
1 scallion (green onion)
¾ cup plain yogurt, preferably
   nonfat
1 teaspoon Dijon mustard
Freshly ground black pepper

1. Bring a large pot of salted water to a boil. Add the pasta and cook until it is tender but still firm to the bite, about 10 minutes.

2. Meanwhile, drain the salmon and transfer it to a large mixing bowl. Flake the salmon with a fork. Core, peel, and cut the apple into chunks. Rinse the dill and pat it dry. Trim the scallion and cut it into large pieces.

3. Combine the apple chunks, dill, scallion, yogurt, and mustard in a blender or food processor and process until smooth. Season to taste with salt and pepper. Transfer the mixture to the mixing bowl.

4. When the pasta is cooked, drain it thoroughly, then run cold water over it to cool it. When it is cool, drain it again thoroughly, pat it dry, and add it to the mixing bowl. Toss all the ingredients together and adjust the seasoning. Serve immediately, or cover and refrigerate until later.

VARIATIONS

Party Version with Sour Cream: Substitute ½ cup mayonnaise mixed with ¼ cup sour cream for the yogurt. Use fresh salmon or another firm fresh fish.

Dilled Ham: Substitute 1½ cups cubed smoked ham for the salmon, and be sure to include the apple in the dressing.

Margherita Pasta with Smoked Salmon and Cucumbers

PASTA: *Fancy strands*
MAKES: *4 servings*
TIME: *20 to 30 minutes*

Try this recipe on a work night, when you're entertaining guests. Even small portions of smoked salmon in a creamy sauce give it a rich taste and elegant look. This is a good example of how the judicious use of luxurious ingredients can turn a humble pasta into something festive.

Pastel-hued, bright-tasting, and crisp, diced raw cucumber and fresh tomato provide contrast for the delicate salmon and cream. Simmer the vegetables in the cream just long enough to heat them through—any more and you'll alter the texture and flavor of the dish.

Another smoked fish such as smoked trout or sable could stand in for the smoked salmon. To complete the meal, serve a watercress and fresh mushroom salad to start and a lemon sorbet for dessert.

Salt
¾ pound Margherita pasta or fusilli
    lunghi, or 1 pound fresh linguine
2 medium-size or 4 plum tomatoes
2 small or 1 medium-size cucumber
2 scallions (green onions), or 2 bunches
    fresh chives (½ cup loosely packed,
    when minced)
½ pound mild smoked salmon
1 cup heavy cream
Freshly ground black pepper

1. Bring a large pot of salted water to a boil. Add the pasta and cook until it is tender but still firm to the bite, 3 to 4 minutes for fresh pasta, about 10 minutes for dry.

2. Meanwhile, cut the tomatoes in half and remove the seeds with a spoon. Finely dice the tomatoes and set them aside. Peel, seed, and finely dice the cucumber. Trim the scallions and slice them into very thin rounds (or finely snip the chives). Using a chef's knife, carefully cut the salmon into small pieces.

3. A couple of minutes before the pasta is ready, bring the salmon and heavy cream to a simmer in a large skillet over medium heat. Add the tomatoes, cucumbers, and scallions, and simmer until just heated through, about 1 minute.

4. Drain the pasta and return it to the pot, off the heat. Add the sauce and toss to mix thoroughly. Season lightly with salt and generously with fresh pepper; serve immediately.

VARIATION

Salmon and Cucumber Pasta Salad: Cook the pasta, drain it, and rinse it under cold water; then drain it again and pat dry. Make a sauce of ½ cup sour cream, ¼ cup mayonnaise, 2 tablespoons lemon or lime juice, and if you wish, some freshly grated lemon or lime zest as well. Toss the pasta, the vegetables and salmon, and the sauce together until thoroughly mixed; season to taste with salt and pepper. Serve immediately or cover and chill until later.

Rotelle with Smoked Sardines and Lemon Parsley Sauce

PASTA: *Medium-size fancy shapes*
MAKES: *4 servings*
TIME: *25 to 30 minutes*

The world is divided into people who love sardines and people who loathe them. I fit in with those who love sardines, and I like them served in just about any way.

You are in for a treat with this recipe because it tastes great and it's done in record time—with minimum effort. The hardest part is opening the sardine cans without breaking off the tab with the key!

Ice cream for dessert would be in keeping with the speed and ease of this recipe.

Salt
¾ pound (about 4 cups) rotelle (wagon wheels), radiatore, or medium-size shells
4 cloves garlic
1 cup (packed) fresh parsley leaves
3 cans (4 ounces each) smoked sardines, preferably with bones in
⅓ cup olive oil
2 teaspoons Dijon mustard
1 teaspoon grated lemon zest
6 tablespoons lemon juice
Freshly ground black pepper

1. Bring a large pot of salted water to a boil. Add the pasta and cook until it is tender but still firm to the bite, about 10 minutes.

2. Peel and mince the garlic. Rinse, pat dry, and mince the parsley. Open and drain the cans of sardines.

3. Heat the olive oil in a large skillet over medium heat. Add the garlic and sauté for a few seconds, until you get a whiff of its aroma. Stir in the mustard, lemon zest, lemon juice, and sardines, and simmer until the mixture is hot, 2 or 3 minutes. While this is heating up, break up the sardines with a spoon. Stir the parsley into the sauce, and season to taste with salt and pepper. Keep the sauce warm, covered, off the heat, until the pasta is done.

5. Drain the pasta, ladle some into each bowl, and spoon the sauce over it. Serve immediately.

VARIATION

Sardine Pasta Salad: Cook the pasta, drain it, and rinse it under cold water; drain again and pat dry. Combine the olive oil, lemon zest, lemon juice, mustard, minced parsley, and only 1 minced garlic clove. Toss the sardines and cooled pasta with the dressing, and serve at room temperature.

THE NOSE KNOWS

A good sense of smell is crucial in guiding the cook's creative hand. Many cookbook writers describe how something should look before, during, and after cooking while we neglect to describe its aroma. The nose knows when onions are not cooked enough, because they emit a faintly acrid raw aroma, or when garlic is properly cooked because it smells sweet, and when broccoli is overdone because it gives off a powerful odor.

If you begin to match the way things smell with the way they look, your nose will become as effective a guide as your eyes.

Rosy Creamed Sole Tossed with Fedelini

PASTA: *Thin strands*
MAKES: *4 servings*
TIME: *30 minutes*

Here a cream sauce, colored rose with tomato paste, carries the delicate taste of the sole to the pasta.

To make your life simpler, and for a lusher dish, simmer 1 cup of heavy cream until it has reduced to ½ cup, then poach the fish (with the tomato paste) in it until it is cooked through. Toss this sauce over the pasta, and dinner is done.

Serve steamed asparagus either with the pasta or before it, and follow with fresh strawberries.

> *Salt*
> *1½ pounds skinless sole fillets*
> *½ cup fresh mint leaves*
> *¾ pound fedelini, vermicelli, or*
> *spaghettini*
> *2 tablespoons butter*
> *2 tablespoons all-purpose*
> *flour*
> *2 cups milk*
> *2 tablespoons tomato paste*
> *Freshly ground black pepper*

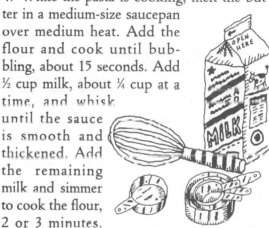

1. Bring a large pot of salted water to a boil for the pasta.

2. Remove any stray bones from the fish with tweezers. Then cut the fish into thin strips about ½ inch wide and 2 inches long. Rinse, pat dry, and mince the mint leaves.

3. Add the pasta to the boiling water and cook until it is tender but still firm to the bite, 6 to 8 minutes.

4. While the pasta is cooking, melt the butter in a medium-size saucepan over medium heat. Add the flour and cook until bubbling, about 15 seconds. Add ½ cup milk, about ¼ cup at a time, and whisk until the sauce is smooth and thickened. Add the remaining milk and simmer to cook the flour, 2 or 3 minutes. Whisk in the tomato paste, and then add the fish strips. Cook, uncovered, until the fish is just cooked through, about 2 minutes. Add the minced mint, season to taste with salt and pepper, and remove from the heat. Keep warm, covered, off the heat, until the pasta is done.

5. Drain the pasta, and divide it among four shallow bowls. Ladle the fish sauce over each portion, and serve immediately.

Note: If you already have white sauce in your freezer, defrost it and then reheat it over low heat. Add the tomato paste and fish, and cook until done. Add the mint, and pour the sauce over the cooked pasta.

SECOND TIME AROUND

Leftovers can be turned into soup. Add chopped stewed tomatoes, tomato juice, or fish stock to the remains of the dish, and reheat until hot.

Swordfish over Fresh Linguine

PASTA: *Fresh ribbons*
MAKES: *4 servings*
TIME: *20 to 25 minutes*

The contrast of the "meaty" swordfish, tangy tomatoes, and fresh cilantro is wonderful against the tender texture of fresh egg noodles. Ordinarily, I don't favor broiling fish but I make an exception in this case, because the charred flavor is important to the overall taste of the dish.

Salt
¾ pound fresh linguine, tagliatelle, or
    fettuccine
1½ pounds swordfish steak, in a single
    piece
¼ cup olive oil, plus additional for
    brushing the swordfish
1 clove garlic
½ cup (packed) fresh cilantro, mint, or
    basil leaves
2 tablespoons lemon juice
2 medium-size tomatoes, or 6 plum
    tomatoes

1. Bring a large pot of salted water to a boil for the pasta. Cut the linguine strands in half (so the pasta will be easier to toss with the swordfish and sauce later on).

2. While the water is heating, brush the swordfish with olive oil, and broil the fish, for about 10 minutes per inch of thickness, turning it over once. Broil the fish as close to the heat source as possible, so you develop some charred taste.

3. Meanwhile, peel the garlic clove, and rinse and pat dry the cilantro. Combine the garlic, cilantro, ¼ cup olive oil, and the lemon juice in a blender or food processor and process until smooth. Transfer this mixture to a glass or porcelain serving bowl.

4. Halve the tomatoes, scoop out the seeds and juices with a spoon, and cut the tomatoes into ½-inch pieces. Add the tomatoes to the cilantro sauce. When the fish is done, re- move it from the heat. Cut the fish into ½-

inch cubes, and add them to the bowl with the tomatoes.

5. When the water is boiling, add the pasta and cook until it is tender but still firm to the bite, 2 or 3 minutes. Drain the pasta and immediately add it to the mixing bowl with the fish, tomatoes, and sauce. Toss thoroughly and season to taste with salt and pepper. Serve warm or at room temperature.

VARIATION

Keep this recipe in mind if you have leftover grilled fish (fresh tuna or mako work well, too) from a summer Sunday barbecue. Follow the recipe, but serve the dish at room temperature, making sure you have rinsed and chilled the noodles before assembling the recipe.

SECOND TIME AROUND

Try leftovers of this swordfish and pasta dish with a plain or an Anchovy Mayonnaise (see Index), seasoned with chopped fresh herbs.

Fresh Tuna and Sun-Dried Tomatoes with Shells

PASTA: *Medium-size fancy shapes or tubes*
MAKES: *4 servings*
TIME: *30 to 35 minutes*

This is the fresh-fish version of one of my favorite recipes in the *Monday-to-Friday Cookbook*. The "second time around" dish is so good that you may want to make a double batch just so you can be sure of having some leftovers.

Salt
¾ pound (about 4 cups) medium-size shells, penne, or fusilli
1 large onion
4 medium-size carrots
¾ pound fresh tuna, monkfish, mako, or swordfish
¼ cup (packed) sun-dried tomatoes in oil, or 2 tablespoons sun-dried tomato paste or tapenade
1 cup fresh parsley leaves
⅓ cup olive oil
2 tablespoons black olive paste (see Note)
½ to 1 teaspoon dried red pepper flakes

1. Bring a large pot of salted water to a boil for the pasta.

2. While the water is heating, peel and thinly slice the onion. Peel the carrots and

slice them into ¼-inch-thick rounds. Cut the fish into ½-inch chunks. Finely julienne the sun-dried tomatoes. Rinse, pat dry, and mince the parsley.

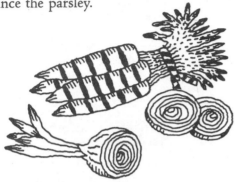

3. Heat the oil in a large skillet over medium heat. Add the onion and carrots, and sauté until somewhat softened, about 5 minutes. Add the sun-dried tomatoes and fish, reduce the heat, cover, and cook until the carrots and onions are completely tender and the fish is cooked through, 6 to 8 minutes.

4. Meanwhile, add the pasta to the boiling water and cook until it is tender but still firm to the bite, about 8 minutes.

5. Add the black olive paste and red pepper flakes to the sauce, and cook just a couple of minutes to evenly distribute the olive paste. Stir in the parsley, and season to taste with salt.

6. Drain the pasta and spoon some into each bowl; then ladle the sauce over the pasta and serve immediately.

Note: If you don't have black olive paste, pit and mince ½ cup flavorful black olives, such as Kalamata, in step 2. Add them to the sauce with the red pepper flakes in step 5.

VARIATION

Omit the fresh fish and substitute 2 cans (7 ounces each) tuna fish, drained. Add the tuna to the sauce in step 5, right before you add the black olive paste. Cook just to heat the tuna through, about 2 minutes.

SECOND TIME AROUND

Leftovers are terrific when they are mixed with chopped fresh parsley, chopped bell pepper, and either a basic vinaigrette or an Anchovy Mayonnaise (see Index).

Pasta with Meat

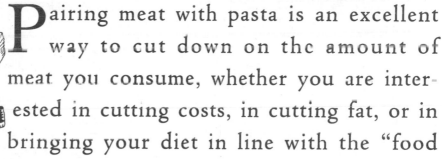

Pairing meat with pasta is an excellent way to cut down on the amount of meat you consume, whether you are interested in cutting costs, in cutting fat, or in bringing your diet in line with the "food pyramid" guidelines.

If you have ever actually weighed 3 ounces of meat (the recommended size of one portion), you know how little it is and how forlorn such a small amount looks on a dinner plate. However, mixed in a sauce and served over pasta, 2 or 3 ounces of meat is plentiful.

Whether it's beef, lamb, or pork, the best cuts to cook with pasta are those that cook the fastest. These fall into two groups: ground meats and cuts that are tender enough to be sliced into strips for stir-fries and sautés. And of course a pasta sauce is a superb way to use up leftover Sunday roast, also.

GROUND MEATS

Beef: Choose the leanest, such as ground round or sirloin. Ground chuck might be good for hamburgers, where you need a higher fat content for a juicier burger, but it is not the best choice for a pasta sauce.

Just about everything blends well with beef; in fact, you can substitute ground beef for ground veal, lamb, or sausage in any of these recipes. I happen to enjoy beef, especially with Asian seasonings but also with quintessential American seasonings.

Veal: When buying ground veal, look for the palest pink-colored meat. Use it in the more subtle and delicate pasta sauces, such as those enriched with cream or mild cheeses. Veal marries well with the spring flavors of asparagus and peas and is also a great match for sauces with Italian, Hungarian, and French seasonings—olives and sage, paprika and dill, tarragon and chives.

Lamb: Although plain ground lamb isn't easy to find in supermarkets, lamb patties are, especially during barbecuing season. These are nothing more than lightly seasoned ground lamb shaped into patties, sometimes topped with a sprig of parsley. These do just fine for sautés and pasta sauces.

When I combine pasta with ground lamb, I tend to add assertive flavors: sweet dried

fruits, salty green olives, pickles, anchovies, and the more exotic spices and herbs of the Middle and Far East, such as cumin, coriander, curry, and mint. Also good with lamb are the familiar Western flavors of wild mushrooms, lentils, citrus, tarragon, thyme, and rosemary.

Pork: Supermarkets occasionally offer ground pork. But if you can't find any when you want the flavor of pork in a pasta sauce, squeeze fresh sausage meat out of its casing and proceed as you would with ground meat. To rid the sauce of excess fat, sauté the sausage until it is well done, drain the rendered fat, return the drained meat to the skillet, and then proceed with the recipe.

Be sure the type of sausage you select is appropriate for the dish you intend to cook. Some sausages are meant to be eaten for dinner, whereas others are intended for breakfast. Some sausages are spicy and hot, others mild.

With pork I like sauerkraut and mustard, or red wine and oregano, as well as pickles and corn, allspice and anise, or caraway and rosemary. Pasta sauces made with sausage are a happy accompaniment to lentils, potatoes, chestnuts, and greens.

CUTS FOR STIR-FRIES AND OTHER SAUTES

Beef: When you want strips or cubes of beef for sautés and stir-fries, choose tender steaks because they cook quickly. The most tender are sirloin steaks. Flank steak is a lot cheaper and just fine as long as you cook it very rare; otherwise it toughens.

Avoid the packaged "stir-fry" cuts. The various pieces might come from different parts of the animal, and if so they would probably cook at an uneven rate. Also pass by the boneless cubes of beef that are recommended for stewing; they take lots of cooking time (which you don't have) to become tender.

Remember that in a pasta sauce you can always substitute leftover roast beef, cut into strips, for fresh steak. Cook the leftovers just enough to reheat them—no longer.

Veal: Loin or rib chops and veal scallops are perfect for stir-fries and quick sautés. Avoid buying veal shoulder; although boneless, it has too much fat and sinew to be of any use in quick-cooking methods.

Lamb: Lamb for stir-fries and sautés should come from the tender cuts, just as with beef and veal. The best comes from rib or loin chops. If it seems a shame to buy an expensive cut and then cut the meat off the bone to use in a sauté, think of it another way: You can get away with using the meat of one small lamb chop per person in a pasta dish. Imagine serving a single chop any other way!

Pork: If you want to create a quick pasta dish with strips or cubes of pork, buy pork chops cut from the loin or rib, also known as "center-cut" chops. These are sold bone-in or boneless, and they are cut thick or thin. Whatever you choose, they are ideal for sautéing and stir-frying because they cook quickly without drying out or turning tough.

Ham: I prefer ham over raw pork for many of my pasta dishes because I get more for my money. A little lean smoked ham goes a long way in flavoring a sauce. There are many types of ham to choose from: baked, smoked, and cured. Experiment with them, because each variety will infuse your dish with a different flavor.

If you are concerned about fat and cholesterol, look for hams that are 95% or more fat-free. These leaner hams release more water in the skillet than the fattier ones, but this is obscured in pasta sauces and does not affect chilled pasta dishes, where the ham is added uncooked.

Cured meats: Although it's high in fat, bacon is perfection with pasta. A couple of strips of bacon, cooked until the fat is rendered, diced, and stirred into a sauce will add a tremendous amount of flavor at little cost and without too many calories.

Bacon-lovers on serious fat-restricted diets should substitute turkey bacon for the real stuff.

PAIRING PASTA WITH MEATS

The rules of matching meat with pasta shapes are almost identical to those of matching poultry or seafood with pasta. The finer the meat is cut, the more it becomes part of the texture of the sauce, and the easier it is to eat it with strand or ribbon pasta. Ground meat sauces are also great with small short pasta, such as elbows or small shells.

If the meat is cut into chunks, it should be matched with medium to large short shapes, such as penne or fusilli. The larger the dice of meat, the larger the pasta shape.

All meat sauces harmonize with semolina pasta, but much can be made of the stronger-tasting whole-grain pastas if you pair them with a spicy or exotically seasoned sauce. A buckwheat noodle, for example, can stand up to a curried lamb sauce, whereas ordinary fettuccine might be lost under such strong seasonings.

LEFTOVER MEATS FOR PASTA DISHES

What better way to use up a leftover roast than to slice or cut it up for a pasta dish? Simply remove all the fat and cut the meat into thin strips or small dice. Bring a pasta sauce, either homemade or store-bought, to a simmer and gently reheat the meat in it for a couple of minutes before tossing it over the cooked noodles.

Or you can stir-fry some fresh vegetables, add the diced leftover meat at the last minute to reheat it, and then stir this into the cooked pasta. Finally, you can always make a dressing and turn the mixture into a pasta salad.

There are many ways of combining pasta, leftover meat, and one or two pantry ingredients for a speedy and satisfying meal.

Beef: Leftover roast beef is marvelous combined with pasta and corn kernels, petite peas, crushed tomatoes, stewed tomatoes, green or black olives, pickles, capers, soy sauce, Worcestershire sauce, barbecue sauce, hoisin sauce, or chili paste with garlic.

Veal: Leftover veal is wonderful over pasta. Season it with sun-dried tomatoes, crushed tomatoes, white wine, pesto, marinated artichoke hearts, black olive tapenade, chopped spinach, or dried porcini mushrooms.

Lamb: Try combining leftover lamb and pasta with tomatoes, hoisin sauce, chili paste with garlic, anchovies, prepared eggplant appetizer (caponata), thawed frozen lima beans, Indian chutney, or pickles.

Pork or ham: If you have leftover roasted pork or ham in the house, combine it with corn kernels, sauerkraut, mustard, dried fruit, nacho or jalapeño peppers, pimientos, or fried peppers with onions.

All-American Barbecued Beef with Noodles

PASTA: *Medium-size or large tubes*
MAKES: *6 servings*
TIME: *25 minutes*

This simple recipe lends itself to a world of variations—all of them flavorful. There is more sauce here than I ordinarily pair with pasta because the hollow pasta has a lot of surface area for trapping the sauce.

You can add steamed fresh or thawed frozen vegetables to the meat to round out the meal, or serve a side of carrots, corn, or anything else in season. Good cheeses to serve with this are aged Monterey Jack or crumbled sharp Cheddar.

Salt
1 pound ziti or rigatoni
1 onion
1 tablespoon vegetable oil
2 tablespoons Worcestershire sauce
1 pound ground round
3 to 4 tablespoons barbecue sauce
1 can (11½ ounces) crushed tomatoes
4 to 6 drops Tabasco sauce (optional)

1. Bring a large pot of salted water to a boil. Cook the pasta until it is tender but still firm to the bite, 10 to 12 minutes.

2. Meanwhile, peel and finely slice the onion.

3. Heat the oil in a large skillet over medium-high heat. Add the onions and sauté just to coat them with oil, about 1 minute. Reduce the heat to medium, add the Worcestershire sauce, and cover the skillet. Cook until the onions are tender, 4 to 5 minutes.

4. Uncover the skillet, add the beef, and cook, stirring to break up the lumps, just until it is no longer pink, about 1 minute. Add the barbecue sauce and crushed tomatoes.

Simmer, stirring occasionally, until the mixture is hot, about 3 minutes. Season to taste with salt and Tabasco sauce.

5. Drain the pasta and divide it among six shallow bowls. Spoon the sauce over each portion, and serve immediately.

VARIATIONS

■ In step 4, when you add the crushed tomatoes, also add 2 cups of diced freshly steamed vegetables or 1 package of frozen corn, sliced carrots, or petite peas, thawed.
■ Substitute 4 minced garlic cloves for the onions.
■ Sauté ½ pound sliced mushrooms along with the onions.

THE GROUND CHICKEN ALTERNATIVE

For people on low-fat or low-calorie diets, ground chicken is a terrific substitute for ground beef. (When you make this substitution, keep in mind that poultry cooks more quickly than beef.)

Ground chicken should look moist, and if it's prepackaged, there should be no liquid in the bottom of the package. Because it is so perishable, you should either use it on the same day you buy it or freeze it (wrap the chicken in 4-ounce portions; it should keep for a month).

Gingered Beef with Glass Noodles

PASTA: *Mung bean or rice noodles, or thin strands*
MAKES: *4 servings*
TIME: *30 to 45 minutes*

In this stir-fry of beef and vegetables, the glass, or cellophane, noodles make for a pleasant textural change from ordinary pasta.

If you don't care for the texture of cellophane noodles, however, you can substitute cooked thin noodles. Chop them into short lengths so they'll be easier to stir into the other ingredients.

This is delicious served hot, at room temperature, and even chilled, so it's a good choice for one of those coming-and-going evenings.

An exotic fruit salad of pineapple and kiwi, or mango mixed with bananas and seedless grapes, sprinkled with coconut, would fit in with the Asian nature of this dish.

¼ pound cellophane noodles, or
    2 to 3 cups cooked thin strands
2 cloves garlic
2 quarter-size slices fresh ginger
4 scallions (green onions)
½ to ¾ pound sirloin beef or
    leftover roast beef
½ pound fresh mushrooms
¼ cup vegetable oil
1 package (10 ounces) frozen petite peas,
    thawed
¼ cup soy sauce
¼ cup water
1 teaspoon sugar
Salt and freshly ground black pepper

1. Place the cellophane noodles in a large mixing bowl, add boiling water to cover them well, and let them soften, 20 to 30 minutes. When they are soft, cut them into 2-inch lengths. (If you are using other cooked noodles, cut them into 2-inch lengths.)

2. Meanwhile, peel and mince the garlic and ginger. Trim 2 inches off the scallion tops, then thinly slice the rest. Cut the beef into ½-inch cubes. Wipe the mushrooms clean with a damp paper towel, trim ¼ inch off the stems, and thinly slice them.

3. Heat the oil in a large skillet over medium-high heat. Add the garlic and ginger and sauté until you get a whiff of the garlic, about 10 seconds.

4. Reduce the heat to medium and add the mushrooms, peas, beef, scallions, soy sauce,

CUTTING THROUGH THE TANGLE

It can be awkward to cut cellophane noodles once they are softened because they can become quite tangled. Here's an easy way to handle them: Set the softened noodles in one bowl, and set an empty bowl or large plate next to it. Lift a small handful of strands out of the bowl and using kitchen shears, cut them into 2-inch lengths that will drop into the waiting empty bowl.

They won't all be exactly the same length, but it doesn't matter—they will be more manageable and blend with the other ingredients.

and water. Stir until the ingredients are well combined. Add the plumped noodles and the sugar and season with salt and pepper, and cover. Simmer over low heat until the ingredients are hot, about 3 minutes. Serve immediately if you wish, or cover the dish loosely and serve at room temperature. After a couple of hours at room temperature, cover the dish and chill it.

SECOND TIME AROUND

This is delicious the next day, freshened with a little fresh lime or lemon juice, or with diced fresh tomatoes and minced fresh chile peppers added.

STUCK-UP NOODLES

Egg noodles stick to each other even more tenaciously than ordinary noodles, so be sure that your sauce is ready by the time the noodles are cooked.

If you do wind up with clumped noodles and can't manage to unstick them, you can still make use of them: Using a sharp knife, cut the mass of stuck-together noodles into pieces or shreds and add them to a soup, where the shape and consistency won't matter much.

Or cut up the mass and add it to a stir-fry of meat, poultry, or vegetables at the end of the cooking time. As you toss the cut-up noodles in the stir-fry, they will reheat and come somewhat unstuck.

Sweet and Spicy Beef with Egg Noodles

PASTA: *Wide or medium-size egg noodles or ribbons*
MAKES: *4 servings*
TIME: *25 minutes*

This ground beef sauce has a Middle Eastern flavor. Although the seasonings might seem exotic, they appeal to children as long as you omit the fiery chile.

The spicy-sweet meat is delightful over the soft egg noodles, and the tartness of the yogurt or cheese, added at the end, provides a nice counterpoint. If you have the time, make a double batch of this and turn half into a Middle Eastern lasagne (see below). It's wonderful for a buffet supper.

A good vegetable side dish to serve with this would be broccoli, string beans, or carrots. Frozen fruit ice or sherbet would be fine for dessert.

Salt
1 large onion
1 clove garlic
1 small fresh green chile, or ½ teaspoon dried red pepper flakes (optional)
½ teaspoon ground allspice
¾ teaspoon ground cinnamon
1½ teaspoons ground cumin
¾ pound wide or medium egg noodles or fettuccine
2 tablespoons vegetable oil
2 teaspoons sugar
¾ to 1 pound ground round
¾ cup tomato purée or Michèle's Tomato Sauce (page 245)
About ½ cup plain yogurt, sour cream, or crumbled feta or Asiago cheese (optional)

1. Bring a large pot of salted water to a boil for the pasta.

2. While the water is heating, peel and finely chop the onion. Peel and mince the garlic. Seed and mince the fresh chile. In a small

bowl, combine the allspice, cinnamon, cumin, and the red pepper flakes if you are not using the fresh chile. Set the bowl aside.

3. Add the pasta to the boiling water and cook until it is tender but still firm to the bite, about 6 to 10 minutes (depending upon the type of pasta).

4. Meanwhile, heat the oil in a large skillet over medium-high heat. Add the onions and the garlic and sauté to coat them with the oil, about 1 minute. Reduce the heat to medium and continue to cook, stirring now and then, until the onions are tender, 4 to 5 minutes.

5. When the onions are cooked, stir in the mixture of spices, the fresh chile if you are using it, and the sugar. Using your fingers, crumble the meat into the onions. Sauté until the meat is no longer pink, about 2 minutes. Add the tomato purée and bring to a simmer. Season to taste with salt, and continue to cook over low heat until the noodles are done.

6. Drain the noodles and return them to the pot, off the heat. Add the sauce, toss well, and serve immediately. If you wish, top each portion with some yogurt, sour cream, or crumbled cheese.

VARIATION

Middle Eastern Lasagne: Make the sauce as directed in the main recipe, and cook the noodles. Toss the noodles with ¼ cup ricotta cheese (this will keep them from sticking). Spread half of the sauce in a 9-inch-square baking dish and top it with half of the noodles. Sprinkle the noodles with ¼ cup crumbled feta cheese. Repeat with the remaining sauce, noodles, and another ¼ cup feta cheese. Cover with aluminum foil and set aside in the refrigerator for a couple of days, or in the freezer for a couple of weeks. Thaw if needed, then bake in a 375°F oven until thoroughly hot, about 1 hour.

ESPECIALLY GOOD FOR CHILDREN

If you are convinced that your kids will not eat the Sweet and Spicy Beef with these seasonings, you can turn half of the recipe into a milder-flavored dish.

Reduce by half the quantities of the spices, chile, and sugar, and don't add those ingredients in step 5. Just crumble in the meat and add the tomato purée. Then transfer half of this mixture to a small saucepan and keep it warm. Stir the reduced quantities of the spices, chile, and sugar into the sauce remaining in the skillet, and heat through. Toss half the noodles with the kids' sauce and half with yours.

Burgundy Steak with Penne

PASTA: *Medium-size tubes*
MAKES: *4 to 6 servings*
TIME: *30 to 35 minutes*

Here is a terrific way to get the flavor of beef stew without all the work: Cook carrots, onions, and mushrooms in wine and stock, add strips of beef, and toss over pasta. Voilà—a hearty meat and pasta meal!

The only tricky part is selecting the right cut of meat. Choose a good-quality steak, which does not need a long cooking time; ordinary stewing beef requires long simmering to become tender.

Think of this as a model recipe that you can vary for any number of pasta-and-beef dishes.

Salt
1 medium-size onion
4 medium-size carrots
½ pound fresh mushrooms
2 tablespoons vegetable oil
1 teaspoon dried thyme
½ cup dry red wine
½ cup beef broth
1 pound penne
¾ to 1 pound boneless rib eye or sirloin steaks
Freshly ground black pepper

1. Bring a large pot of salted water to a boil for the pasta.

2. While the water is heating, peel and finely chop the onion. Peel the carrots and cut them into thin rounds. Stem the mushrooms and cut the caps into thin slices. (You'll save time if you cut these vegetables in a food processor fitted with the slicing disk.)

3. Heat the oil in a large skillet over medium-high heat. Add the onions and cook, stirring occasionally, until they soften and turn golden, about 5 minutes. Add the carrots, mushrooms, thyme, red wine, and beef broth. Bring to a simmer, cover, and cook gently over low heat for 5 minutes. Remove the cover, and cook over high heat until almost all of the liquid has evaporated; about 5 minutes.

4. While the vegetables are cooking, add the pasta to the boiling water and cook until it is tender but still firm to the bite, about 10 minutes.

5. Remove any fat from the steaks and cut the meat into strips about 1 inch long, ½ inch wide, and ¼ inch thick.

6. When most of the liquid has evaporated from the skillet, add the steak strips and

cook them over high heat, stirring constantly, until they turn gray, about 1 minute. Remove the skillet from the heat, season to taste with salt and pepper, and keep covered until the pasta is done.

7. Drain the pasta and divide it among four to six shallow bowls. Spoon some meat, vegetables, and sauce over each portion, and serve immediately.

VARIATIONS

Asian Steak with Penne: Substitute sesame oil for the vegetable oil, and instead of the thyme use 1 teaspoon chili paste with garlic. Replace the red wine with ¼ cup soy sauce and ¼ cup hoisin sauce.

Tex-Mex Steak with Penne: Instead of the thyme, season the vegetables with 2 teaspoons chili powder, 1 teaspoon ground cumin, and ½ teaspoon dried oregano. In step 3, add one 4-ounce can chopped green chiles and 1 chopped jalapeño pepper to the onions. Top each serving with some sour cream, sliced scallions, and shredded sharp Cheddar cheese, if you wish.

Curried Steak with Penne: Instead of the thyme, season the dish with 1 teaspoon ground cumin, 1 teaspoon ground coriander, 1 teaspoon ground turmeric or curry powder, and ½ teaspoon dried red pepper flakes. Omit the red wine and beef broth, and substitute 1 can (14 ounces) crushed tomatoes. Serve with plain yogurt, if you wish.

CLEANUP TIP

You'll find that you can be more patient about cooking if you use the waiting time to accomplish other small tasks. For example, if I say to cook something "until tender, about 5 minutes," you won't become impatient and cheat on the cooking time if you wash a couple of utensils while you wait. And since much of the tedium in getting dinner on the table lies in cleaning up afterward, using those spare minutes to wash up as you go makes the after-dinner chores less onerous.

Creamed Veal and Apples over Fettuccine

PASTA: *Fresh ribbons*
MAKES: *4 servings*
TIME: *25 minutes*

This is an unbelievably speedy party dish for midweek entertaining.

Apples love cream, as does tender veal, and both are well served by butter. The low-fat alternative (see the following page) is good but different, so every once in a while indulge in the real thing. McIntosh apples are the choice here because they are sweet and juicy and will almost dissolve into the sauce, whereas most other apple varieties keep their shape.

To complete the meal, precede this with fresh artichokes, or an asparagus or beet salad, and follow it with a chocolate or nut dessert.

Salt
1 shallot, or ½ small onion
2 McIntosh apples
¾ pound veal scallops
2 tablespoons butter
¼ cup Madeira, hard cider, or
*   dry white wine*
1 pound fettuccine or linguine,
*   preferably fresh*
½ cup chicken broth
½ cup heavy cream
Freshly ground black pepper
¼ cup minced fresh chives or thinly sliced
*   scallions (green onions)*

1. Bring a large pot of salted water to a boil for the pasta.

2. Meanwhile, mince the shallot. Peel, core, and chop the apples into ½-inch dice. Cut the veal into strips about ¼ inch wide and 1½ inches long.

3. Melt the butter in a large skillet over medium-high heat. Add the shallots and sauté until they sizzle and begin to wilt, about another 30 seconds. Add the apples

and sauté until they have absorbed the butter and are just beginning to turn tender, about 1 minute. Add the Madeira, cover, and simmer over low heat until the apples are tender, about 2 minutes.

4. At this point add the pasta to the boiling water and cook until it is tender but still firm to the bite, 3 to 4 minutes.

5. Uncover the skillet, turn the heat up to high, and add the veal strips. Cook, stirring continuously, until the strips are mostly gray, 1 to 2 minutes. Add the chicken broth and heavy cream, and cook over high heat until the veal is cooked through and the cream has thickened somewhat, about 2 minutes. Season to taste with salt and pepper, and add the chives or scallions.

6. Drain the pasta, return it to the pot, off the heat, and add the veal-apple cream sauce. Toss the ingredients together until thoroughly combined, and taste for seasoning. Serve immediately.

ESPECIALLY GOOD FOR DIETERS *Substitute 1 tablespoon vegetable oil for the butter, and cook the dish in a nonstick skillet. Omit the cream. When the sauce is cooked, add plain or low-fat yogurt (the nonfat variety is just too lean) and immediately remove the skillet from the heat so the yogurt does not curdle. Add the chives or scallions, toss with the fettuccine, and serve.*

Veal with Olives and Penne

PASTA: *Ribbons or medium-size tubes or fancy shapes*
MAKES: *4 servings*
TIME: *30 minutes*

Veal accommodates itself to any number of flavors. In this dish, the green olives add a bright accent.

To turn this into a more complete meal, add a cup or so of cooked carrots or stir in some peas. A lemony dessert would be in keeping with the style of this pasta dish.

You'll have an easier time cutting the veal into strips if the cutlets have not already been pounded into thin scallops.

Salt
½ pound medium-wide egg noodles, or penne, or rotini
¾ pound veal cutlets
½ medium-size onion
½ pound fresh mushrooms
½ cup (2½-ounce jar) pitted green olives ("martini olives")
¼ cup olive or vegetable oil
¼ cup dry white wine
½ cup chicken broth
Freshly ground black pepper

1. Bring a large pot of salted water to a boil. Add the pasta and cook until it is tender but still firm to the bite, 8 to 10 minutes.

2. Meanwhile, cut the veal into strips about 2 inches long, ½ inch wide, and ¼ inch thick. Peel and finely chop the onion. Wipe the mushrooms clean with a damp paper towel, remove the stems (reserve them to chop into soups or stews), and thinly slice the caps. Drain the olives and chop them fine.

3. Heat the oil in a large skillet over medium-high heat. Add the onions and mushrooms and cook, stirring continuously, until they sizzle and begin to wilt, about 1 minute. Add the white wine, cover, and simmer over low heat until the mushrooms have softened, about 3 minutes.

4. Remove the lid from the skillet, turn the heat up to high again, and evaporate any remaining liquid. When the onions and mushrooms are sizzling again, add the veal and cook, stirring continuously, until the meat is no longer pink, about 2 minutes. Stir in the olives and chicken broth, and cook just long enough to bring the liquid to a full simmer

(don't overdo this or you will boil the veal). Remove the skillet from the heat, and season to taste with salt and pepper. If the pasta is not done, keep the veal warm in the skillet, covered and off the heat.

5. When the pasta is done, drain it. If you are using short pasta, return it to the pot, off the heat, and toss it with the veal and sauce. If you are serving this over ribbon noodles, divide them among four shallow bowls and then top the noodles with veal and sauce. Serve immediately.

VARIATIONS

▪ This is a wonderful way to reheat strips of leftover Thanksgiving turkey, roasted pork, and even beef. Just substitute 2 cups of left-over meat or poultry for the veal, and add it in step 4 along with the olives and broth. Simmer until heated through, about 2 minutes.

▪ To turn this into a more substantial dish, add 1 package (10 ounces) frozen petite peas, thawed, when you add the green olives in step 4. Cook for a minute or so just to heat the peas.

Paprika Veal and Peppers with Fusilli

PASTA: *Medium-size fancy shapes or tubes*
MAKES: *4 to 6 servings*
TIME: *25 to 30 minutes*

Here's a recipe for pasta tossed with ground veal seasoned in a Hungarian style.

When serving this in the fall, precede it with a light broth, such as chicken with herbs. When serving it in the spring, an asparagus salad would be a fine beginning. A light fruit dessert completes the meal perfectly any time of the year.

> *Salt*
> *1 small onion*
> *1 green bell pepper*
> *2 tablespoons vegetable oil*
> *¾ pound ground veal*
> *1 tablespoon paprika*
> *1 teaspoon caraway seeds*
> *1 can (14½ ounces) stewed tomatoes*
> *2 cups fusilli, radiatore, or penne*
> *Freshly ground black pepper*
> *¼ cup sour cream (optional)*

1. Bring a large pot of salted water to a boil for the pasta.

2. While the water is heating, finely chop the onion. Core, seed, and finely chop the bell pepper.

3. Heat the oil in a large skillet over medium-high heat. Add the onions and peppers and cook, stirring occasionally, until they begin to soften, about 2 minutes. Stir in the veal and cook until the meat has turned a white-gray color and is well crumbled, 2 to 3 minutes. Reduce the heat to medium and add the paprika, caraway, and stewed tomatoes. Using a wooden spoon, mash the tomatoes against the sides of the skillet to break them up. Cover the skillet and cook over low heat for 10 to 15 minutes.

4. Meanwhile, add the pasta to the boiling water and cook until it is tender but still firm to the bite, about 10 minutes.

5. Remove the skillet from the heat and stir in the sour cream. Adjust the seasoning.

6. Drain the pasta and return it to the pot, off the heat. Add the sauce and mix until thoroughly combined. Serve immediately.

ESPECIALLY GOOD FOR DIETERS

Use just 1 tablespoon of oil and a nonstick skillet. For the veal substitute 2 cups cooked black beans (or one 19-ounce can, drained).

SECOND TIME AROUND

If you have about 2 cups of leftover sauce and pasta, you can create another meal: Slice 4 to 6 medium-size carrots, and sauté them until tender. Add the leftovers and ½ cup chicken broth, and simmer until hot. This will loosen the pasta, and add some flavor and texture, without turning the dish into a soup.

TWO TASTES FROM ONE RECIPE

How can you create two separate dishes without having to prepare two recipes? Easy. Here's what I did when I was a chef in a corporate dining room and had to serve this recipe to four meat eaters and two vegetarians.

I doubled the quantities of everything except the veal. I cooked half of the onions, peppers, tomatoes, and flavorings in each of two skillets, adding veal to one skillet and black beans to the other. Then, after the pasta was done, I divided it into two separate mixing bowls, adding the veal sauce to one and the black bean sauce to the other.

Leftovers of the two were combined and reheated together—a third dish!

Tangled Veal, Scallions, and Tagliatelle

PASTA: *Medium-size fresh ribbons*
MAKES: *4 servings*
TIME: *30 minutes*

This nest of tagliatelle and strips of veal is seasoned with rounds of scallions, flecks of hot pepper, and a touch of hoisin sauce. It is a surprising way to serve veal, but it works well—and it works with strips of lamb or beef too.

Salt
¾ pound veal cutlets or 4 veal
    chops
2 bunches scallions (green onions)
2 tablespoons vegetable oil
2 tablespoons soy sauce
1 tablespoon hoisin sauce
¼ cup beef or chicken broth
1 teaspoon dried red pepper flakes
1 pound fresh tagliatelle or Chinese
    egg noodles

1. Bring a large pot of salted water to a boil for the pasta.

2. While the water is heating, cut the veal into strips about 2 inches long, ½ inch wide, and ¼ inch thick. (If you are using veal chops, remove the meat from the bone, trim off the fat, and cut the meat into strips.) Trim 3 inches off the tops of the scallions, and slice the rest into thin rounds.

3. Heat the oil in a large skillet over high heat. Add the veal strips and sauté until they turn gray, about 1 minute. Add the soy sauce, hoisin, and broth, and bring to a simmer. Add the scallions and red pepper flakes, and simmer until the veal is just cooked through, about 1 minute. Remove the skillet from the heat, season to taste with salt, and keep warm.

4. Add the pasta to the boiling water and cook until it is tender but still firm to the bite, 3 to 4 minutes.

5. When the pasta is done, drain it. Place a portion of noodles in each plate, top them with the veal and sauce, and serve immediately.

VARIATIONS

This is a wonderful way to cook strips of steak or lamb, or to reheat strips of leftover cooked meat.

Ginger-Spiked Lamb and Fusilli

PASTA: *Medium-size fancy shapes*
MAKES: *4 to 6 servings*
TIME: *30 to 35 minutes*

Lamb is sturdy enough to stand up to the heat of ginger and the piquancy of garlic. And combined with spaghetti twists and shards of green beans, it provides a satisfying meal any night of the week.

In urban produce markets it has become increasingly easy to find French haricots verts, which I prefer to American green beans because they are reed-thin, never woody, and sweet-tasting. This dish will work fine with regular green beans if you cut them into 1-inch lengths (the short length obscures any stringiness).

Pineapple is especially pleasing after this pasta dish.

Salt
¾ pound boneless loin of lamb
½ pound green beans, preferably haricots verts
4 cloves garlic
Piece of fresh ginger, about 1 inch long and 1 inch in diameter
1 medium-size onion
¾ pound fusilli, spaghetti twists (gemelli), or rotelle (wagon wheels)
¼ cup olive or vegetable oil
¼ cup dry white wine
1 cup beef or chicken broth
Freshly ground black pepper

1. Bring a large pot of salted water to a boil for the pasta.

2. While the water is heating, cut the lamb into strips about 1 inch long, ½ inch wide, and ¼ inch thick. (If you are using lamb chops, remove the meat from the bone, cut off the fat, and cut the meat into strips.) Trim off the stem ends and cut the green beans (regular and haricots verts) into ¾- to 1-inch lengths. Peel and mince the garlic. Peel and mince the ginger. Peel and finely chop the onion. (You may, if you wish, chop the garlic, ginger, and onion in the food processor.)

3. Add the pasta to the boiling water and cook until it is tender but still firm to the bite, 8 to 10 minutes.

4. Meanwhile, heat the oil in a large skillet over high heat. Add the garlic, ginger, and onions. Stir-fry over high heat, stirring con-

tinuously, until the onions begin to soften, about 2 minutes. Add the lamb and sauté until the meat is no longer pink, about 30 seconds. Add the white wine and cook until it has almost evaporated, about 30 seconds. Then add the green beans and beef broth. Cover the skillet, reduce the heat, and simmer until the beans are tender and the lamb is cooked through, about 5 minutes. Season to taste with salt and pepper.

5. When the pasta is done, drain it and portion it out. Top each portion with lamb, green beans, and sauce. Serve immediately.

VARIATIONS

■ With tomatoes: For the beef stock substitute 1 can (14½ ounces) stewed tomatoes, drained and chopped, or crushed tomatoes.
■ With Middle Eastern spices: In step 4, after you stir-fry the onions, ginger, and garlic, stir in 1 teaspoon each of ground cumin and ground coriander. Then add the lamb and proceed with the recipe.
■ With Asian seasonings: Substitute sesame oil for the olive oil, rice or white wine vinegar for the white wine, and ¼ cup soy sauce mixed with ¼ cup hoisin sauce for ½ cup of the beef stock (keep the other ½ cup beef stock).

Middle Eastern Lamb over Twists

PASTA: *Small tubes and fancy shapes*
MAKES: *4 servings*
TIME: *25 to 30 minutes*

This recipe showcases a robust Middle Eastern blend of lamb, onions, tomatoes, cumin, mint, and yogurt. A side dish of steamed green beans would round out the meal nicely, as would a first course of green bean and shallot salad.

If you can't find plain ground lamb, substitute lamb patties (the same thing only shaped into ovals, lightly seasoned, and dotted with parsley). You could also substitute ground beef or even sausage meat for the lamb.

Salt
1 medium-size onion
½ cup (firmly packed)
  fresh cilantro, mint, or
  parsley leaves
2 tablespoons vegetable oil
1 pound ground lamb
¾ pound elbow macaroni, pipe rigati, or
  spaghetti twists (gemelli)
1½ teaspoons ground cumin
1 teaspoon dried mint or oregano
⅛ to ¼ teaspoon cayenne pepper
¾ cup tomato purée or crushed tomatoes
⅓ cup plain yogurt (preferably nonfat)

1. Bring a large pot of salted water to a boil for the pasta.

2. While the water is heating, peel and finely chop the onion. Rinse, pat dry, and mince the cilantro.

3. Heat the oil in a medium to large skillet over medium-high heat. Crumble the lamb into the oil and cook, stirring continuously to break up the meat, until it has lost all traces of pink, about 5 minutes. Using a slotted spoon, transfer the lamb to a sieve placed over a bowl (to catch the juices).

4. Add the onions to the skillet, cover, and cook over medium heat, stirring occasionally, until they are tender, about 5 minutes.

5. While the onions are cooking, add the pasta to the boiling water and cook until it is tender but still firm to the bite, 10 minutes.

6. When the onions are tender, stir in the cumin. Rub the mint between your fingers, and add it to the skillet along with the cayenne pepper. Return the lamb to the skillet (leaving any juices in the bowl), and add the tomato purée. Cover, and simmer over medium-low heat until all the ingredients are heated through, about 5 minutes. Keep the lamb covered, off the heat, until the pasta is ready. Right before the pasta is done, add the yogurt and cilantro to the lamb, and season to taste with salt.

7. Drain the pasta and divide it among four shallow bowls. Ladle a portion of lamb and sauce over each pasta portion, and serve.

VARIATION

Middle Eastern Red Kidney Beans over Twists: Omit the lamb (and most of step 3). In step 6, substitute 2 cups cooked or 1 can (16 to 19 ounces) red kidney beans, drained, for the cooked lamb.

RUBBING HERBS

It helps to release the flavor of dried herbs if, right before you add them to the saucepan, you rub them between your fingers.

Pork and Cabbage over Rigatoni

PASTA: *Large or medium-size tubes*
MAKES: *4 to 6 servings*
TIME: *30 to 35 minutes*

This hearty combination of pork, beans, cabbage, and pasta is a perfect and extremely satisfying winter dish. Keep it in mind when the weather turns snowy, and comfort food is the only answer.

The brief, gentle cooking coaxes out the sweetness of the cabbage yet preserves its firm texture. The flavors of the pork and cabbage are highlighted by the assertive garlic and the subdued pasta.

Salt
¾ pound boneless pork loin, or 4 medium-size pork chops
¼ head of cabbage
4 cloves garlic
1 pound rigatoni or ziti
¼ cup olive or vegetable oil
2 tablespoons dry white wine
1 can (14½ ounces) stewed tomatoes
1 can (16 ounces) red kidney beans, drained
½ teaspoon dried red pepper flakes

1. Bring a large pot of salted water to a boil for the pasta.

2. While the water is heating, cut the pork into strips about 1 inch long, ¼ inch wide, and ¼ inch thick. (If you are using pork chops, remove the meat from the bone, cut off the fat, and cut the meat into strips.) Core the cabbage and cut it into thin shreds. Peel and mince the garlic.

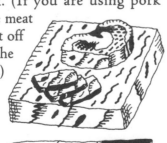

3. Add the pasta to the boiling water and cook until it is tender but still firm to the bite, about 10 minutes.

4. Meanwhile, heat the oil in a large skillet over high heat. Add the garlic and the pork strips, and cook, stirring continuously, until the meat turns white, about 2 minutes. Reduce the heat to medium and add the white wine and tomatoes. Break up the tomatoes by pressing them against the sides of the skillet with a wooden spoon. Add the beans and cabbage, and bring to a boil over high heat.

5. Cover the skillet and simmer over medium-high heat until the cabbage begins to wilt, about 5 minutes. Stir, reduce the heat, and simmer, covered, over low heat until the cabbage is almost tender, another 5 minutes. Season to taste with salt and the red pepper flakes. Remove the skillet from the heat and keep warm, covered, until the pasta is ready.

6. When the pasta is done, drain it and return it to the pot, off the heat. Stir in the pork, beans, cabbage, and all of the sauce, and mix until thoroughly combined. Adjust the seasoning and serve immediately.

SECOND TIME AROUND

This dish provides leftovers that are perfect to turn into soup. Simply add enough chicken broth or water to reach the desired consistency, and bring the soup to a simmer. Stir in some grated Parmesan or diced mozzarella, and cook over low heat until the cheese has barely melted, about 2 minutes. Serve immediately.

Another way to recycle the leftovers is to place them in a greased baking dish, top the dish with diced mozzarella, cover, and bake in a preheated 350°F oven just until the cheese has melted and the pasta is hot, about 20 minutes.

Hammed-Up Elbows with Sour Cream

PASTA: *Small tubes*
MAKES: *4 servings*
TIME: *25 minutes*

A bowl of macaroni tossed with mushrooms, ham, and caraway seeds is simplicity itself—but oh, so good. Steamed asparagus would make a good side dish, as would green beans and shallots.

Although not really designed as a dish to serve to guests, this is something to keep in mind for those nights when you will be entertaining, because you can make it in advance: Assemble the finished pasta and sauce in an ovenproof dish the day before, and bake it the following night under a thin blanket of bread crumbs, as described in the "Second Time Around" that follows.

Salt
¾ pound elbow macaroni
½ pound fresh mushrooms
⅓ pound smoked ham (Black Forest would be a good choice) in a single slice
2 tablespoons butter, margarine, or vegetable oil
1 teaspoon caraway seeds
Freshly ground black pepper
½ cup sour cream

1. Bring a large pot of salted water to a boil. Add the pasta and cook until it is tender but still firm to the bite, about 8 minutes.

2. Meanwhile, remove the mushroom stems (reserve them for another use), wipe the caps clean with a damp paper towel, and cut the caps into thin slices. Dice the ham.

3. Melt the butter in a medium-size saucepan over medium heat. Add the mushrooms and sauté them until tender, about 3 minutes. Add the caraway seeds and ham, and continue to sauté until the ham is

warmed through, about 3 minutes. Season to taste with salt and pepper.

4. Drain the pasta and return it to the pot, off the heat. Add the sour cream and the mushroom-ham mixture, and toss until thoroughly mixed. Adjust the seasoning and serve immediately.

VARIATION

■ Leaner version: Substitute smoked turkey for the ham and either nonfat yogurt or part-skim ricotta cheese for the sour cream. In step 3, cook the mushrooms in ¼ cup chicken broth instead of the butter.

SECOND TIME AROUND   *Place the leftovers in a lightly greased baking dish. Top with ¼ cup bread crumbs mixed with 2 tablespoons grated Parmesan cheese. Dot with 2 tablespoons butter and bake at 350°F until thoroughly hot, about 20 minutes.*

Summer Ham and Vegetable Orecchiette

PASTA: *Medium-size flat shapes or ribbons*
MAKES: *4 servings*
TIME: *25 to 30 minutes*

Orecchiette blend beautifully with the diced ham and zucchini here, but I love this sauce over thin ribbon pasta as well.

> *Salt*
> *¾ pound orecchiette, bow-ties (farfalle),*
>   *tagliatelle or linguine*
> *2 ounces prosciutto*
> *4 to 6 fresh sage or basil leaves*
> *2 medium-size tomatoes*
> *2 cloves garlic*
> *¾ pound smoked ham (preferably*
>   *Black Forest) in a single slice*
> *2 medium-size zucchini*
> *¼ cup olive oil*
> *¼ cup dry white wine*
> *Freshly ground black pepper*

1. Bring a large pot of salted water to a boil. Add the pasta and cook until it is tender but still firm to the bite, 8 to 10 minutes.

2. Meanwhile, slice the prosciutto into fine shreds or cut it into fine dice, and set it in a large mixing bowl. Cut the sage leaves into fine shreds and add them to the mixing bowl. Halve the tomatoes and scoop out the seeds

with a spoon. Cut the tomatoes into small cubes and add them to the bowl.

3. Peel and mince the garlic. Trim any fat from the ham; then cut it into ½-inch cubes. Trim the zucchini and cut it into small dice.

4. Heat the oil in a large skillet over medium-high heat. Add the garlic and sauté for a few seconds, until you get a good whiff of its aroma. Add the diced ham and zucchini. Then add the wine and cover the skillet. Simmer over low heat until the zucchini is tender, 3 to 4 minutes. Taste for seasoning, and stir in the tomato mixture. Keep warm, off the heat.

5. Drain the pasta and divide it among four shallow bowls. Top each portion with some of the ham and vegetables, and serve immediately.

SECOND TIME AROUND

These leftovers are best when served as a salad. Toss them with an olive oil and lemon juice vinaigrette or a dressing of mayonnaise and lemon juice. If you wish, add diced red bell peppers or watercress leaves.

Chic Chorizo and Peppers over Pasta

PASTA: *Medium-size fancy shapes or ribbons*
MAKES: *4 servings*
TIME: *30 to 35 minutes*

This dish is perfect as it stands. Don't bother with it if you have to cut down on fat because it doesn't adapt well to alterations. It is rich, so reserve it for special occasions when you're having company over during the week or when you're having a mini family celebration.

If I have room for dessert, I follow this with a plateful of sliced fresh pineapple splashed with port wine or dotted with fresh mint.

Salt
½ to ¾ pound chorizo or hot Italian sausage
1 onion
2 red bell peppers
½ pound fresh mushrooms
2 tablespoons vegetable oil
½ pound rotelle (wagon wheels) or radiatore, or spinach fettuccine
1 teaspoon caraway seeds
2 tablespoons water
Freshly ground black pepper
½ cup sour cream

1. Bring a large pot of salted water to a boil for the pasta.

2. While the water is heating, thinly slice the chorizo. Peel and finely chop the onion. Core and seed the peppers, and cut them into thin strips. (Or finely chop the onion and peppers together in a food processor.) Stem the mushrooms (reserve the stems for another use), wipe the caps clean with a damp paper towel, and cut them into very thin slices.

3. Heat the oil in a large skillet over high heat. Add the chorizo and sauté until both sides are slightly brown and crisp around the edges, 2 to 3 minutes. With a slotted spoon, transfer the chorizo to a bowl and set it aside.

4. Add the pasta to the boiling water and cook until it is tender but still firm to the bite, 8 to 10 minutes.

5. While the pasta is cooking, add the onions, mushrooms, and peppers to the remaining fat in the skillet and cook, stirring continuously, until the onions and peppers are somewhat tender, about 3 minutes. Add the caraway seeds, water, and the cooked chorizo. Cover, and simmer over low heat until all the vegetables are tender, 5 to 10 minutes. Stir the mixture occasionally so it doesn't scorch. Season to taste with salt and pepper.

6. Drain the pasta and return it to the pot, off the heat. Add the chorizo mixture and the sour cream, and toss the ingredients together. Adjust the seasoning and serve immediately.

Hot Sausage and Sweet Currants over Whole-Wheat Pasta

PASTA: *Ribbons or medium-size fancy shapes*
MAKES: *4 servings*
TIME: *30 to 35 minutes*

Ribbon pasta is not the best choice with this coarse-textured sauce, but I love the whole-wheat taste with the spicy sausage and sweet currants, and whole-wheat short shapes can be hard to find. If you have a source for whole-wheat short shapes, by all means use them. They're ideal.

If you don't care for whole-wheat pasta,

serve this with semolina fusilli or rotelle—more appropriate shapes for this type of sauce anyway.

If you want to round out the meal or add more visual appeal, just include the spinach. This is such a hearty dish that you won't need dessert, but if you do want it, fresh fruit finishes the meal perfectly.

> Salt
> ½ pound fresh mushrooms
> ½ pound fresh spinach, or 1 package (10 ounces) frozen chopped spinach, thawed (optional)
> ¾ pound whole-wheat linguine or plain or whole-wheat fusilli, rotelle (wagon wheels), or radiatore
> ¾ pound hot Italian sausages
> ⅓ cup dry white wine
> ¼ cup currants, or ½ cup raisins
> Freshly ground black pepper
> ¼ cup ricotta cheese or sour cream (optional)

1. Bring a large pot of salted water to a boil for the pasta.

2. While the water is heating, stem the mushrooms (reserve the stems for another use), wipe the caps clean with a damp paper towel, and thinly slice them. If you are going to use fresh spinach, stem, rinse, and coarsely chop it. If you are using frozen spinach, squeeze it with your hands to remove as much water as possible.

3. Add the pasta to the boiling water and cook until it is tender but still firm to the bite, about 10 minutes.

4. Meanwhile, empty the sausages from their casings, squeezing the meat into a large skillet. Sauté the sausage over medium-high heat, breaking it up with a spoon until the meat is crumbly, about 2 minutes. Add the mushrooms, cover, and simmer over low heat until the mushrooms are soft and the sausage is cooked, about 5 minutes. Then add the white wine and currants, (and spinach if you are using it), and cook until the wine has evaporated somewhat, about 1 minute (or until the spinach has just wilted and is hot, about 2 minutes). Season to taste with salt and pepper, cover, and set aside, off the heat, until the pasta is done.

5. Drain the pasta and return it to the pot, off the heat. Add the sausage mixture and toss the ingredients well. Serve immediately, topping each portion with a tablespoon of ricotta cheese or sour cream if you wish.

ESPECIALLY GOOD FOR CHILDREN

Omit the mushrooms and spinach. Substitute sweet Italian sausage for the hot sausage, and tomato sauce or chicken broth for the white wine. Be sure to stir in the ricotta cheese or sour cream to finish.

Beans and Grains with Pasta

While we are familiar with such classics as *pasta e fagioli* (a soup of white beans and pasta) and kasha varnishkes (bow-tie noodles with kasha), the full range of possibilities for combining pasta with beans or grains represent unexplored territory for most of us.

In different cuisines we find many bean-and-grain matches but few pasta-and-bean or pasta-and-grain partnerships. And yet what better way to introduce grain- and bean-shy diners to their delectable qualities than to combine them with an old friend like pasta?

Even if you can accept the notion of beans with pasta, you might not be as sanguine about grains. After all, pasta is made from grain (wheat), so why combine one grain with another? You'll discover the answer when you experience, for example, the nutty crunch of quinoa, melded with seasonings and blended with pasta.

Anyone interested in concentrating on the base of the food pyramid—in eating healthily, in other words—or in eating cheaply, or in taking a culinary adventure will be surprised and delighted by these new pasta recipes, which make the most of the richness and complexity of grains and beans.

BEANS

When it comes to Monday-to-Friday cooking, any beans you choose have to be ready to heat up at a moment's notice. There's no time for soaking and cooking dried beans for 2 hours before you get down to the business of making dinner. This means relying on canned beans or, if you're a purist, on beans that you have cooked on the weekend and stored in the fridge or the freezer.

If you decide on canned beans, your best bet is the health- food-store variety because they taste less salty, their flavor is fresher, and their texture is firmer. You can also find a range of canned beans in a health food store that you can't in an ordinary supermarket: tiny plum-hued adzuki beans, fava beans, oval navy beans. When you open these cans, don't be startled by the black flecks of what look like debris; these are pieces of seaweed used as seasoning.

There are three basic ways of combining beans and pasta. The first is the stew method: You cook some seasoning vegetables such as onions and carrots, then add the beans, pasta, and enough liquid to season and simmer the beans and soften the pasta. For these types of stews, I prefer small or medium-size short shapes such as elbow macaroni, small shells, or orzo. The second way is to create a separate bean sauce and toss it over the cooked pasta. The third way is to add beans to pasta in cold salads.

LENTILS

Because dried lentils take less time to cook than dried beans, they are a distinct Monday-to-Friday possibility. With a simple sauce, dinner can be ready in 35 or 40 minutes.

The least expensive and most commonly available lentil in this country is the brown lentil. True, it tends to lose its shape when cooked, but I think its comforting quality and sturdy flavor are real assets to pasta.

In some gourmet stores you can find a French variety of dried green lentil (*lentilles du Puy*). When cooked, these lentils are firmer than the standard brown ones, which makes them a good choice for pasta salads. They are more expensive, however.

Also available in some gourmet and health food stores is the red lentil. While it cooks in half the time of the other lentils, it isn't ideal because it does not have the same earthy flavor.

GRAINS

Some grains complement the flavor and texture of pasta, I have discovered, and others do not.

The grains I do like with pasta are those that take no longer than 15 minutes to cook and add a distinctive flavor or texture. These include buckwheat groats (kasha), millet, quinoa, cracked wheat, and wild rice (a grass really, not a grain). Wild rice is not exactly a staple in my household, but pairing it with pasta is one way of getting the most out of this expensive ingredient, and its texture and color are very pleasing with pasta.

Basil-Flecked Red Beans for Spaghettini

PASTA: *Thin strands or ribbons*
MAKES: *6 servings*
TIME: *25 minutes*

This is a perfect dish for vegetarians: It's very filling and very fast to prepare.

If you wish, serve a side dish of sautéed mushrooms and peppers or steamed broccoli or cauliflower.

Salt
1 pound spaghettini or linguine fine
24 medium-size fresh basil leaves
6 cloves garlic
12 sun-dried tomatoes
     (packed in olive oil), drained
4 cups cooked red kidney beans, or 2 cans
     (16 ounces each) red kidney beans,
     drained
½ cup olive oil
1 cup water or chicken broth
Freshly ground black pepper or
     dried red pepper flakes
Grated Parmesan cheese, for serving
     (optional)

1. Bring a large pot of salted water to a boil. Add the pasta and cook until it is tender but still firm to the bite, 8 to 10 minutes.

2. Meanwhile, cut the basil leaves into fine shreds. In a food processor, mince the garlic with the sun-dried tomatoes; set aside. If you are using canned beans, rinse and drain them. Chop the beans.

3. Heat the olive oil in a medium-size saucepan over medium heat. Stir in the garlic and sun-dried tomatoes, and cook until you can smell the aroma of the garlic, about 10 seconds. Add the beans and water, and simmer until the beans are heated through, about 2 minutes. Remove the skillet from the heat and stir in the basil. Season to taste with salt and black pepper or red pepper flakes. Keep warm, covered, off the heat, until the pasta is ready

4. Drain the pasta and divide it among six shallow bowls. Top each portion with some of the bean sauce, and serve immediately. Pass the cheese separately.

VARIATION

Mix in either 2 cups sliced steamed carrots or ½ cup finely shredded prosciutto after you add the garlic in step 3.

SECOND TIME AROUND

Add chicken broth or tomato juice to the leftovers and turn them into soup. To thicken and flavor it, stir in diced mozzarella or grated Parmesan cheese at the end.

Bow-Tie Noodles with Kasha and Onions

PASTA: *Medium-size flat shapes or small tubes*
MAKES: *6 servings*
TIME: *30 minutes*

I love a bowl of kasha with noodles, made my grandmother's way—cooked with onions and served with sour cream. But I have discovered that the earthy taste of kasha also works with curry and apple (see the variations that follow).

When you're serving this as the main course, precede it with a cabbage salad.

Salt
1 medium-size onion
1 cup medium-grind kasha
*   (roasted buckwheat groats)*
1 egg, beaten
1¾ cups chicken or beef broth or water
2 tablespoons vegetable oil
3 cups bow-tie (farfelle) noodles or elbow
*   macaroni*
1 teaspoon sugar
1 tablespoon white wine vinegar
Freshly ground black pepper
Sour cream (optional)

1. Bring a large pot of salted water to a boil for the pasta.

2. While the water is heating, peel and mince the onion. Mix the kasha with the egg in a small bowl until the grains are thoroughly coated.

3. Heat the oil in a medium-size skillet over medium heat. Add the onions and sauté until they are coated with the oil. Cover the skillet and cook the onions over low heat until they are tender, 4 to 5 minutes.

4. While the onions are cooking, add the pasta to the boiling water and cook until it is tender but still firm to the bite, about 10 minutes. Bring the broth to a boil in a microwave or in a small saucepan. Then, set it aside.

5. When the onions are tender, add the sugar and vinegar, and then stir in the egg-coated kasha. Sauté over low heat until the kasha smells toasty and begins to stick to the skillet, about 3 minutes. Add the hot broth and bring the liquid to a boil. Stir, cover, and simmer over low heat until the kasha is just tender, 5 to 8 minutes. Stir again, and season to taste with salt and pepper. Keep warm, covered, off the heat, until the pasta is ready.

6. When the pasta is done, drain it and return it to the pot, off the heat. Add the kasha mixture, toss thoroughly, and serve immediately. Top each portion with sour cream, if you wish.

VARIATIONS

Cholesterol-Free Kasha: Use only 1 tablespoon oil, and omit the sour cream. In step 2, mix the kasha with just the egg white instead of the whole egg. (In this version the kasha will taste good but the texture will be softer than when it's cooked with whole egg.)

Apple and Curry Kasha: In step 2, peel, core, and mince 1 red apple. Sauté the apple with the onion in step 3 and stir in ½ teaspoon curry powder. Serve with sour cream or plain nonfat yogurt.

Coriander-Scented Lentils with Spaghettini

PASTA: *Thin strands*
MAKES: *4 servings*
TIME: *35 to 40 minutes*

Earthy as well as easy to make, these subtly seasoned lentils evoke the flavors of the Middle East. You might want to make a double batch and save half for later in the week, when you can turn it into a soup. I like to serve grated or steamed parsnips or carrots with this pasta-and-lentil dish.

2 small onions
1 clove garlic
1 quarter-size slice of fresh
   ginger, or ¼ teaspoon
   ground dried ginger
¼ cup vegetable oil
1 tablespoon wine vinegar (white or red),
   if needed
¾ teaspoon ground coriander
½ teaspoon ground cumin
1 cup lentils
2 cups chicken broth or water
Salt
1 pound spaghettini
1 cup (firmly packed) fresh mint leaves
¼ cup extra-virgin olive oil or butter,
   (optional)
Freshly ground black pepper

1. Peel and finely chop the onions. Peel and mince the garlic and fresh ginger.

2. Heat the oil in a medium-size saucepan over medium heat. Add the onions and cook, stirring occasionally, until they begin to wilt, about 3 minutes. Add the garlic and fresh ginger, if you are using it, and sauté until you can smell the aroma of the garlic, about 30 seconds. (If any of this begins to stick to the pan, add the vinegar and continue to sauté.)

3. Stir in the coriander, cumin, and dried ginger, if you are using it, then the lentils and broth. Bring to a boil, reduce the heat to medium-low, and simmer, covered, until the lentils are tender, about 25 minutes.

4. While the lentils are cooking, bring a large pot of salted water to a boil. Add the pasta and cook until it is tender but still firm to the bite, about 8 minutes. While this is cooking, rinse, pat dry, and mince the mint leaves.

5. Drain the pasta and return it to the pot, off the heat. If you wish, toss the pasta with the olive oil or butter. Season the lentils to taste with salt and pepper, add them to the spaghettini, and toss well.

6. Ladle the pasta and lentils into deep bowls, and sprinkle each portion with mint.

VARIATIONS

■ Cut the cooking time by 15 minutes by substituting red lentils for the brown. If you do this, be sure to begin boiling water for the pasta sooner.

■ In addition to the mint, top each portion with a dollop of plain nonfat yogurt, crumbled feta cheese, or chopped fresh tomatoes.

■ Prepare the lentils a couple of hours in advance through step 3. Reheat them, covered, for 10 to 15 minutes in a 300°F oven or for

3 to 4 minutes in the microwave. The lentils will have absorbed all of the moisture while they were standing, so you definitely will need the suggested olive oil or butter in step 5.

SECOND TIME AROUND

LENTIL SOUP: *For 2 cups of leftovers, add 1 can (14½ ounces) crushed or stewed tomatoes and about 2 cups (one 14-ounce can) chicken broth. Add 1 cup cooked vegetables (perhaps leftover parsnips, carrots, or spinach), or 1 cup diced smoked meat, to turn this into a main-course soup. Bring it to a simmer and cook until all of the ingredients are heated through, about 5 minutes. You can finish the soup with ¼ cup minced fresh herbs such as mint, or parsley, or cilantro.*

Cumin-Brushed Tofu over Shells

PASTA: *Medium-size fancy or flat shapes*
MAKES: *4 servings*
TIME: *25 to 30 minutes*

I love this recipe because it is so easy to prepare, plus it's light and fresh. It makes a perfect late evening meal.

Salt
½ to ¾ pound medium-size shells
4 cloves garlic
*½ pound tofu, preferably
    firm*
4 medium-size carrots
2 tablespoons vegetable oil
1 tablespoon ground cumin
¼ cup lemon juice
½ cup chicken broth
½ cup fresh parsley leaves
Freshly ground black pepper

1. Bring a large pot of salted water to a boil. Add the pasta and cook until it is tender but still firm to the bite, about 10 minutes.

2. Meanwhile, peel and mince the garlic. Cut the tofu into ¼-inch cubes. Peel and thinly slice the carrots.

3. Heat the oil in a medium-size saucepan over medium-high heat. Add the garlic and carrots and sauté for about 1 minute. Then add the tofu, cumin, lemon juice, and chicken broth. Bring to a simmer, cover, and cook until the carrots are tender, about 5 minutes.

4. Meanwhile, rinse, pat dry, and mince the parsley. When the carrots are tender, add the parsley and season to taste with salt and pepper.

5. Drain the pasta and return it to the pot, off the heat. Add the tofu mixture, toss it well, and adjust the seasoning. Serve immediately.

VARIATIONS

■ Seasonings: Instead of the cumin, season the dish with chili powder. Or substitute chopped fresh herbs, such as basil, dill, or mint, for the cumin; stir them in at the end of step 4.

■ Vegetables: Instead of the carrots, use 2 cups corn kernels or chopped green beans or red bell peppers.

Garlicky White Beans and Sage with Orecchiette

PASTA: *Medium-size fancy shapes or tubes*
MAKES: *4 servings*
TIME: *25 minutes*

This dish has a heady flavor, comforting on cold winter nights and well into the cool evenings of spring. It's also fast, fast, fast, but if you want to cut the preparation time even more, use fresh fettuccine, which takes only 2 to 3 minutes to cook.

To round out the meal in early fall, serve sliced tomatoes with a vinaigrette dressing before or after the pasta and beans. In winter, broccoli or cauliflower would be a natural accompaniment.

Salt
½ pound (3 cups) orecchiette, fusilli, radiatore, or penne
6 medium-size fresh sage leaves, or 1 teaspoon dried crushed sage
2 cloves garlic
½ cup (packed) fresh parsley leaves
2 cups cooked white beans, or 1 can (19 ounces) white beans, drained
⅓ cup olive oil
¼ cup dry white vermouth or dry white wine
Freshly ground black pepper
Grated Parmesan or Asiago cheese, for serving

1. Bring a large pot of salted water to a boil. Add the pasta and cook until it is tender but still firm to the bite, 8 to 10 minutes.

2. Meanwhile, cut the fresh sage leaves into fine shreds. Peel and mince the garlic. Rinse, pat dry, and finely chop the parsley. If you are using canned beans, rinse and drain them.

3. Heat the olive oil in a medium-size saucepan over medium heat. Stir in the garlic and sage, and cook until you can smell

the aroma of the garlic, about 10 seconds. Add the vermouth and cook until some has evaporated, about 1 minute. Add the beans, cover, and simmer until they are heated through, about 2 minutes. Remove the saucepan from the heat and add the parsley; season to taste with salt and pepper. Keep warm, covered, off the heat, until the pasta is ready.

4. When the pasta is done, drain it and return it to the pot, off the heat. Add the bean mixture, toss well, and serve immediately. Pass the cheese separately.

VARIATIONS

Smoky White Beans and Sage: In step 3, after you have added the beans, add 2 ounces finely shredded or diced prosciutto, smoked ham, or turkey.

Low-Fat White Beans and Sage: In step 3, cook the garlic and sage in just 1 tablespoon olive oil. Then add ½ cup chicken broth after you have added the vermouth.

Lemon White Beans and Sage with Butter: In step 3, cook the garlic and sage in 2 tablespoons butter. Instead of the vermouth, substitute ½ teaspoon grated lemon zest, ¼ cup lemon juice, and ¼ cup chicken broth.

Gingered Tofu and Carrots with Rotini

PASTA: *Medium-size fancy shapes, or rice or buckwheat noodles*
MAKES: *4 servings*
TIME: *30 to 35 minutes*

To build a dinner around this fragrant and filling pasta dish, all you need is a simple dessert of sliced nectarines tossed with blueberries or a dish of vanilla ice cream.

Salt
½ pound tofu, preferably firm
1 nickel-size slice of fresh ginger, or ½ teaspoon ground dried ginger
6 medium-size carrots
2 scallions (green onions)
2 tablespoons sesame oil
2 tablespoons rice vinegar or white wine vinegar
2 tablespoons soy sauce, preferably low-sodium
1 teaspoon sugar
⅓ cup water
½ to ¾ pound rotini, fusilli, buckwheat noodles (soba), or thin rice noodles
Freshly ground black pepper

1. Bring a large pot of salted water to a boil for the pasta.

2. Meanwhile, cut the tofu into ½-inch dice. Peel and mince the fresh ginger. Peel and thinly slice the carrots. Trim 3 inches off the scallion tops and thinly slice the rest.

3. Combine whichever ginger you are using, sesame oil, rice vinegar, soy sauce, sugar, and water in a medium-size saucepan, off the heat.

4. Add the pasta to the boiling water and cook until it is tender but firm to the bite, about 10 minutes for the semolina pasta. Follow package directions for buckwheat or rice noodles.

5. While the pasta is cooking, bring the soy sauce mixture to a hard boil over high heat. Add the tofu and carrots, cover, and simmer over medium-high heat until the carrots are tender, about 4 minutes. Remove the saucepan from the heat and add the scallions. Season to taste with salt and pepper. Keep warm, covered, off the heat, until the pasta is ready.

6. When the pasta is done, drain it and return it to the pot, off the heat. Add the tofu mixture and toss well. Adjust the seasoning and serve immediately.

VARIATIONS

■ Substitute ½ to ¾ pound diced parsnips or white turnips for the carrots.
■ To change the dish into a more "Western" one, substitute vegetable oil for the sesame oil, white wine vinegar for the rice vinegar, and Worcestershire for the soy sauce.

SECOND TIME AROUND

Create a soup by adding 2 cups chicken broth to each 2 cups of leftovers. Add 2 tablespoons minced fresh herbs, such as cilantro or parsley, and maybe ¼ pound fresh seafood, such as shelled shrimp or crab, or chunks of fish fillet.

Peppered and Spiced Black Beans with Pasta

PASTA: *Flavored fancy shapes or ribbons*
MAKES: *4 to 6 servings*
TIME: *25 to 30 minutes*

This peppery pasta and black bean dish will appeal to folks who appreciate sharply flavored foods. Wonderful when freshly made, it is also delicious the next day, baked with tomatoes or served as a salad (see the Second Time Around that follows).

I like to serve this over a green or red-hued pasta because the black beans look prettier against pasta that has some color. For a contrasting flavor, serve a sweet vegetable side dish, such as carrots or fresh corn.

Salt
4 cloves garlic
2 jalapeño peppers, preferably fresh
2 green bell peppers
¾ pound flavored pasta, such as
    red pepper rotini, saffron-hued
    linguine, or spinach linguine
¼ cup vegetable oil
1 can (16 to 19 ounces) black beans,
    drained
1 cup fresh cilantro or parsley leaves
1½ teaspoons chili powder
2 tablespoons red wine vinegar
½ cup plain nonfat yogurt

1. Bring a large pot of salted water to a boil for the pasta.

2. While the water is heating, peel and mince the garlic. Stem, seed, and mince the jalapeños. Core, seed, and chop the bell peppers. (You could do all of the chopping at once in a food processor.)

3. Add the pasta to the boiling water and cook until it is tender but still firm to the bite, 8 to 10 minutes.

4. Meanwhile, heat the oil in a large skillet over medium heat. Add the garlic, jalapeños, and bell peppers. Sauté until you can smell the garlic aroma and the peppers are beginning to soften, 2 to 3 minutes. Cover, and cook over very low heat until the peppers are soft, 4 to 5 minutes.

5. While the peppers are cooking, rinse the beans and finely chop them. Rinse, pat dry, and finely chop the cilantro.

6. When the peppers are soft, add the chili powder, vinegar, and beans. Cover and simmer over low heat until the beans are heated through, 3 to 4 minutes. Remove the skillet from the heat, and stir in the cilantro and yogurt. Mix well, and season to taste with salt. Keep warm, covered, off the heat, until the pasta is ready.

7. When the pasta is done, drain it and return it to the pot, off the heat. Add the black bean mixture and toss until thoroughly combined. Taste for seasoning and serve immediately.

SECOND TIME AROUND

Usually there are no leftovers after I make this because we love spicy food. However, if you don't finish it all at one sitting, toss what's left (at least 1 cup) with 1 chopped fresh tomato, spoon it into a baking dish, cover, and bake at 300°F until hot, about 15 minutes.

Or turn it into a cold pasta salad by moistening the leftovers with additional yogurt; serve it with shredded romaine lettuce.

GETTING A HANDLE ON CHILES

Take care when handling fresh chiles. As soon as you are through seeding and chopping the peppers, wash your hands thoroughly. The volatile oils from the peppers could linger on your fingers and will irritate the tiniest cut or sting your eyes if you touch them.

Red-Hot Chick-Peas with Rigatoni

PASTA: *Large or medium-size tubes*
MAKES: *4 to 6 servings*
TIME: *25 minutes*

On nights when you are even more harried than usual, think of this recipe. It is amazingly delicious, especially given how little work is involved.

Serve a side dish of stir-fried mushrooms and bell peppers, or follow this with steamed broccoli or cauliflower dressed with a vinaigrette.

Salt
4 cloves garlic
4 jalapeño peppers, preferably fresh
1 pound rigatoni, ziti, or mezzani
½ cup extra-virgin olive oil
2 cans (14½ ounces each) crushed
*   tomatoes*
2 cans (16 ounces each) chick-peas,
*   drained*
1 teaspoon dried oregano

1. Bring a large pot of salted water to a boil for the pasta.

2. While the water is heating, peel and mince the garlic. Stem, seed, and mince the jalapeño peppers.

3. Add the pasta to the boiling water and cook until it is tender but still firm to the bite, about 10 minutes.

4. Meanwhile, heat the oil in a large skillet over medium heat. Add the garlic and jalapeños, and sauté for a few seconds, until you can smell the garlic aroma. Stir in the crushed tomatoes and cook until somewhat thickened, about 1 minute. Add the chick-peas and oregano and simmer, uncovered, until the pasta is done.

5. Drain the pasta and return it to the pot, off the heat. Add the chick-peas and sauce, and toss until thoroughly combined. Season to taste with salt, and serve immediately.

VARIATIONS

With just a simple shift in proportions, you can create slightly different dishes. If you want more of a pasta taste, then reduce the chick-peas to 1 cup. Or conversely, if you want a richer chick-pea flavor, follow the recipe but serve it with only half the amount of pasta.

Speckled Quinoa and Orzo

PASTA: *Tiny shapes*
MAKES: *4 to 6 servings*
TIME: *20 minutes*

·············

S imply flavored with garlic and Parmesan, this dish makes a fine dinner when served with a braised vegetable, or a wonderful accompaniment alongside roasted meats. Sun-dried tomatoes add a note of acidity, and toasted quinoa contributes crunch.

When serving this as a main course, I usually choose a side of braised fennel or celery root. When there are only two of us, so washing the leaves is not so onerous, I'll serve braised fresh spinach.

If you can't find quinoa, a delicious and highly nutritious grain that's generally available in health food stores, then substitute millet, cracked wheat, or even kasha.

2 cloves garlic
8 to 10 sun-dried tomatoes, preferably packed in olive oil
⅓ cup olive oil
¾ cup quinoa
1¼ cups orzo, acini de pepe, or tubettini
3 cups chicken broth or water
Salt and freshly ground black pepper
¾ cup grated Parmesan cheese

1. Peel and mince the garlic. Mince the sun-dried tomatoes.

2. Heat the olive oil in a medium-size saucepan over medium-high heat. Add the quinoa and orzo and cook, stirring constantly, until the quinoa turns golden brown, about 1 minute. Add the garlic and sun-dried tomatoes, and continue to sauté until you can smell the garlic, about 30 seconds.

3. Add the chicken broth and bring to a simmer. Then reduce the heat to low, cover the pan, and cook gently until the orzo is tender, 12 to 15 minutes. There will be a little liquid that has not been absorbed by the pasta (when you add the cheese, the liquid will be absorbed and the dish will become creamy, somewhat like risotto). Season to taste with salt and pepper. Remove the saucepan from the heat and stir in the Parmesan. Serve immediately.

VARIATIONS

■ Dried porcini or other wild mushrooms are a natural in this recipe. Bring 3 cups of chicken broth to a boil and pour it over ½ ounce dried mushrooms; soak for 30 minutes. Strain the reconstituted mushrooms through a cheesecloth-lined sieve, reserving the broth. Rinse the mushrooms, mince them, and then add them to the reserved broth. Omit the sun-dried tomatoes, and substitute the mushroom-laced broth for the plain chicken broth in the recipe.

■ Right before stirring in the cheese in step 3, add a bunch of arugula leaves or a cupful of shredded radicchio.

■ Change the liquid: Substitute ½ cup of dry white wine or dry vermouth for ½ cup of the chicken broth, or substitute ¼ cup of vodka for ¼ cup of the broth.

Sweet and Spicy Chick-Peas with Elbows

PASTA: *Small tubes*
MAKES: *4 servings*
TIME: *30 to 35 minutes*

These chick-peas freeze well without the pasta, so make a double batch and you'll have another meal ready in no time.

Serve a side dish (or a first course) of steamed broccoli to make the meal complete. For a dramatic presentation, pile cooked broccoli florets in the middle of a shallow bowl and surround them with the pasta and chick-peas.

Salt
1 onion
2 cloves garlic
½-inch slice of fresh ginger
3 carrots
¼ cup (packed) fresh
   cilantro or parsley leaves
2 tablespoons vegetable oil
1 teaspoon ground coriander
1 teaspoon ground cumin
½ teaspoon anise or fennel seeds
¼ teaspoon cayenne pepper
1 can (14½ ounces) stewed tomatoes
2 cups cooked chick-peas, or
   1 can (19 ounces) chick-peas, drained
½ pound elbow macaroni
2 tablespoons lime juice
½ cup sour cream or plain yogurt
   (optional)

1. Bring a large pot of salted water to a boil for the pasta.

2. Meanwhile, peel and finely chop the onion. Peel and mince the garlic and the ginger. Peel and thinly slice the carrots. Rinse, pat dry, and mince the cilantro.

3. Heat the oil in a medium-size saucepan over medium heat. Add the onions, garlic, and ginger and cook until the onions turn lightly golden, 4 to 5 minutes.

4. Stir in the ground coriander, cumin, anise, and cayenne along with the stewed tomatoes and the carrots. Bring to a simmer, cover, and cook until the carrots are almost tender, about 5 minutes.

5. Add the chick-peas to the tomatoes and carrots and simmer, covered, until they are hot, about 10 minutes. (You can cook them longer; they'll just absorb more of the flavor of the other ingredients.)

6. While the chick-peas are cooking, add the pasta to the boiling water and cook until it is tender but still firm to the bite, about 10 minutes.

7. When the chick-peas are hot, stir in the lime juice and season to taste with salt. Remove the pan from the heat.

8. Drain the pasta and divide it among four shallow bowls. Ladle the chick-peas and sauce over the pasta and top with the minced cilantro. Pass the sour cream or yogurt separately if you wish.

VARIATIONS

■ In step 4, add ½ to 1 cup chicken broth or water to make a soupier mixture.

■ You'll be amazed to see how easily you can go from an Indian flavor to an Italian one just by switching some of the seasonings around: Substitute a fruity olive oil for the vegetable oil, and omit the ginger. Instead of the ground coriander and cumin, use ½ teaspoon dried rosemary and ¼ teaspoon dried red pepper flakes. Substitute lemon juice for the lime juice, and ½ cup chopped parsley leaves for the cilantro. If you have any on hand, add 1 teaspoon black olive or anchovy paste in step 4.

SECOND TIME AROUND

SWEET AND SPICY CHICK-PEA SALAD: *Chill the chick-pea mixture (without the pasta) and serve it as is over a bed of sliced cucumbers, or toss it first with plain yogurt (1 tablespoon for each cup of chick-peas).*

CHICK-PEA SOUP: *For each cup of leftover chick-peas and pasta, add ½ cup water, chicken broth, or tomato juice, and simmer until hot.*

Pasta with Vegetables

Steamed fresh vegetables, a handful of pasta, a drizzle of fragrant olive oil, and a sprinkling of fresh herbs is all you need for a quick, delicious meal any night of the week, any time of the year.

Spring, summer, and fall are my favorite seasons for making a meal of vegetables and pasta because that's when the vegetables are at their peak. However, there are quick-cooking methods even for winter vegetables, resulting in hearty dishes for the coldest nights.

When I pass a produce store and the vegetables look particularly appealing, I'll buy some, often without a specific recipe in mind. When I get home, I plan menus so that the most perishable vegetables are eaten within the first couple of days, leaving the longer-lasting ones for the end of the week. And because I make it a habit never to be without my pantry staples—onions, carrots, and bell peppers—there are always dinner possibilities in the vegetable crisper; even on the most harried evenings.

In this chapter, I give a range of recipes for the most commonly used fresh vegetables—with enough variations and suggestions so that you can devise a pasta recipe for almost any vegetable you can get your hands on.

TURN COOKED VEGETABLES INTO A SMOOTH PASTA SAUCE

For 2 portions of pasta: In a food processor or blender, combine 1 cup cooked vegetables, ¼ to ½ cup chicken broth, ½ teaspoon flavoring such as anchovy or black olive paste, pesto sauce, or Indian pickle, and ¼ to ½ teaspoon additional spice. Enrich this with 2 tablespoons cream or 1 to 2 tablespoons olive oil, if you wish, and purée.

Note that fibrous vegetables, such as broccoli or asparagus, will yield a coarser mix than one made from carrots or green peas.

Beets and Walnuts with Dilled Fedelini

PASTA: *Thin ribbons or strands*
MAKES: *4 servings*
TIME: *25 minutes*

I grate the beets for this light and delicious springtime dish, so they cook in record time. They aren't as sweet this way as when they are baked or boiled—you may want to add a jot of sugar.

If you like, follow this with a meat dish—perhaps veal scallopine or broiled lamb chops.

Salt
1 pound fedelini, linguine fine, vermicelli, or fine egg noodles
6 medium-size beets, green tops removed
½ cup fresh dill, or 2 tablespoons dried dill weed
2 small bunches fresh chives, or 4 scallions (green onions)
½ cup shelled walnuts
3 tablespoons butter, at room temperature
2 tablespoons lemon juice
4 tablespoons chicken broth
Freshly ground black pepper
½ teaspoon sugar (optional)

1. Bring a large pot of salted water to a boil. Add the pasta and cook until it is tender but still firm to the bite, about 8 minutes.

2. Meanwhile, peel the beets and grate them in a food processor. Rinse, pat dry, and mince the dill and the chives or finely slice the scallions (you should have ½ cup) and chop the walnuts. In a large mixing bowl, combine 2 tablespoons of the butter, lemon juice, 2 tablespoons of the chicken broth, and the minced dill; set it aside.

3. Melt the remaining 1 tablespoon butter in a large skillet over medium heat. Add the grated beets and sauté just to heat them through, about 1 minute. Add the remaining 2 tablespoons chicken broth, cover the skil-

let, and simmer until the beets are almost tender, 2 to 3 minutes. Add the walnuts and chives, and season to taste with salt and pepper. Taste the beets; if they are not sweet enough, stir in the sugar. Remove the skillet from the heat and keep warm, covered, off the heat.

4. Drain the pasta and toss it in the bowl with the dill mixture. Season to taste with salt and pepper. Using tongs, arrange a wreath of pasta around the outside edge of individual shallow bowls. Spoon the beets and walnuts in the middle, and serve immediately.

VARIATIONS

■ Other vegetables: This is also delicious when made with grated carrots, celery root, or parsnips.

Baked Beets with Fedelini: If you have baked whole beets on hand, use them instead of the fresh beets. Peel the baked beets, cut them into ½-inch dice, and proceed with the recipe.

Canned Beets with Fedelini: If you substitute canned beets, you don't even have to cook them. Dice the beets, and in step 2, combine

them with all of the butter, lemon juice, chicken broth, dill, chives, and walnuts in the mixing bowl. Toss this with the cooked pasta—the heat of the noodles will melt the butter and warm the other ingredients. Season to taste with salt and pepper.

ESPECIALLY GOOD FOR DIETERS

Omit the walnuts and butter. In step 2, combine the lemon juice and dill with chicken broth. And in step 3, cook the beets in 4 tablespoons chicken broth in a nonstick skillet.

Thai-Style Broccoli with Rice Noodles

PASTA: *Rice or mung bean noodles, thin strands or ribbons*
MAKES: *4 servings*
TIME: *30 minutes*

I f you have trouble finding any of the slightly exotic ingredients, take a look at the variations that follow to create your own version of broccoli and pasta. If you decide to give the broccoli a Western-style presentation, serve it with linguine instead of glass noodles.

Serve a dessert containing pineapple or another tropical fruit.

6 cups water
¼ pound rice noodles (rice sticks) or
    vermicelli
1 small head broccoli
3 small cloves garlic
½ cup unsalted roasted peanuts (optional)
½ cup fresh cilantro leaves
2 tablespoons ketchup
2 tablespoons oyster sauce
¼ cup lime juice
1 teaspoon dried red pepper flakes
1 tablespoon sugar
½ cup chicken broth
⅓ cup vegetable oil
Salt

1. Bring the water to a boil. Place the rice noodles in a large mixing bowl, pour the hot water over them, and let them soften, about 15 minutes. (If using vermicelli, bring a large pot of salted water to a boil. Add the pasta and cook until it is tender but still firm to the bite, 6 minutes.)

2. Meanwhile, trim the broccoli, removing about 4 inches of stem. Slice the remaining stems into ⅛-inch-thick rounds, and finely chop the florets (you need about 6 cups). Peel and mince the garlic. Finely chop the peanuts if you will be using them. Rinse, pat dry, and mince the cilantro. In a bowl or measuring cup, combine the ketchup, oyster sauce, lime juice, red pepper flakes, sugar, and chicken broth.

3. When the noodles are soft, drain them and cut them with kitchen scissors into 2-inch lengths.

4. Heat the oil in a large skillet (or wok) over high heat. Add the garlic and stir-fry until you get a whiff of its aroma, about 10 seconds. Add the broccoli and stir-fry until it turns bright green, about 1 minute. Add the ketchup mixture, and stir with a wooden spoon until well blended.

5. Add the cut rice noodles. Stir, tossing the noodles and broccoli together (use two forks, chopsticks, or two spoons, if needed) until the ingredients are combined and the noodles have taken on an even reddish color. Cover and simmer until the broccoli is barely tender, 2 to 3 minutes. Season with salt and serve immediately. Sprinkle some of the cilantro and peanuts over each portion.

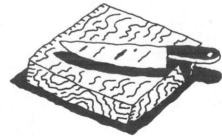

VARIATIONS

Thai-Style Broccoli and Beef: Use only half the amount of broccoli. Cut ½ pound of sirloin beef into strips ("stroganoff pieces"). In step 4, stir-fry the beef for about 1 minute before you add the garlic; then proceed with the recipe.

Italian-Style Broccoli with Fedelini: Cook ¾ pound fedelini instead of the rice noodles. Drain a small can (2 ounces) anchovies, mince them, and add with the broccoli in step 4. Omit the peanuts, and substitute parsley for the cilantro. Substitute olive oil for the vegetable oil, and ¼ cup white wine for the oyster sauce, lime juice, and sugar. Serve the sauced broccoli over the fedelini.

French-Style Broccoli with Linguine: Cook ¾ pound linguine instead of the rice noodles. Substitute olive oil for the vegetable oil, parsley for the cilantro, and ¼ cup white wine plus 1 teaspoon dried thyme for the chicken broth. Omit the peanuts, ketchup, oyster sauce, lime juice, dried red pepper flakes, and sugar.

Mediterranean-Style Broccoli with Spaghetti: Cook ¾ pound spaghetti instead of the rice noodles. Omit the peanuts, and substitute fresh mint or parsley for the cilantro. Omit the ketchup, oyster sauce, and lime juice. Substitute ¼ cup lemon juice for the lime juice, and add ¼ teaspoon each of ground cumin and cinnamon to the chicken broth. Serve the broccoli and spaghetti topped with plain yogurt, if you wish.

SECOND TIME AROUND

This is fantastic served chilled the next day. Although the lime juice will turn the broccoli dark, the flavor won't be compromised.

Cardamom Carrot Threads with Spaghetti Twists

PASTA: *Fancy or plain strands*
MAKES: *4 servings*
TIME: *30 minutes*

This is a lovely vegetarian dish of shredded carrots seasoned with cardamom, ginger, and garlic and creamed with yogurt. Try it over lentils, rice, or baked potatoes as well as pasta.

A salad of tropical fruits would be in keeping with the character of this recipe.

Salt
¾ pound spaghetti twists (gemelli) or spaghettini
3 small cloves garlic
3 quarter-size slices of fresh ginger
1 pound carrots
2 tablespoons vegetable oil
1 teaspoon ground cardamom
½ teaspoon ground cumin
½ cup chicken broth
½ cup plain nonfat yogurt

1. Bring a large pot of salted water to a boil. Add the pasta and cook until it is tender but still firm to the bite, 8 to 10 minutes.

2. Meanwhile, peel and mince the garlic and ginger. Peel the carrots, and grate them in a food processor.

3. Heat the oil in a large skillet over high heat. Add the garlic and ginger, and stir-fry just until you get a whiff of the garlic aroma, about 10 seconds. Then add the carrots, cardamom, cumin, and chicken broth. Bring to a simmer, cover, and cook gently over low heat until the carrots are just tender, about 4 minutes. Remove the skillet from the heat and stir in the yogurt. Season to taste with salt and pepper and keep warm, off the heat, until the pasta is done.

4. Drain the pasta and return it to the pot, off the heat. Mix in the carrots and sauce, and serve immediately.

VARIATION

■ The seasoning for the carrots is also good with boiled or steamed green beans, cauliflower, or parsnips (you'll need 4 cups, chopped).
■ I like this also served chilled and tossed with a yogurt salad dressing.

Spicy Hot Cauliflower over Elbows

PASTA: *Medium-size or small tubes or medium-size fancy shapes*
MAKES: *4 servings*
TIME: *25 to 30 minutes*

When you've read over this recipe and its many variations, you'll know how to make a meal out of pasta and steamed vegetables. It is a terrific dinnertime solution for all seasons and all types of vegetables. The flavors are simple and straightforward, yet with a well-stocked pantry you can create more complex dishes too.

Here I have broken my own Monday-to-Friday rule of never using more than two pots to make dinner. I steam the cauliflower before reheating it in the olive oil because I don't want the cauliflower to have that "fried" taste.

I prefer steaming vegetables to boiling them because the method is quicker and the vegetables do not become waterlogged. (If you do not own a steamer, however, then go ahead and boil the vegetables. But remember that boiling will take longer than steaming.)

Salt
1 head cauliflower
3 cups pipe rigate (elbow twists), elbow macaroni, radiatore, rotelle (wagon wheels), or fusilli
1 clove garlic
6 tablespoons olive oil
1 teaspoon dried red pepper flakes
½ cup grated Parmesan cheese, for serving

1. Bring a large pot of salted water to a boil.

2. While the water is heating, cut the cauliflower into florets (you should have 5 to 6 cups). In a large saucepan, bring 2 inches of water to a boil. Place a vegetable steamer in the pot, add the cauliflower to the steamer, cover, and steam until barely cooked through, 3 to 4 minutes.

3. Meanwhile, add the pasta to the boiling water and cook until it is tender but still firm to the bite, 8 to 10 minutes.

4. While the pasta is cooking, peel and mince the garlic. Cut the steamed cauliflower into small pieces.

5. About 5 minutes before the pasta will be done, heat 4 tablespoons of the olive oil in a large skillet over medium-high heat. Add the garlic and red pepper flakes, and stir-fry until the garlic and pepper are evenly dispersed in the oil, about 10 seconds. Add the cauliflower and cook, stirring frequently, until it is well coated with the oil. Cover, and simmer over low heat until the cauliflower is heated through, about 1 minute. Season to

taste with salt. Keep warm in the skillet, covered, off the heat.

6. Drain the pasta and return it to the cooking pot, off the heat. Toss it with the remaining 2 tablespoons olive oil. Add the cauliflower, and toss all the ingredients together until well blended. Season to taste with salt. Serve immediately, and pass the Parmesan on the side.

VARIATIONS

Seasoning Additions:

■ In step 5, right after the garlic and red pepper flakes, add 1 tablespoon prepared mustard or 1 to 2 tablespoons anchovy paste or tomato paste. Or omit the garlic and add pesto, olive paste, or sun-dried tomato tapenade (which already contain garlic).

If you don't have these seasonings in paste form, add 2 tablespoons minced sun-dried tomatoes, ¼ cup minced pitted imported black olives, or a 2-ounce can of anchovies, drained and minced.

■ In step 5, add 2 tablespoons minced capers when you add the garlic. (You can add the capers in addition to the seasonings listed above.)

■ In step 6, toss the pasta with ¼ cup olive oil and 2 tablespoons lemon juice.

■ In step 6, toss the pasta with ¼ cup olive oil and ¼ cup minced fresh herbs, such as parsley, basil, or mint.

Vegetable and Seasoning Combinations:

■ Asparagus and artichoke hearts: Season additionally with black olive paste or fresh basil.

■ Broccoli and cauliflower: Season additionally with anchovy paste, capers, or fresh parsley or basil.

■ Brussels sprouts, green beans, and petite peas: Season additionally with tomato paste or fresh mint.

■ Lima beans, corn kernels, and carrots: Season additionally with sun-dried tomatoes and fresh parsley.

Other Cheeses:

■ Pecorino Romano, ½ cup grated; good with green beans and carrots

■ Dry chèvre or feta cheese, ½ cup crumbled, good with asparagus, artichokes, and peas

■ Sharp Cheddar, ¾ cup grated; good with corn and lima beans

■ Ricotta, ½ to ¾ cup; good with carrots and Brussels sprouts

■ Blue cheese, ½ cup crumbled; good with cauliflower and broccoli

ESPECIALLY GOOD FOR CHILDREN

If your kids like vegetables with pasta, they'll love the Spicy Hot Cauliflower recipe if you omit the dried red pepper flakes.

Ravioli with Curried Cauliflower

PASTA: *Stuffed pasta*
MAKES: *4 to 6 servings*
TIME: *30 to 35 minutes*

This recipe, full of heady aromas and spicy flavors, will delight lovers of Indian food. I often serve a meat-filled ravioli, so I include a vegetable in the sauce for a dinner-in-one-dish. However, you could make the sauce without the cauliflower and serve a vegetable course either after or alongside the pasta.

This sauce is also useful for reheating leftover poultry or meat and then serving over plain linguine or macaroni.

Salt
1 head cauliflower
1 medium-size onion
4 cloves garlic
½ teaspoon dried red pepper flakes
1 teaspoon ground cumin
1 teaspoon ground cinnamon
1½ teaspoons ground coriander
½ teaspoon ground ginger
½ teaspoon curry powder or ground
 turmeric
¼ cup vegetable oil
1 can (14 ounces) crushed red tomatoes
1 pound ravioli stuffed with meat or
 vegetables
Freshly ground black pepper
Plain yogurt (optional)

1. Bring a large pot of salted water to a boil for the pasta.

2. While the water is heating, cut the cauliflower into small pieces. Peel and finely chop the onion. Peel and mince the garlic. Measure the spices and mix them together in a small bowl; set it aside.

3. Heat the oil in a large skillet over high heat. Add the onions and garlic, reduce the heat to medium, and cook, stirring occasionally, until tender, about 5 minutes. Stir in the spices, tomatoes, and cauliflower. Mix well, cover, and simmer over medium heat until the cauliflower is just tender, about 10 minutes.

4. Meanwhile, add the ravioli to the boiling water and cook until they are tender, 5 to 10 minutes, depending upon the size and freshness of the ravioli.

5. Drain the ravioli and return them to the pot, off the heat. Mix in the cauliflower sauce, and season to taste with salt and pepper. Serve immediately, topping each portion with a small spoonful of yogurt if you wish.

VARIATIONS

You can vary this recipe endlessly by changing the vegetables. Select ones that go well with these particular spices, such as green beans, okra, or carrots. (When making the substitution, figure that you'll need about 3 cups of diced fresh vegetables.)

**ESPECIALLY
GOOD FOR
CHILDREN**

This recipe is just terrific for families with picky eaters. After the ravioli are cooked, separate out the children's portions; toss them with olive oil and sprinkle with Parmesan. Serve the sophisticated vegetable sauce with the adult's servings.

Eggplant "Chinoise" with Penne

PASTA: *Medium-size tubes*
MAKES: *4 servings*
TIME: *30 to 35 minutes*

 s illustrated by this quick recipe for eggplant with pasta, a well-stocked pantry makes a huge difference in cooking dinner. I prefer to offer this as a main course with steamed broccoli or a quick sauté of carrots and mushrooms, but it would also work well as a side dish (by itself or mixed with the pasta) with full-flavored meats and poultry, such as lamb, pork, or turkey.

2 medium-size eggplants
    (2 pounds total)
Salt
4 cloves garlic
¼ cup hoisin sauce
¼ cup water
¼ cup lemon juice
1 pound penne
2 tablespoons sesame oil
2 tablespoons vegetable oil
½ teaspoon dried red pepper flakes
    (optional)

1. Cut the eggplants in half, then into ½-inch dice. Toss them in a colander with 2 teaspoons salt, and set aside. Bring a large pot of salted water to a boil for the pasta.

2. While the water is heating, peel and mince the garlic. Combine the hoisin sauce, water, and lemon juice in a small mixing bowl, and set aside.

3. Add the pasta to the boiling water and cook until it is tender but still firm to the bite, 8 to 10 minutes.

4. Meanwhile, heat the sesame and vegetable oils in a large skillet over medium heat. Add the garlic and immediately start to add the eggplant, taking it by the handful and squeezing out as much water as possible, then stirring it into the oil and garlic. (This will require about four batches.)

5. When all the eggplant has been added, stir in the hoisin mixture. Cover, and simmer over medium heat until the eggplant is soft and tender, 5 to 7 minutes. Season with the dried red pepper flakes and salt to taste.

6. Drain the pasta and return it to the pot, off the heat. Add the braised eggplant and toss it with the pasta until thoroughly combined. Check the seasonings, adding more salt and red pepper flakes if necessary.

VARIATIONS

■ Instead of the eggplant substitute 1½ pounds mushrooms (caps only, sliced), 1 pound diced French haricots verts, or 1 pound sliced carrots.

Eggplant and Shrimp with Penne: In step 5, after you add the hoisin mixture, stir in ½ pound chopped, peeled, deveined shrimp.

SECOND TIME AROUND

To recycle this recipe, just add lemon juice and a sprinkling of chopped fresh cilantro or mint leaves, and serve chilled or at room temperature.

Eggplant with Two Cheeses over Shells

PASTA: *Small or medium-size fancy shapes or tubes*
MAKES: *4 servings*
TIME: *30 to 35 minutes*

Eggplants come in all sizes and shapes. In my neighborhood in early summer, I can find my favorites, a non-bitter variety, small and roundish, about 5 inches long and 2 inches in diameter. Although harder to find, there are also the skinny long "Chinese" eggplants. And finally there is the common eggplant, usually large and weighing a pound at least. Stay away from the truly gigantic ones—their flavor can be a bit acrid.

Eggplant is flavorful and aromatic enough so that you don't need a lot of other ingredients to make it taste good. That, of course, means less work for you!

Although I serve this pasta dish alone, as a one-dish meal, I could see serving an additional course such as a watercress, romaine, and cucumber salad in summer, or a light seafood soup in fall and winter.

This way of preparing eggplant is also a terrific Monday-to-Friday way of making a vegetable side dish, without the pasta, to serve with meat or poultry.

1 medium or 6 small eggplants
  (1¼ pounds total)
Salt
2 cloves garlic
1 can (14½ ounces) "pasta-style chunky" or "Italian-style" stewed tomatoes, drained
¾ pound (3 cups) medium-size shells, elbow macaroni, or penne
¼ cup olive oil
½ teaspoon dried red pepper flakes, or more to taste
⅓ to ½ cup (loosely packed) grated Parmesan or Pecorino Romano cheese
¼ cup part-skim ricotta cheese (optional)

1. Cut the eggplants in half, then into ½-inch dice. Toss them in a colander with 1 teaspoon salt, and set aside.

2. Bring a large pot of salted water to a boil for the pasta.

3. While the water is heating, peel and mince the garlic, and chop the tomatoes.

4. Add the pasta to the boiling water and cook until it is tender but still firm to the bite, 8 to 10 minutes.

5. Meanwhile, heat the oil in a large skillet over medium heat. Add the eggplant, taking it by the handful and squeezing out as much moisture as possible, then stirring it into the oil. (This will require about four batches.) When all the eggplant has been added, stir in the garlic and sauté until you can smell its aroma, about 15 seconds. Add the tomatoes, cover, and simmer over low heat until the eggplant is just tender, 5 to 7 minutes. Season to taste with red pepper flakes and salt.

6. Drain the pasta and return it to the pot, off the heat. Add the tomato-eggplant sauce along with the grated cheese, and toss until thoroughly combined. Season with more salt and red pepper flakes if necessary. Serve immediately, topping each portion with a small spoonful of ricotta cheese if you like.

VARIATIONS

Middle Eastern Eggplant with Shells: Omit the Parmesan cheese. Instead, core, seed, and finely dice 1 green or red bell pepper. In step 5, after you have added the eggplant and garlic, add the diced pepper, ½ teaspoon ground cinnamon, and ¼ teaspoon ground allspice or nutmeg. Then, after you add the tomatoes, add ½ cup raisins. Serve with ricotta cheese.

Asian Eggplant: Omit the tomatoes, Parmesan, and ricotta. Peel, seed, and cut into ½-inch dice either 4 Kirby cucumbers or 2 medium-size standard cucumbers. Substitute 2 tablespoons each of sesame oil and vegetable oil for the olive oil. In step 5, after you have added the eggplant and garlic, stir in 2 tablespoons soy sauce, 2 tablespoons rice vinegar, and 1 teaspoon sugar. In step 6, when you toss the pasta with the eggplant, add the cucumbers.

Asian Eggplant Noodle Salad: Cook ½ pound rice or mung bean noodles and let them cool to room temperature. Cut the noodles into 2-inch lengths. Prepare the Asian eggplant (above) and let the sauce cool to room temperature. Toss the sauce with the noodles, and if you like, drizzle the salad with a squeeze of fresh lemon juice or add a sprinkling of minced fresh cilantro.

SECOND TIME AROUND

If you plan to save some of this eggplant dish for the following day, set aside a portion in step 6 and don't add the cheeses to it. Instead add some olive oil, lemon juice, and fresh parsley to the cheese-free leftovers.

Far Eastern Mixed-up Vegetables with Spaghettini

PASTA: *Thin strands or ribbons*
MAKES: *4 servings*
TIME: *25 to 30 minutes*

Versatility could be this recipe's middle name. On its own, it is a perfectly flavorful vegetarian main course. Served in smaller portions, it becomes an ideal side dish to poultry and beef. What's more, this is just as delicious at room temperature or chilled as it is when eaten hot. This flexibility means the dish is an ideal choice for nights when everyone's eating at a different time, what I call eating "seriatimly."

Salt
¼ pound fresh mushrooms, preferably
   shiitake
2 medium-size carrots
2 cloves garlic
1 quarter-size slice of fresh ginger
½ pound spaghettini or linguine
2 tablespoons sesame oil
2 tablespoons vegetable oil
2 tablespoons soy sauce, preferably
   low-sodium
2 tablespoons rice or white wine vinegar
½ cup chicken broth
2 cups (loosely packed) bean sprouts
Freshly ground black pepper

1. Bring a large pot of salted water to a boil for the pasta.

2. While the water is heating, stem the mushrooms (reserve the stems for another use) and thinly slice the caps. Peel the carrots and cut them into ⅛-inch-thick rounds. Peel and mince the garlic and ginger.

3. Add the pasta to the boiling water and cook until it is tender but still firm to the bite, about 8 minutes.

4. Meanwhile heat the sesame and vegetable oils in a large skillet over high heat. Add the carrots, garlic, and ginger and stir-fry until you can smell the garlic, about 15 seconds. Add the mushrooms and stir-fry for a few more seconds, until they are coated with the oil. Add the soy sauce, vinegar, and chicken

CUTTING TECHNIQUES FOR CUTTING TIME

Keep your knives as sharp as possible so you can cut, dice, and mince faster. If you are dicing strips of vegetables into smaller cubes or pieces, you can work faster if you stack or align several strips on a cutting board and cut across them with a single stroke of the knife.

broth. Reduce the heat to medium, cover, and simmer until the carrots are tender, about 4 minutes. Add the bean sprouts and continue to simmer, uncovered, until they are heated, about 1 minute longer. Season to taste with salt and pepper.

5. When the pasta is done, drain it and divide it among four shallow bowls. Top each portion with vegetables and sauce. Serve immediately or at room temperature. Or chill to serve later.

Note: If you know in advance that you are not going to eat the pasta right away, rinse it under cold water and drain it before you add the vegetables and sauce. This keeps the noodles from continuing to cook and becoming too soft.

VARIATION

■ Other vegetables that work with these seasonings are peas, asparagus, broccoli, green beans, and carrots.

SECOND TIME AROUND

Any leftovers can be tossed with a dressing made by combining a spoonful of mayonnaise, a tad of lemon juice, a touch of hoisin sauce, a touch of Chinese chili paste. Sliced Kirby cucumbers would be lovely with this salad.

Pasta Primavera

PASTA: *Small or medium-size fancy shapes or tubes*
MAKES: *6 servings*
TIME: *30 minutes*

P asta Primavera is an elegant dish, one that usually consists of linguine tossed with a sauce of minuscule cubed vegetables bound with a touch of tomato and cream. As it is done in restaurants, it takes a lot of work because each vegetable is cooked separately.

In the *Monday-to-Friday Cookbook*, I offered a simplified version of Pasta Primavera that involved sautéing the vegetables in sequence, beginning with the ones that take the longest to cook and ending with the quicker-cooking ones.

In this book, I am giving more versions of this dish because it is such a superb way to match vegetables with pasta, at any time of the year.

Because the sauce is replete with small pieces of vegetables, I think a short curly pasta is a better choice than linguine. This Pasta Primavera combines fusilli with an abundance of asparagus, that hallmark of spring, along with carrots and corn.

Salt
1 medium-size onion
3 carrots
16 asparagus spears
1 pound short pasta such as fusilli, penne, elbow macaroni, or cavatappi
¼ cup vegetable oil
¼ cup dry white wine
1 can (14½ ounces) crushed tomatoes
1 package (10 ounces) frozen corn kernels, thawed
2 tablespoons extra-virgin olive oil
Freshly ground black pepper
Grated Parmesan cheese, for serving

1. Bring a large pot of salted water to a boil for the pasta.

2. Meanwhile, peel and finely chop the onion. Peel and cut the carrots into ¼-inch cubes. Snap off the tough ends of the asparagus stems (about 3 inches from the bottom), and cut the spears into ¼-inch-thick rounds.

3. Add the pasta to the boiling water and cook until it is tender but still firm to the bite, about 10 minutes.

4. While the pasta is cooking, heat the vegetable oil in a large skillet over medium heat. Add the onions and carrots and cook, stirring frequently, until slightly wilted, about 2 minutes. Add the white wine, cover, and simmer over low heat until the vegetables start to become tender, about 3 minutes. Add the crushed tomatoes and bring to a simmer. Add the asparagus, cover, and simmer over medium heat until the asparagus are barely tender, 3 to 4 minutes. Then add the corn kernels, cover, and simmer just until the corn is heated through, about 1 minute.

5. Drain the pasta and toss it with the olive oil in a mixing bowl. Ladle a portion onto each plate, and spoon some vegetables and sauce in the center. (Or return the pasta to the cooking pot, off the heat, and toss it with the oil and sauce until well mixed.) Serve the grated Parmesan on the side.

VARIATIONS

Herbed Pasta Primavera: In step 2, mince ½ cup (packed) herbs such as dill, basil, or parsley leaves. In step 5, toss the pasta, sauce, and oil with the minced herbs.

Creamy Pasta Primavera (especially good for company): In step 4, after you have added the corn, add either 4 tablespoons butter or ½ cup heavy cream, and simmer the sauce until the butter has melted in or the cream is heated up, about 1 minute. Omit the olive oil in step 5.

Low-Fat Creamy Pasta Primavera: In step 4, after you have added the corn, finish the sauce with ¾ cup evaporated skim milk. Simmer until it is heated through, about 1 minute. Omit the olive oil in step 5.

No-Tomato Pasta Primavera: Omit the crushed tomatoes and substitute 1 cup chicken broth. In step 5, toss the pasta with 2 tablespoons softened butter instead of the olive oil. You could also add ½ cup minced fresh herbs or ½ cup finely diced red bell pepper when you add the butter.

SECOND TIME AROUND

If you're cooking for two people, cook just enough pasta for two but make the entire amount of vegetable sauce, reserving half of it for the following day. The next day, combine the reserved sauce and some water or chicken broth in a food processor or blender, and create a fresh-tasting vegetable soup in an instant.

Pasta Estiva

PASTA: *Fresh ribbons*
MAKES: *4 servings*
TIME: *30 minutes*

My basic recipe for pasta with summer vegetables is nothing more than a selection of vegetables—cucumbers, radishes, and squash—bound with an uncooked sauce of diced fresh ripe tomatoes, olive oil, and chives. I don't think this dish needs cheese,

but if you want some, crumble in a dry goat cheese, or add a dice of fresh mozzarella to the tomatoes before tossing the noodles with the steamed vegetables.

Although the dice of vegetables is easier to eat when served with short pasta, I prefer the tender chewiness of fresh linguine.

> *Salt*
> *1 medium-size (8 ounces) zucchini*
> *1 medium-size (8 ounces) yellow squash*
> *4 Kirby or 2 medium-size cucumbers*
> *8 radishes*
> *2 ripe tomatoes*
> *2 small bunches fresh chives or 4 scallions (green onions), with green tops*
> *¼ cup olive oil*
> *Freshly ground black pepper*
> *1 cup water*
> *1 pound fresh linguine (green spinach or squid-ink linguine are attractive here)*

1. Bring a large pot of salted water to a boil for the pasta.

2. While the water is heating, cut the zucchini and yellow squash in half lengthwise. Using a small spoon, scrape out the seeds. Cut the squash into ¼-inch dice. Peel, seed, and cut the cucumbers into ¼-inch cubes. Trim the radishes and cut them into cubes.

3. Halve the tomatoes, scoop out the seeds with a spoon, and cut the tomatoes into a fine dice (or blend briefly in a food processor to finely chop them). Place the tomatoes

in a large serving bowl. Rinse, pat dry, and mince the chives or finely slice the scallions; add them to the tomatoes along with the olive oil. Season the tomatoes with salt and pepper, and set aside.

4. Add the pasta to the boiling water and cook until it is tender but still firm to the bite, 3 to 5 minutes for fresh pasta, longer for dry.

5. Meanwhile, bring the 1 cup water to a boil in a large skillet. Add the diced vegetables, cover, and boil hard until they are barely tender, 1 to 2 minutes. Drain and add them to the tomatoes in the serving bowl.

6. Drain the pasta, add it to the bowl, and toss with the vegetables. Season with salt and pepper, and serve immediately.

VARIATIONS

■ Vary the vegetables: All you need is about 3 cups of fresh vegetables, cut into small dice so they cook 2 to 3 minutes.

■ Change the sauce: Omit the tomatoes and create a sauce with ⅓ cup olive oil mixed with fresh herbs and a splash of lemon juice; or simply mix the herbs with 2 to 3 tablespoons softened plain or seasoned butter (see page 39).

Or thin a couple of tablespoons of pesto or black olive paste with lemon juice. Reserve ¼ cup of the pasta cooking water and add it to the cooked pasta and vegetables to make the ingredients spread more evenly over the pasta.

SECOND TIME AROUND

Leftovers lend themselves to a couple of recycling possibilities. In keeping with the season, it makes sense to create a salad: Toss 2 cups of leftover pasta and vegetables with 2 tablespoons yogurt dressing, curry mayonnaise, or basic vinaigrette. You can add a fresh ingredient or two, such as cooked chick-peas, grilled vegetables, baked ham, smoked turkey, or leftover grilled fish.

Or recycle the leftovers into a soup: Heat 2 cups of leftovers with 1 cup chicken broth and 1 cup tomato or vegetable juice. Presto!

Pasta d'Autunno

PASTA: *Medium-size fancy shapes*
MAKES: *4 to 6 servings*
TIME: *30 minutes*

This recipe marries pasta with fall vegetables—here, green beans and fresh mushrooms. I love a touch of goat cheese crumbled over the finished dish, but the mix also works well with Parmesan, Romano, and aged Gouda cheeses.

Baked apples, poached pears, or bananas and grapes would be a good dessert choice, in keeping with the fall season.

Salt
1 onion
2 red bell peppers
½ pound fresh mushrooms, preferably
    shiitake or wild mushrooms
¾ pound medium-size shells
¼ cup olive oil
½ pound green beans
10 fresh sage leaves, or ½ teaspoon
    dried sage
1 cup chicken or vegetable
    broth
Freshly ground black pepper
¼ cup dry goat cheese
    (optional)

1. Bring a large pot of salted water to a boil for the pasta.

2. While the water is heating, peel and finely chop the onion. Core, seed, and chop the red peppers. Wipe the mushrooms clean with a damp paper towel, remove the stems (reserve them for another use), and thinly slice the caps.

3. Add the pasta to the boiling water and cook until it is tender but still firm to the bite, about 10 minutes.

4. Meanwhile, heat the oil in a large skillet over medium-high heat. Stir in the onions and peppers, cover, and reduce the heat. Simmer until the vegetables are tender, about 5 minutes. While this is cooking, trim the green beans and cut them into ½-inch pieces. Rinse, pat dry, and mince the sage leaves.

5. Add the chicken broth, mushrooms, green beans, and sage to the skillet. Cover and simmer over low heat until all the vegetables are tender, about 5 minutes. Season to taste with salt and pepper.

6. Drain the pasta and portion it out. Ladle some of the vegetables and sauce over each portion, and crumble the goat cheese on top if you wish. Serve immediately.

VARIATIONS

■ Vary this recipe by substituting another vegetable for the green beans—perhaps 1 cup of finely diced Brussels sprouts, cauliflower, broccoli, or cooked winter squash, such as acorn squash or pumpkin. (You could omit the mushrooms if the sauce feels too vegetable-heavy, but I think they add a characteristic autumnal touch.)

■ To turn this into a meal that would also appeal to meat eaters, toss in 1 cup diced smoked turkey, ham, or roasted veal or chicken when you add the green beans. You could even add 1 cup diced fresh seafood, in which case you should substitute clam juice for the chicken broth.

SECOND TIME AROUND

Pasta d'Autunno leftovers, if they have not been tossed with goat cheese, are best recycled as a soup. Combine 2 cups of leftovers with 1 cup chicken broth and 1 cup tomato or vegetable juice. And if you like, add shreds of romaine lettuce, diced meat or poultry, or 1 cup additional sliced mushrooms.

Leftovers with cheese should be placed in a greased casserole, topped with bread crumbs mixed with grated Parmesan cheese, and baked at 350°F until heated through.

ABOUT THOSE MUSHROOM STEMS

If you have accumulated 2 cups or more of mushroom stems, it is time to turn them into a light soup. Sauté the stems, ¼ cup chopped onion, and 1 minced garlic clove in 2 tablespoons olive oil. When the onions and mushrooms are tender, add 2 cups chicken broth or crushed tomatoes and ¼ cup orzo or rice. Bring to a simmer and cook until all the ingredients are tender, about 15 minutes.

Pasta d'Inverno

PASTA: *Thick strands or soba noodles*
MAKES: *4 to 6 servings*
TIME: *30 to 35 minutes*

This pasta is plain but supremely satisfying and just right for a cold winter night. The tender sweet cabbage acts as a foil for the luxurious cheeses that envelop the strands of pasta.

Ordinarily I wouldn't indulge in such a rich sauce. However, the dish just would not taste as terrific with less cheese, so I reserve it for a special occasion or for a frigid night when I feel deserving of something particularly luscious.

Salt
2 onions
1 small head cabbage (1½ pounds)
¾ pound bucatini, perciatelli, spaghetti, or soba
⅓ cup olive oil
½ teaspoon dried red pepper flakes
¾ cup water
1 cup ricotta cheese (whole-milk or part-skim)
1 cup grated Parmesan cheese

1. Bring a large pot of salted water to a boil for the pasta.

2. While the water is heating, peel and finely chop the onions. Core and thinly slice the cabbage.

3. Add the pasta to the boiling water and cook until it is tender but still firm to the bite, about 10 minutes.

4. Meanwhile, heat the oil in a large skillet over medium-high heat. Add the onions and sauté for about 1 minute. Add the cabbage, red pepper flakes, and water. Cover the skillet, reduce the heat, and simmer until the vegetables are tender, about 10 minutes. Season to taste with salt.

5. While the vegetables are cooking, combine the ricotta and Parmesan in a large mixing bowl.

6. Drain the pasta and transfer it to the mixing bowl with the cheeses. Add the vegetables and their juices, and mix the ingredients thoroughly to combine. Adjust the seasoning and serve immediately.

VARIATIONS

■ To keep this dish seasonal, substitute winter vegetables for the cabbage—such as 2 pints Brussels sprouts, cored and sliced into thin rounds, or 1 pound white turnips, rutabagas, carrots, or parsnips, peeled and thinly sliced or cut into matchstick strips.

■ Keep the ricotta, but substitute crumbled feta, Kashkaval, or a dry goat cheese for the Parmesan.

PASTA D'INVERNO THE SUNDAY START-UP WAY

There is a way to prepare Pasta d'Inverno in advance so that it's ready in the refrigerator when you get home too tired to chop and peel. I do the prep work on a Sunday when I have more time. Covered, the dish keeps for 2 days in the fridge.

Cook the pasta (use ¾ pound penne for this version), toss it lightly with olive oil, and set it aside. Braise the cabbage and onions as described in step 4. Oil a shallow rectangular baking dish (about 13 x 9 inches), and arrange half the pasta in the bottom. Scatter cubes or slices of a melting cheese such as fontina, taleggio, or mozzarella over the pasta and then add some Parmesan. Spread the cabbage over the cheese, arrange the remaining pasta over that, and top with more melting cheese and Parmesan. Cover and refrigerate until the day you're serving the dish. Then, bake, covered, at 350°F for 30 minutes; uncover and bake for another 15 minutes.

New Potatoes with Olives and Bow-Tie Pasta

PASTA: *Medium-size flat shapes*
MAKES: *4 to 6 servings*
TIME: *35 to 40 minutes*

This recipe takes a few more minutes than others in this book because of the potatoes, which add a bit to the cooking time. Here I take the trouble to pit and mince black olives instead of relying on black olive paste because there is precious little other preparation involved. The white wine sharpens the other flavors, but you could substitute 1 or 2 tablespoons cider or white wine vinegar if you prefer.

This is so good and filling that it is plenty for dinner. Still, you might want to complete the meal with a simple dessert. If you plan to make this a side dish, serve it with roasted veal or grilled chicken.

8 small (1 pound) new red potatoes
Salt
½ pound (about 4 cups) bow-ties (farfalle)
    or orecchiette
4 large romaine lettuce leaves
12 Kalamata or Spanish green olives, or
    1 or 2 tablespoons black or
    green olive paste
3 scallions (green onions)
6 tablespoons grated Parmesan cheese
½ cup olive oil
¼ cup dry white wine
Freshly ground black pepper

1. Scrub the potatoes clean with a vegetable brush; then place them in a medium-size saucepan and cover them with 1 quart of water. (If any of the potatoes are substantially larger than the rest, cut them in half or even quarters.) Bring the water to a boil, reduce the heat to medium, partially cover the saucepan, and cook until the potatoes are just tender, 15 to 20 minutes.

2. Once the potatoes are cooking, bring a large pot of salted water to a boil. Add the pasta and cook until it is tender but still firm to the bite, 8 to 10 minutes.

3. Meanwhile, rinse the lettuce leaves, pat them dry, and cut them crosswise into shreds. Place the shredded romaine in a large mixing bowl. Pit and chop the olives, and add them to the mixing bowl. Trim the scallions and cut them into thin slices. Add them to the mixing bowl along with the Parmesan, olive oil, and white wine. Toss the ingredi-

ents together, and season to taste with salt and pepper.

4. Drain the pasta, add it to the other ingredients in the bowl, and mix thoroughly.

5. Drain the potatoes, set them on a cutting board, and carefully (so you don't burn yourself) cut each one into 8 to 12 chunks. Add these to the pasta, season with salt and pepper, and toss well. Serve immediately or at room temperature.

SECOND TIME AROUND

Serve leftovers of this pasta as a salad. To each 2 cups of leftovers add a generous tablespoon of Basic Vinaigrette Dressing (see Index).

SALT AND POTATOES

Potatoes absorb great amounts of salt without tasting salty, and this means that for this dish to taste just right, you will need to use more salt than you might ordinarily.

Spinach with Fusilli Lunghi

PASTA: *Fancy strands or short shapes*
MAKES: *2 servings*
TIME: *20 to 25 minutes*

I make this dish only when I'm cooking for two, because who wants to wash volumes of fresh spinach? This recipe just doesn't work with frozen spinach, so if you are even less inclined than I am to wash gritty greens, you might substitute watercress or romaine lettuce.

I usually serve this as a main course, and I round out the meal with an easy starter such as sliced tomatoes or cucumbers vinaigrette.

Salt
2 bunches (1¼ to 1½ pounds) fresh
    spinach, mustard greens, turnip greens,
    kale, broccoli rabe, or Swiss chard
¼ pound fresh mushrooms
2 cloves garlic
1 pound fusilli lunghi, Margherita, short
    fusilli, or rotini
2 tablespoons olive oil
2 tablespoons water
Freshly ground black pepper

1. Bring a large pot of salted water to a boil for the pasta.

2. Stem the spinach, place it in a large bowl,

cover it with cold water, and set it aside. Remove the mushroom stems and thinly slice the caps. Peel and mince the garlic. Then swish the spinach around in the water, lift the leaves out of the water, and using your hands, squeeze out the excess moisture. Chop the leaves coarsely.

3. Add the pasta to the boiling water and cook until it is tender but still firm to the bite, 8 to 10 minutes.

4 About 5 minutes before you think the pasta will be done, heat the oil in a large skillet over high heat. Stir in the mushrooms. Add the water and reduce the heat to medium. Cover the skillet and simmer until the mushrooms are tender, about 2 minutes. Uncover, add the garlic, increase the heat to high again, and sauté just until you get a whiff of the garlic, about 30 seconds.

5. Add half the spinach and stir until it has wilted somewhat, about 15 seconds. Add the remaining spinach and continue to stir until it is wilted but still bright green, about 2 minutes. Remove the skillet from the heat, season the spinach to taste with salt and pepper, and keep warm, covered, off the heat, until the pasta is done.

6. Drain the pasta and return it to the pot, off the heat. Add the spinach mixture and mix thoroughly. Adjust the seasoning, and serve immediately.

VARIATIONS:

Spinach, Pine Nuts, and Raisins with Fusilli: Substitute 2 tablespoons each of pine nuts and currants or raisins for the mushrooms. In step 4, sauté them just to heat, about 1 minute.

Spinach and Feta Cheese with Fusilli: In step 5, mix ¼ pound crumbled feta or dry goat cheese with the pasta and spinach mixture.

Spinach and Anchovy with Fusilli: In step 5, mix 1 tablespoon anchovy paste with the pasta and spinach mixture.

Labor Day Tomatoes with Orecchiette

PASTA: *Small or medium-size flat or fancy shapes*
MAKES: *4 to 6 servings*
TIME: *25 to 30 minutes*

This would be a terrific selection for a Labor Day picnic because it makes the most of the season's tomatoes. You can serve this right after it is made, but it will taste even better if you allow it to cool a bit and serve it slightly warm or at room temperature. And it's fine chilled, the day after the pasta's been cooked.

Serve this with corn on the cob or steamed zucchini.

> Salt
> 4 large vine-ripened tomatoes
>   (2 to 2½ pounds)
> 4 cloves garlic
> ½ cup (packed) fresh basil leaves
> 1 pound orecchiette, bow-ties (farfelle), or
>   gnocchi pasta
> ⅓ cup olive oil
> Freshly ground black pepper

1. Bring a large pot of salted water to a boil for the pasta.

2. While the water is heating, halve the tomatoes and remove the seeds with a spoon. Finely chop the tomatoes by hand. (Don't do this in a food processor because it will make them too watery.) Peel and mince the garlic. Rinse, pat dry, and cut the basil leaves crosswise into thin shreds.

3. Add the pasta to the boiling water and cook until it is tender but still firm to the bite, 10 to 12 minutes.

4. Meanwhile, heat the oil in a large skillet over high heat. Add the garlic and sauté for a few seconds, until it is about to turn golden. Add the tomatoes and cook, stirring constantly, to heat them through, about 1 minute. Remove the skillet from the heat, add the basil, and season to taste with salt and pepper.

5. Drain the pasta and toss it with the warm tomato mixture. Cool to room temperature before serving.

VARIATION

With one slight change you can create a dish that is more filling and higher in protein: Use half the amount of pasta. After you have tossed the tomatoes and pasta together in step 5, add ½ pound finely diced fresh mozzarella.

SECOND TIME AROUND

Leftovers are delicious mixed with shreds of fresh romaine lettuce and tossed with Basic Vinaigrette Dressing (see Index).

Vegetarian's Delight

PASTA: *Medium-size ribbons or stuffed pasta*
MAKES: *4 to 6 servings*
TIME: *30 to 35 minutes*

....

T he tender bite of the barely cooked zucchini against the silkiness of the white sauce and the crunch of the walnuts makes this dish a study in subtle contrasts. I'd wager that meat eaters will revel in the deliciousness of this pasta dish as much as vegetarians will.

A bracing green salad or a crisp, tangy dice of fresh fruit would be lovely after this filling meal.

> Salt
> 1 pound (2 medium-size) zucchini or
>   yellow squash
> 4 scallions (green onions)
> ½ cup shelled walnuts or pecans
> ¾ pound fettuccine, or 1 pound cheese- or
>   mushroom-stuffed pasta
> 2 tablespoons butter
> 2 tablespoons all-purpose flour
> 1½ cups low-fat milk
> ½ cup raisins, preferably golden
> Freshly ground black pepper

1. Bring a large pot of salted water to a boil for the pasta.

2. While the water is heating, rinse the zucchini, trim off the ends, and grate it by hand or in a food processor. Trim and thinly slice the scallions. Finely chop the nuts.

3. Add the pasta to the boiling water and cook until it is tender but still firm to the bite, 8 to 10 minutes.

4. Meanwhile, melt the butter in a nonreactive medium-size saucepan over medium heat for a few seconds, until it is bubbly. Add the scallions and sauté for a few seconds; then whisk in the flour. Whisk just until the flour

and butter are combined, about 10 seconds, making sure the whisk reaches all around the edge of the saucepan.

5. Slowly add the milk, by tablespoonfuls at first, whisking constantly to make sure the flour paste absorbs the milk without creating lumps. When about 1 cup of milk has been added and you have a smooth mass, you may add the milk at a faster rate, but continue to whisk constantly.

6. When all the milk has been added, increase the heat to bring it just to a boil. Whisk constantly, although not frantically, watching carefully so that the milk does not scorch on the bottom of the saucepan. Add the raisins and zucchini, cover the pan, and simmer over low heat until the zucchini is warmed through but still crunchy, about 3 minutes. Season to taste with salt and pepper.

7. Drain the pasta and return it to the pot, off the heat. Add the zucchini sauce, and toss until well combined. Spoon out the portions, and top each one with some of the chopped nuts.

SECOND TIME AROUND

Leftovers are easily turned into soup by adding 1 can (14½ ounces) stewed tomatoes for each 2 cups of "Delight."

Pasta Salads

A pasta salad, prepared with the right type of noodle and coupled with a few fresh ingredients, can be as satisfying as any hot pasta dish.

These salads are perfectly suited to Monday-to-Friday cooking. For the harried cook, they also provide an elegant means of using up leftovers and a way of preparing a meal in advance for those nights when you won't have any time to cook.

THE BEST PASTAS FOR SALADS

DRY PASTA

I like to make salads with thin ribbons or small shapes of durum wheat pasta. Pasta that is too thick or too large tastes pasty and chewy when served cold. For simple pasta salads dressed with a vinaigrette, I recommend small shapes such as orzo or tubettini, or skinny shapes such as vermicelli or linguine fine. The small shapes are good for side-dish salads, the long noodles for first- or main-course salads.

For more complex salads that include a number of other ingredients along with the pasta, I like fusilli, rotelle, gemelli, or penne—shapes that are small enough that they do not become gluey but large enough to match the size and shape of the other ingredients.

FRESH EGG NOODLES

Believe it or not, Chinese egg noodles are the best type of fresh pasta for salads because they hold their shape well after boiling and

stand up to dressings. However, I know that freshly made Chinese noodles aren't always easy to find; thin fresh linguine make a good substitute.

OTHER PASTA TYPES

Of all the exotic non-semolina noodles, I like mung bean starch noodles or rice flour noodles best for all-purpose salads. I reserve buckwheat noodles for the more assertively flavored salads. The transparent mung bean ("cellophane") noodle has a pleasant slippery texture with little of its own flavor, which makes it an excellent vehicle for the dressing and other ingredients.

STUFFED PASTAS

Please don't use stuffed pastas, such as tortellini or ravioli, in salad. The fat in the meat or cheese fillings hardens and tastes unpleasant when served cold.

HOW TO COOK PASTA FOR SALAD MAKING

If you are cooking only half a pound of pasta, then boil the pasta until it is perfectly al dente; do not undercook it. Drain it immediately, rinse it thoroughly under cold water, and drain again. (Rinsing with cold water stops the cooking process.)

However, when you are cooking a pound of pasta or more, undercook it very slightly. This amount of pasta will continue to cook a little after draining because the larger mass retains the heat longer. Drain, rinse, and drain again. Then pat the pasta dry with paper towels.

DRESSING THE PASTA

Some people like to dress pasta while it's still hot because it absorbs more of the flavor of the dressing. But since the pasta isn't rinsed in cold water, it softens more. If you like to taste the pasta in your salad as well as the dressing, then add the dressing to cooled pasta. The choice is yours.

In any event, when a pasta salad stands for a couple of hours, it soaks up the dressing and appears dry. To freshen and moisten it, you need either to toss the pasta with the dressing that has sunk to the bottom of the bowl or to add more dressing. When you make a pasta salad, dress it, toss it, and serve it immediately. You end up using a lot less dressing than when you dress the salad in advance.

STORING AND SERVING PASTA SALADS

My favorite pasta salads are those that are made no longer than an hour before serving. That way they taste spritely, the texture of the pasta is perfect, and they can be served at room temperature, which allows all the flavors to come through.

However, there are times when you want the convenience of serving a cold pasta salad you've prepared the night before. If at all possible, prepare most of the salad ingredients the night before, but wait to cook and cool the pasta, and then toss it with the prepared ingredients close to serving time.

If this is not possible, then prepare and cook all the salad elements in advance, but keep them separate. Cook, drain, and cool the noodles, then toss them with just enough oil so that they don't stick together. Keep everything, separate and covered, in the refrigerator until the following day. To serve the salad, remove all of the ingredients from the refrigerator an hour or two before you want to eat, so that the chill wears off and the full flavor of the ingredients comes through. If you are adding green vegetables to the salad, do so at the last possible moment (if left on too long, the acid in the dressing will turn the green a dull olive color).

If you are serving leftover pasta salad, remove it from the refrigerator an hour before serving to revive the flavors. Try to add one fresh ingredient to pick up the taste and color of the salad, and if the salad looks dry, add a little more dressing before serving.

HOW TO CREATE A PASTA SALAD WITH LEFTOVERS

For Two People

Cooked pasta	2 cups
Other ingredients, such as cooked vegetables, meat, beans, or poultry	2 cups
Dressing	2 to 4 tablespoons

MATCHING INGREDIENTS WITH DRESSINGS

Pasta salads that include meat and poultry are terrific with mustard vinaigrettes or with mayonnaise- or yogurt-based dressings, such as Rich and Creamy Dressing (page 217).

Seafood pasta salads are delicious with my Basic Vinaigrette Dressing or Citrus Dressing (pages 213, 216) or Anchovy Mayonnaise (page 215).

Pasta salads with cheese work best with vinaigrettes that include mustard, fresh herbs, or chopped tomatoes (see the Basic Vinaigrette variations, page 214).

Bean and lentil pasta salads marry nicely with my Citrus Dressing or Tart and Sweet Balsamic Dressing (both page 216).

Fresh vegetable pasta salads taste best with the citrus or vinaigrette dressings—they enhance the flavor of the vegetables.

Chicken Salad with Wagon Wheels

PASTA: *Medium-size fancy shapes*
MAKES: *4 servings*
TIME: *35 minutes*

Delicious, refreshing, elegant, simple— all are apt descriptions of this salad. Follow it with a berry dessert or start with a cold soup, such as gazpacho.

Salt
2 ribs celery
1 scallion (green onion)
¾ pound skinless, boneless chicken or
  turkey breasts
½ pound (3 cups) rotelle (wagon wheels)
  or radiatore
1 tablespoon dried tarragon
⅓ cup lemon juice
⅓ cup mayonnaise (regular or low-fat)
⅓ cup sour cream or low-fat yogurt
Freshly ground black pepper
Boston or Bibb lettuce leaves, for serving

1. Bring a large pot of salted water to a boil for the pasta.

2. Meanwhile, cut the celery into ¼-inch dice. Trim off 1 inch of the scallion top and cut the rest into very thin slices. Cut the chicken into 1-inch dice.

3. When the water comes to a boil, add the pasta and cook until it is almost done, about 7 minutes. Add the chicken chunks and boil until cooked through, 2 to 3 minutes. Drain the pasta and chicken in a large colander. Then transfer the pasta and chicken to a plate, cover lightly with aluminum foil, and refrigerate to cool off quickly, about 10 minutes.

4. In a large mixing bowl, whisk together the tarragon, lemon juice, mayonnaise, and sour cream. Season to taste with salt and pepper.

5. When the pasta is cool, toss it with the dressing in the mixing bowl, cover lightly with foil, and refrigerate for another 10 minutes. Serve the salad over lettuce leaves. Or chill it thoroughly, about 1 hour, and then serve.

VARIATION

Chicken Waldorf Pasta Salad: Add 1 McIntosh apple, cored and cut into ½-inch dice, and ½ cup chopped walnuts.

Chinese Chicken and Pasta Salad

PASTA: *Medium-size fancy shapes or fresh egg noodles*
MAKES: *6 servings*
TIME: *30 to 35 minutes*

Noodles combined with poached chicken and Chinese seasonings makes for a delicious, original salad that appeals to children as well as adults. It is wonderful as part of a barbecue or buffet.

When I have the energy, I wash a few spinach leaves to serve with this salad for a deep green contrast to the pale tan dressing. Sliced tomatoes or cucumbers also make a good accompaniment. This salad tastes best at room temperature. If you do chill it and serve it later, it might need more seasoning or a touch of vinegar to liven it up.

After the powerful flavors of this main course, stick with a simple seasonal fruit for dessert.

Salt
¾ to 1 pound skinless, boneless chicken or turkey breasts
1 pound fusilli, rotini, Chinese egg noodles, fettuccine, or broad egg noodles
4 scallions (green onions)
1 teaspoon sugar
2 tablespoons soy sauce, preferably low-sodium
2 tablespoons sesame oil
2 tablespoons rice or white wine vinegar
2 teaspoons chili paste with garlic
¼ cup peanut butter
Spinach or romaine lettuce leaves, for serving (optional)

1. Bring a large pot of salted water to a boil, for the pasta.

2. Meanwhile, cut the chicken into strips about 2 inches long and ½ inch wide.

3. When the water comes to a boil, add the chicken and simmer until it is just cooked through, 2 to 3 minutes. Using a sieve or slotted spoon, fish the chicken strips out of the water and set them in a colander to drain. Bring the water back to a boil, skim off any surface foam, and add the pasta. Cook until it is tender but still firm to the bite, 8 to 10 minutes.

4. While the pasta is cooking, trim the scallions and cut them into pieces. In a food processor or blender, combine the scallions, sugar, soy sauce, sesame oil, vinegar, chili paste, and peanut butter. Process until

smooth. Season to taste with salt, and transfer to a mixing or serving bowl.

5. Drain the pasta and rinse it under cold water to cool it completely. Drain the pasta again, pat it dry, and add it to the mixing bowl along with the chicken. Toss the salad with the dressing, and adjust the seasoning if necessary. Serve over spinach or romaine lettuce leaves, if you wish.

VARIATION

Sesame Chicken and Pasta Salad: Substitute 3 tablespoons sesame paste for the peanut butter and 2 teaspoons hoisin sauce for the sugar. Add ½ cup chopped fresh cilantro leaves to the dressing ingredients in step 1.

Crab Salad with Pizzoccheri

PASTA: *Ribbons made of buckwheat or whole-wheat, or flavored, or tubes*
MAKES: *4 servings*
TIME: *25 minutes*

Pizzoccheri, slightly twisted charcoal gray-brown buckwheat ribbons—a specialty of northern Italy—taste much like Japanese soba. The texture of buckwheat noodles is a lot less chewy than that of semolina, which is what makes them so good in cold summertime salads.

Salt
¾ *pound pizzoccheri, Japanese soba noodles, or spinach penne*
½ *cup mayonnaise*
¼ *cup lime juice*
½ *cup (packed) fresh parsley leaves*
2 *scallions (green onions)*
⅛ *to ¼ teaspoon cayenne pepper*
4 *plum tomatoes*
¾ *to 1 pound fresh or frozen lump crabmeat (thawed if frozen)*

1. Bring a large pot of salted water to a boil. Add the pasta and cook until it is tender but still firm to the bite, 8 to 10 minutes.

2. Meanwhile, whisk the mayonnaise and lime juice together in a mixing bowl. Rinse, pat dry, and mince the parsley, and add it to the mayonnaise. Trim the scallions, thinly slice them, and add them to the mixing bowl along with cayenne. Halve the tomatoes and remove the seeds with a spoon. Chop the tomatoes into small dice and add them to the mayonnaise. Mix well, add the crabmeat, and mix again.

3. Drain the noodles and rinse them under cold water to cool them thoroughly. Drain again. Add the noodles to the salad and mix

all the ingredients together. Season to taste with salt and serve immediately. Or chill, covered, in the refrigerator for 2 hours or as long as overnight.

VARIATIONS

■ Substitute leftover grilled fish steaks—such as swordfish, tuna, mako, or even salmon fillets—for the crabmeat. You'll need about 2 cups cubed cooked fish.
■ This is also terrific with scallops or shrimp. Simmer the scallops or shrimp in the pasta water for 2 to 3 minutes, and then retrieve them with a sieve. Drain, and cool to room temperature before adding to the salad.
■ An addition of 1 cup cooked corn kernels would be a natural in this salad.

Fiery Shrimp, Avocado, and Gnocchi Salad

PASTA: *Medium-size fancy shapes or tubes*
MAKES: *4 servings*
TIME: *25 minutes*

The tender avocado and soft pasta balance the shrimp and crunchy vegetables, and act as a perfect foil for the heat of the Tabasco.

Salt
½ pound gnocchi pasta, fusilli, or penne
¾ pound shrimp, peeled and deveined, sea scallops, or lump crabmeat
2 scallions (green onions)
1 rib celery
1 green bell pepper
¼ cup vegetable oil
2 tablespoons red wine vinegar, or 3 tablespoons lemon juice
½ teaspoon dried thyme
¼ teaspoon Tabasco sauce
2 ripe avocados, preferably Hass
Freshly ground black pepper

1. Bring a large pot of salted water to a boil. Add the pasta and cook until it is tender but still firm to the bite, 8 to 10 minutes.

2. Meanwhile, if you are using sea scallops, first remove the rubbery appendage on the side of each scallop. In a large skillet, bring an inch of water to a simmer. Add the shrimp or scallops, cover, and simmer gently over low heat until the seafood is cooked through, 3 to 4 minutes. Drain and let cool. (If you are using crabmeat, pick it over and discard any bits of shell or debris; do not cook.)

3. Trim 1 inch off the scallion tops and cut the rest into 2-inch lengths. Cut the celery into chunks. Core, seed, and cut the green pepper into chunks. Then combine the scallions, celery, peppers, oil, vinegar, thyme, and Tabasco in a food processor and blend until smooth.

4. Drain the pasta and rinse it under cold water to cool it thoroughly. Drain again and pat it dry.

5. Peel and pit the avocados, and dice them. Combine the pasta, seafood, and avocados in a mixing bowl, and toss well with the dressing. Season to taste with salt, and serve immediately at room temperature. Or chill, covered, in the refrigerator for 2 hours or as long as overnight.

VARIATION

This is terrific with leftover grilled fish, such as swordfish, tuna, mako, or even salmon fillets. You'll need about 2 cups of cubed leftover fish; add it to the salad in step 5.

ADVANCE PREPARATION

When you want to prepare a pasta salad ahead, here is how you can keep it looking fresh: To avoid discoloring any green ingredient, make the dressing without the acid element (vinegar or lemon juice) and toss the salad with that acid-free dressing. Just before you are ready to serve the salad, add the vinegar or lemon juice and toss again.

Also, do not combine a particularly perishable ingredient, such as avocados, with the others in advance. Add the fragile ingredient right before you serve the salad.

Smoked Salmon, Sugar Snap Peas, and Ziti

PASTA: *Medium-size tubes or fancy shapes*
MAKES: *4 servings*
TIME: *30 to 35 minutes*

Other smoked fish can stand in for the salmon here. Even smoked sardines will work in this salad. The sweet sugar snap peas and the sharp dressing contrast felicitously with the smoky fish.

If you are serving this to guests, precede the salad with a chilled cream soup and follow it with a berry dessert.

Salt
¾ pound (3 cups) sugar snap peas or snow peas, or 2 cups shelled fresh peas
1 shallot or 2 scallions (green onions)
½ recipe Basic Vinaigrette Dressing (see page 213)
½ pound (3 cups) ziti, penne, or fusilli
½ pound smoked salmon, or canned smoked mussels, oysters, or sardines
½ cup (packed) fresh parsley leaves
Freshly ground black pepper

1. Bring a large pot of salted water to a boil for the pasta.

2. While the water is heating, snap off the ends of the snap peas or snow peas and pull off any strings. Discard any yellow or bruised ones. Peel and mince the shallot (or trim 1 inch off the scallion top and cut the rest into very thin slices). Make the dressing in a large mixing or serving bowl, and add the shallots or scallions to it.

3. When the water comes to a boil, add the sugar snap or snow peas and cook until they are crisp-tender, about 1 minute. Using a sieve, retrieve them from the water and run cold water over them to stop the cooking. Set them aside to drain.

4. Add the pasta to the boiling water and cook until it is tender but still firm to the bite, 8 to 10 minutes.

5. While the pasta is cooking, cut the smoked salmon into ½-inch pieces and add them to the dressing in the mixing bowl. (Or drain the canned smoked fish, pat it dry, cut it into pieces, and add them to the mixing bowl.) Rinse, pat dry, and mince the parsley, and add it to the mixing bowl. Pat dry the snap peas and add them to the mixing bowl.

6. Drain the pasta and rinse it under cold water to cool it. Drain it again, pat it dry with a kitchen towel, and add it to the mixing bowl. Toss well and season to taste with freshly ground pepper (the smoked salmon will make it salty enough).

VARIATIONS

Instead of the sugar snap peas, use 4 Kirby cucumbers, peeled, seeded, and diced. Or try the salad with 2 ripe tomatoes, seeded and cut into small dice.

Beef and Fusilli Salad with Horseradish Dressing

PASTA: *Medium-size fancy shapes or tubes*
MAKES: *4 to 6 servings*
TIME: *30 to 35 minutes*

I developed this recipe using leftover roast beef, but you don't need to cook a roast before you can enjoy it. Just go to the deli counter at your market, buy a thick slice of roast beef, and voilà, the work is done!

Salt
½ pound (3 cups) fusilli, rotini, or ziti
½ cup mayonnaise (regular or low-fat)
2 tablespoons white wine vinegar or
*　　cider vinegar*
¼ cup prepared white horseradish
¾ pound boneless roasted beef or leftover
*　　cooked beef, such as filet or sirloin,*
*　　fat removed*
1 clove garlic
½ cup pitted green olives
8 leaves romaine lettuce
Freshly ground black pepper

1. Bring a large pot of salted water to a boil. Add the pasta and cook until it is tender but still firm to the bite, about 10 minutes.

2. Meanwhile, whisk together the mayonnaise, vinegar, and horseradish in a large mixing bowl. Cut the beef into ½-inch cubes. Peel and mince the garlic. Chop the olives. Rinse the lettuce leaves, pat them dry, and cut them crosswise into thin shreds. Add all of these ingredients to the mayonnaise, and combine thoroughly. Season to taste with salt and pepper.

3. When the pasta is done, drain it and rinse it under cold water to cool it slightly. Drain again and pat dry. Add the pasta to the mixing bowl and toss all of the ingredients together. Adjust the seasoning and serve immediately, or chill, covered, in the refrigerator for 2 hours.

SECOND TIME AROUND

Leftovers of this Beef and Fusilli Salad make a great filling for pita bread sandwiches, especially if you add slices of tomato.

ESPECIALLY GOOD FOR CHILDREN

Except for the horseradish, kids love this salad. Divide the dressing between 2 bowls. Add 2 tablespoons horseradish to one bowl and leave the other dressing plain. Then divide the remaining ingredients between the bowls and you have two salads: one for the kids and one for you.

Zippy Beef with Ziti

PASTA: *Medium-size tubes*
MAKES: *4 to 6 servings*
TIME: *25 to 30 minutes*

To get the maximum flavor, make sure the beef and the dressing are still warm when you toss them with the pasta.

Unfortunately, the acidity of the lime juice turns the zucchini from bright to dull green. So for the salad to look as good as it tastes, be sure to top it with diced red bell pepper.

Salt
¾ pound (3½ cups) ziti, mezzani,
    or penne
½ to ¾ pound boneless beef tenderloin or
    filet, or boneless roasted beef,
    fat removed
2 medium-size zucchini or yellow squash
1 clove garlic
½ cup (packed) fresh mint leaves
½ cup (packed) fresh cilantro or
    parsley leaves
½ medium-size red bell pepper
¼ cup extra-virgin olive oil
1 teaspoon ground cumin
½ teaspoon chili powder
⅓ cup lime or lemon juice
Freshly ground black pepper

1. Bring a large pot of salted water to a boil. Add the pasta and cook until it is tender but still firm to the bite, about 10 minutes.

2. Meanwhile, cut the beef into strips about 1½ to 2 inches long, ½ inch wide, and ¼ inch thick. Rinse the squash and trim the ends. Cut the squash lengthwise into quarters, and cut away most of the seeds. Cut the rest into strips approximately the same dimensions as the beef strips. Peel and mince the garlic. Rinse the herbs, pat them dry, and mince them. Cut the red pepper into a fine dice.

3. Heat the oil in a large skillet, over high heat. Add the garlic and beef strips, and stir-fry until the strips are no longer pink, about 1 minute. Stir in the cumin and chili powder, then add the zucchini strips and lime juice.

Bring to a simmer over medium heat, and cook until the zucchini is barely tender, 1 to 2 minutes. Remove the skillet from the heat, and season to taste with salt and pepper. Transfer the ingredients to a large bowl.

4. When the pasta is done, drain it and rinse it under cold water to cool it slightly. Drain again and pat dry. Add the pasta to the mixing bowl, and toss all the ingredients together. Adjust the seasoning. Right before serving, toss the salad with the minced cilantro and mint. Top each portion with diced red bell pepper.

Ham, Endive, and Apple with Elbows

PASTA: *Small tubes or medium-size fancy shapes*
MAKES: *4 servings*
TIME: *25 to 30 minutes*

This salad is dear to me because it combines ingredients frequently used in Belgium, the country where I spent part of my childhood and where I learned about good food.

Add salt only after all the ingredients have been assembled and you have tasted it for seasoning, because the mustard is salty. I prefer to serve this at room temperature, but it also works well when chilled. So, leftovers can be eaten straight from the fridge.

Salt
¾ pound elbow macaroni,
    fusilli, or shells
½ cup fresh parsley leaves
½ cup mayonnaise
¼ cup Dijon mustard
½ cup dry white wine
¾ pound smoked ham,
    such as Black Forest
2 Belgian endives, or 5 or 6 medium-size
    romaine lettuce leaves
2 McIntosh apples
Freshly ground black pepper

1. Bring a large pot of salted water to a boil. Add the pasta and cook until it is tender but still firm to the bite, about 10 minutes.

2. Meanwhile, rinse the parsley and pat it dry. Purée the parsley with the mayonnaise, mustard, and white wine in a blender or food processor. Place this dressing in a large mixing bowl.

3. Dice the ham and add it to the mixing bowl. Halve the endives lengthwise, cut them into ¼-inch-wide crescents, and add them to the bowl. (If you are using lettuce leaves, tear them into 1-inch pieces.) Wash

and core the apples, cut them into ½-inch chunks, and add them to the bowl.

4. When the pasta is done, drain it well, rinse it under cold water, and drain again. Pat the pasta dry. Add the cooled pasta to the mixing bowl and toss all the ingredients together. Season to taste with salt and pepper and serve.

ESPECIALLY GOOD FOR DIETERS

Substitute ½ cup nonfat yogurt for the mayonnaise, and add 2 tablespoons vegetable oil to the dressing. Instead of the ham, use lean turkey or 2 cups chick-peas (one 19-ounce can, drained).

ON SEASONING SALADS

I recommend that you always do your final seasoning after all the ingredients for a particular recipe are cooked and have been assembled at the temperature you are going to serve them. Chilled salads will need more salt than those served at room temperature, and pasta salads that have been made in advance will need some extra dressing before serving.

Broccoli Penne with Blue Cheese Dressing

PASTA: *Medium-size tubes*
MAKES: *4 to 6 servings*
TIME: *30 to 35 minutes*

....

Separately, the ingredients in this salad might seem ordinary, but when put together they make a fantastic mix, delicious on a spring night—or on any night of the year, for that matter. You don't need much else for dinner, although a rich chocolate dessert couldn't hurt!

Salt
½ pound penne, mezzani, or ziti
1 head broccoli or cauliflower
1 cup cherry tomatoes
½ recipe Blue Cheese Dressing (see page 214)
Freshly ground black pepper

1. Bring a large pot of salted water to a boil. Add the pasta and cook until it is tender but still firm to the bite, 8 to 10 minutes.

2. At the same time, bring a medium-size saucepan of water to a boil for the broccoli. Cut the broccoli into florets, and cook until they are just tender, about 3 minutes. Drain the broccoli and rinse it under cold water. Then drain it again, pat it dry, and set it aside. (If any of the florets seem too big, cut them into smaller pieces.)

3. Halve or quarter the tomatoes. Make the dressing in a large mixing bowl, and add the tomatoes and broccoli.

4. When the pasta is done, drain it, rinse it under cold water, and drain it again. Pat it dry. Add the pasta to the mixing bowl and toss it with the other ingredients. Season to taste with salt and pepper, and serve at room temperature.

VARIATION

Tex-Mex Broccoli Penne Salad: Blend ⅔ cup olive oil with 2 scallions, thinly sliced, 1 jalapeño pepper, seeded and minced, ¼ cup minced fresh cilantro, and ¼ cup lime juice. Toss the pasta and vegetables with this instead of the blue cheese dressing.

Cucumbers with Cool Somen Noodles

PASTA: *Thin strands*
MAKES: *4 to 6 servings*
TIME: *20 minutes*

....

This dish is perfect for summer nights and will keep well for a couple of days. If you do make it in advance, store the cucumbers separately from the noodles.

Because the flavors of this dish are so unusual, I think it is better to serve small portions as a side dish to grilled salmon, tuna, or swordfish, for example, rather than as a full-blown main course.

These Japanese wheat noodles have a stickier quality than Western wheat noodles. If you substitute Western pasta for the somen, you'll need an extra 5 to 10 minutes because they take longer to cook.

Salt
2 carrots
2 scallions (green onions)
½-inch piece of fresh ginger, or
    ¼ teaspoon ground ginger
⅓ cup (packed) fresh mint leaves, or
    1 teaspoon dried mint
2 cucumbers
¼ cup soy sauce (preferably low-salt)
2 tablespoons vegetable oil
¼ cup rice or white wine vinegar
1 teaspoon sugar
Freshly ground black pepper
½ pound somen (Japanese thin wheat
    noodles) or vermicelli

1. Bring a large pot of salted water to a boil for the noodles.

2. Meanwhile, peel the carrots and cut them into thick rounds. Trim the scallions and cut them into 2-inch lengths. Peel the ginger, and rinse the mint leaves and pat them dry. Peel, seed, and cut the cucumbers into ¼-inch dice; set them aside.

3. In a food processor, combine the carrots, scallions, ginger, and mint; process until smooth. Add the soy sauce, oil, vinegar, and sugar, and process until all the ingredients are well blended. Season to taste with salt (added judiciously because of the soy sauce) and pepper, and transfer the mixture to a large mixing bowl.

4. When the water comes to a boil, add the noodles and cook until they are tender but still firm to the bite, 2 to 3 minutes. Drain the noodles and rinse them under cold water until they are completely chilled. Drain again, and pat dry. Add them to the dressing in the mixing bowl. Toss well and chill until serving time. To serve, ladle the portions out and top each one with some of the diced cucumbers.

DRY AND FRESH HERBS

Because fresh herbs don't taste like their dried versions, I use different measures for each one in different recipes. I can't say that as a rule, X amount of dried herbs equals Y amount of fresh—the flavor and aroma of fresh and dried herbs are distinctly different. The only rule I do follow is: Use fresh herbs with abandon but add dried herbs with caution.

Green Bean and Fusilli Salad Française

PASTA: *Medium-size fancy shapes*
MAKES: *4 servings*
TIME: *20 to 25 minutes*

If at all possible, try to buy French haricots verts, which are skinny and sweet and quite unlike the large and fibrous American green beans. If you are unable to find haricots verts, substitute ordinary green beans, split lengthwise and then cut into 1-inch pieces.

Salt
½ pound green beans, preferably French
*   haricots verts*
½ pound (3 cups) fusilli, rotini, or
*   medium-size shells*
2 medium-size tomatoes
1 bunch watercress, stemmed
1 tablespoon black olive paste, or ¼ cup
*   pitted and minced cured black olives*
1 recipe Citrus Dressing (see page 216)
Freshly ground black pepper

1. Bring a large pot of salted water to a boil for the pasta.

2. Trim the green beans and cut them into 1½-inch lengths.

3. When the water comes to a boil, add the pasta and cook for 5 minutes. Add the beans and continue to cook until both the pasta and the beans are tender, another 4 to 5 minutes.

4. Meanwhile, halve the tomatoes, remove the seeds with a spoon, and chop the tomatoes. Rinse the watercress and pat it dry. Using a whisk, blend the black olive paste with the citrus dressing in a large mixing bowl. Then add the tomatoes and watercress leaves.

5. Drain the pasta and green beans, and rinse them under cold water. Drain again, pat dry, and add to the mixing bowl. Toss the ingredients together, and season to taste with salt and pepper.

Fresh Tomatoes with Warm Fedelini

PASTA: *Thin strands or small fancy shapes*
MAKES: *4 servings*
TIME: *20 to 25 minutes*

The perfect way to eat this brightly flavored dish is at room temperature or slightly warm. However, the recipe also works with hot pasta or served chilled. If you intend to serve this cold, whether a few hours or even a day after making the salad, then rinse the pasta under cold water right after draining it, and be sure it is thoroughly chilled before combining it with the tomatoes and dressing.

Salt
3 ripe medium-size or
   8 plum tomatoes
   (1 to 1¼ pounds)
1 cup (packed) fresh basil,
   mint, parsley, arugula, or
   watercress leaves
¼ cup olive oil
3 tablespoons lemon juice
1 pound fedelini, linguine
   fine, or spaghettini, or
   3 cups small bow-ties
   (farfallini)
Freshly ground black pepper

1. Bring a large pot of salted water to a boil. Add the pasta and cook until it is tender but still firm to the bite, 8 to 10 minutes.

2. Meanwhile, halve the tomatoes and remove the seeds with a spoon. Finely chop the tomatoes by hand or in a food processor (don't let them get soupy), and then place them in a large mixing bowl.

3. Rinse the basil (or other herb) and pat it dry. Combine the basil, oil, and lemon juice in the food processor or blender, and process until smooth. Add this mixture to the toma-

toes and toss well. Season to taste with salt and pepper.

4. Drain the pasta and toss it with the tomatoes and dressing. Refrigerate for 20 minutes to cool slightly before serving.

SECOND TIME AROUND

Leftovers are delicious topped with diced fresh mozzarella, freshly grated Parmesan, or crumbled dry goat cheese.

Rotelle à la Grecque

PASTA: *Medium-size fancy shapes or tubes*
MAKES: *4 servings*
TIME: *20 to 25 minutes*

This snappy salad is perfect to serve on a summer evening because the only cooking you have to do is boiling the pasta. Don't limit this to Monday-to-Friday cooking—it's an excellent choice for a weekend summer brunch, as part of a buffet, or for a school potluck supper.

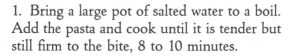

Salt
½ pound (2½ cups) rotelle
   (wagon wheels), fusilli, or penne
¾ pound fresh spinach, or
   1 head romaine lettuce
½ cup olive oil
6 tablespoons lemon juice
2 teaspoons dried oregano
1 clove garlic
1 can (2 ounces) anchovies, drained
1 green bell pepper
2 scallions (green onions)
2 medium-size or 12 cherry tomatoes
¼ to ½ pound feta cheese, or dry goat's-
   milk cheese, to your taste
4 radishes
6 imported black olives, preferably
   Kalamata, or 1 tablespoon
   black olive paste
Freshly ground black pepper

1. Bring a large pot of salted water to a boil.
Add the pasta and cook until it is tender but
still firm to the bite, about 10 minutes.

2. Meanwhile, stem and wash the spinach;
then pat it dry and coarsely chop the leaves.
Set it aside.

3. Combine the olive oil, lemon juice,
oregano, garlic, and anchovies in a food
processor or blender, and process until thoroughly blended. Pour the dressing into a
large mixing bowl.

4. After you prepare each of the following
ingredients, add it to the dressing in the mixing bowl: Core, seed, and cut the green pep-

per into small dice. Trim 3 inches off the
scallion tops and thinly slice the rest. Chop
the tomatoes (or quarter the cherry tomatoes). Crumble the feta cheese. Trim, rinse,
and chop the radishes. Pit and mince the
black olives.

5. When the pasta is done, drain it and rinse
it under cold water. Drain it again and pat it
dry. Add the cooled pasta to the mixing bowl
along with the chopped spinach. Toss the ingredients well, and season the salad to taste
with lots of fresh pepper. (The feta and anchovies will make the salad taste salty
enough.)

Cool Summer
Couscous Salad

PASTA: *Tiny shapes*
MAKES: *6 servings*
TIME: *20 minutes*

A light meal for a hot summer night, this
salad is also great as a side dish with
grilled swordfish, tuna steaks, lamb chops,
and even ham steaks. Think of it too as a
way to use leftover tiny pasta. This will keep,

refrigerated, for 2 days.

A tangy fruit salad made with pineapple, strawberries, and banana would make a good finish to this simple meal.

> 1¾ cups precooked couscous, or 3 cups cooked stelline, acini de pepe, or tubettini
> 2¼ cups boiling water
> ⅓ cup olive oil
> ¼ cup lemon or lime juice
> 1 jar (3 ounces) pimientos, drained
> 1 package (10 ounces) frozen corn kernels, thawed, or 2 cups freshly cooked corn kernels, chilled
> 1 medium-size or 2 small green bell peppers
> Salt and freshly ground black pepper

1. Place the couscous in a large mixing bowl. Pour the boiling water over it and let it stand until the grains have swelled and are softened, about 20 minutes.

2. Meanwhile, combine the oil and lemon juice in a serving bowl. (If you are using leftover pasta, add it to the serving bowl at this point.)

3. Mince the pimientos and add them to the bowl along with the corn kernels. Core, seed, and finely chop the green peppers, and add them to the serving bowl as well.

4. When the couscous has softened, drain it in a sieve to remove any remaining water. Break up any clumps with a fork or your fingers, and add the couscous to the bowl. Mix

all of the ingredients together, and season to taste with salt and pepper. Serve immediately, or cover and chill until serving time.

ESPECIALLY GOOD FOR CHILDREN

I have found that couscous, hot or cold, is a great favorite with my daughter and even with the fussiest eater among her friends. For this salad, I put half the couscous in a separate bowl and mix it with a dressing that she and her friends like, along with the corn kernels and perhaps some diced smoked turkey or ham. The other half of the salad I make as indicated above, adjusting the amount of the remaining ingredients.

Couscous and Lentil Salad

PASTA: *Tiny shapes*
MAKES: *4 servings*
TIME: *20 to 35 minutes*

The time this recipe requires varies—35 minutes if you cook the lentils fresh, only 20 minutes if you happen to have cooked lentils on hand. It's a basic recipe in which you can substitute any variety of cooked legumes for the lentils. Chick-peas are especially delicious.

For a different dressing, just take a look at pages 213 to 217 and substitute ½ cup of another choice.

> 1 cup lentils
> 1 cup precooked couscous, or
>   1½ cups cooked acini de pepe, orzo, or
>   stelline
> 1¼ cups boiling water
> 1 red bell pepper
> ¼ cup olive oil
> ¼ cup balsamic vinegar or another mild,
>   sweet vinegar
> 2 cloves garlic
> 1 teaspoon Dijon mustard
> Salt and freshly ground black pepper

1. Bring 5 cups of water to a boil in a large saucepan. Add the lentils, cover the pan, and cook over medium heat until tender, 20 to 25 minutes.

2. Meanwhile, place the couscous in a large mixing bowl. Pour the boiling water over it and let it stand until the grains have swelled and softened, about 20 minutes.

3. Core, seed, and finely dice the pepper. In a blender or food processor, combine the oil, vinegar, garlic, and mustard, and mix until very well blended.

4. When the lentils are done, drain them and rinse them under cold water. Drain well again and pat dry. Fluff the couscous with a fork, and add the lentils. Pour the dressing through a sieve (to catch the garlic bits) over the lentils and couscous, and add the chopped peppers. Mix thoroughly, and season to taste with salt and pepper.

Note: Don't toss out those bits of garlic. Just add them to another dressing and refrigerate.

VARIATIONS

- Instead of the bell pepper, add 1 cup of a different diced crunchy vegetable, such as fennel or celery.
- Other possible additions include: ¼ cup minced fresh herbs, such as parsley or mint; ½ cup diced cooked ham, chicken, or turkey; ½ of a cup diced cooked vegetable, such as broccoli or asparagus.

Saffron Orzo Salad

PASTA: *Tiny shapes*
MAKES: *4 to 6 servings*
TIME: *10 minutes*

Simply delicious and incredibly easy, this is a beautiful pasta salad to serve with cold veal, salmon, or chicken.

Salt
1 generous cup orzo or tubettini
1 scallion (green onion)
½ cup (packed) fresh parsley leaves
½ cup olive oil
¼ teaspoon powdered saffron
3 tablespoons lemon juice
Freshly ground black pepper

1. Bring a large pot of salted water to a boil. Add the pasta and cook until it is tender, about 10 minutes.

2. Meanwhile, rinse the parsley leaves and pat them dry. Trim the scallion and cut it into pieces. Combine the scallion, parsley, olive oil, saffron, and lemon juice in a blender or food processor, and process until smooth. Season to taste with salt and pepper. Transfer the dressing to a large serving bowl.

3. Drain the pasta, rinse it under cold water, and drain again. Add the cooled pasta to the dressing, toss well, adjust the seasoning, and serve at room temperature.

SECOND TIME AROUND

■ Brighten leftovers with some acidity: for each 2 cups add 1 tablespoon lemon juice.
■ Turn leftovers into a different salad entirely. For 2 cups of leftovers, make a dressing of ¼ cup mayonnaise and ¼ cup crushed tomatoes. Add 2 cups chopped fresh vegetables, such as red peppers or cold steamed asparagus, to the salad.

Spanish Tubetti Salad with Peas and Pimientos

PASTA: *Small tubes*
MAKES: *4 to 6 servings*
TIME: *25 minutes*

Here's a salad that's brimming with vegetables, easy to make, and chock full of flavor. If you turn this into a side dish, serve it with a black bean salad, slices of cold roast pork or baked ham, or grilled tuna or swordfish steaks.

Salt
1 pound tubetti, ditali, or orzo
1 scallion (green onion)
½ cup (4-ounce jar) pimientos, drained
6 tablespoons olive oil
¼ cup lemon juice or white wine vinegar
1 cup (packed) fresh parsley leaves
1 red or green bell pepper
1 package (10 ounces) frozen petite peas, thawed
1 teaspoon dried red pepper flakes (optional)

1. Bring a large pot of salted water to a boil. Add the pasta and cook until it is tender but still firm to the bite, 8 to 10 minutes.

2. Meanwhile, trim about 3 inches off the scallion top and cut the rest into chunks. In a blender or food processor, combine the scallion with the pimientos, olive oil, lemon juice, and parsley leaves. Process until smooth, and season to taste with salt and red pepper flakes. Place this dressing in a large mixing bowl.

3. Core, seed, and cut the bell pepper into ½-inch dice; then add it to the mixing bowl. Pat the peas dry, and add them to the bowl.

4. Drain the pasta and rinse it under cold water until it's thoroughly cooled. Drain the pasta, pat it dry, and add it to the peppers and peas. Toss the ingredients well, adjust the seasoning, and serve at room temperature or chilled.

VARIATIONS

■ Add ½ pound (2 cups) diced smoked turkey or ham.
■ For a more elegant presentation, serve the salad over sliced tomatoes or watercress.

Spinach Fettuccine with Minted Tuna and Yellow Squash

PASTA: *Ribbons or medium-size tubes*
MAKES: *6 servings*
TIME: *30 to 35 minutes*

This main-course salad is such a beauty of a recipe that it is well worth considering for guests. When I expect company, I prepare it the slightly more complicated way described in "Especially Good for Company"—it makes for a festive presentation.

If you do prepare this as part of a special meal, then precede it with gazpacho or chilled asparagus vinaigrette and follow it with a lemon- or orange-flavored dessert.

Salt
1 pound spinach fettuccine or penne
1 large or 2 small yellow summer squash
1 cup mayonnaise
¼ cup white wine vinegar or tarragon vinegar
1 cup (packed) fresh mint, dill, or parsley leaves
1 bunch chives, or 2 scallions (green onions)
3 cans (6 ounces each) tuna, packed in oil or water, or 1 pound grilled or baked fresh skinless tuna fillet
1 large cucumber
Freshly ground black pepper

1. Bring a large pot of salted water to a boil. Add the pasta and cook until it is tender but still firm to the bite, 8 to 10 minutes.

2. Meanwhile rinse the squash and cut it into ½-inch dice. Add water to a depth of 1 inch in a medium-size saucepan and bring to a boil over medium-high heat. Add the squash, cook until just tender, about 2 minutes. (If you have a microwave oven, set the squash in a 10-inch round plate, cover, and cook at full power for 3 minutes.) Once the squash is cooked, drain it and set it aside to cool slightly.

3. In a large mixing bowl, whisk together the mayonnaise and vinegar. Rinse, pat dry, and mince the mint leaves and chives (or scallions). Add them to the mayonnaise. Drain the tuna and add it to the mixing bowl along with the cooled squash. Peel, seed, and finely dice the cucumber and add it to the bowl.

4. Drain the pasta and rinse under cold water. Drain the pasta again, pat it dry, and add it to the mixing bowl. Toss all the ingredients together, and season to taste with salt and pepper.

ESPECIALLY GOOD FOR COMPANY

Divide the mayonnaise and vinegar between two mixing bowls, and whisk them together in each bowl. To one of the bowls, add the mint and chives; to the other add the tuna, squash, and cucumber. Mix the contents of each bowl well.

When the pasta has been drained and cooled, toss it with the minted mayonnaise.

To present the dish, mound the tuna mixture in the center of a large platter or shallow bowl, and form a wreath around it with the dressed spinach pasta. The dish then looks as fabulous as it tastes.

TASTING INDIVIDUAL ELEMENTS OF A DISH

If you are the type of cook (as you should be) who loves to taste every step of the way as you are preparing a recipe, you might notice that the dressings I make for pasta salads seem sharp when tasted alone. But once combined with cooked pasta and the other ingredients, these dressings lose their harshness and the whole dish comes together. Pasta, like potatoes, absorbs seasonings readily, so whatever dressing or sauce you make needs to be overseasoned slightly for the finished dish to taste balanced.

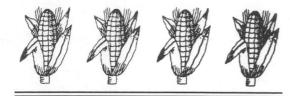

Turkey Pasta Salad with Corn and Pecans

PASTA: *Medium-size fancy shapes*
MAKES: *4 servings*
TIME: *35 minutes*

Because turkey is firmer than chicken and its taste is more pronounced, I tend to use it in dishes that are strongly seasoned. If you prefer a more tender texture, however, go ahead and substitute chicken. The pecans add an unusual flavor and a crunchy note, but you can omit them if you want.

This is a wonderful pasta dish for late summer and early fall, when the days are not yet cool enough to entice you into the kitchen for long but you want to fix something unusual for dinner. In fact this is so good, you could serve it to guests. If you'd like to offer another salad with this, try tomatoes dressed with a vinaigrette. I'd follow this with a plum cake or tart or with a fruit combination that mixes blackberries, plums, and bananas.

Salt
1 rib celery
1 cup shelled pecans
¾ pound skinless, boneless turkey or chicken breasts
¼ cup lime or lemon juice
½ cup mayonnaise (regular or low-fat)
⅛ to ¼ teaspoon cayenne pepper or freshly ground black pepper
2 cups fresh corn kernels, or 1 package (10 ounces) frozen corn kernels, thawed
½ pound (3 cups) radiatore, rotini, or rotelle (wagon wheels)
Romaine lettuce leaves, for serving (optional)

1. Bring a large pot of salted water to a boil for the pasta. In another, medium-size saucepan, bring 1 quart of water to a boil.

2. Meanwhile, cut the celery into ¼-inch dice. Chop the pecans. Cut the turkey into strips about 1½ inches long, ¼ inch wide, and ½ inch thick.

3. In a large mixing bowl, whisk the lime juice, mayonnaise, and cayenne pepper together. Add the celery, pecans, and corn, and set the bowl aside.

4. When the water comes to a boil in the smaller saucepan, reduce the heat and add the turkey strips. Cook at a bare simmer until just done, 1 to 2 minutes (any longer and the turkey will toughen). Drain the turkey strips and pat them dry. Then add them to the mixing bowl and toss.

5. Add the pasta to the large pot of boiling water and cook until it is tender but still firm to the bite, 8 to 10 minutes. Drain the pasta and rinse it under cold water. Drain it again, pat it dry, and then add it to the mixing  bowl. Toss all of the ingredients together and adjust the seasoning. Serve immediately, or cover and chill for a couple of hours. Serve over romaine lettuce if you wish.

Basic Vinaigrette Dressing

MAKES: *1 generous cup*
TIME: *10 minutes*

This dressing is made with more vinegar than you find in salad dressings used for greens. The additional sharpness balances the blandness of the pasta and counteracts the fact that pasta soaks up flavors.

RATIONALIZING LAZINESS: ONE POT OR TWO?

If you really want to avoid washing two pots, you could simmer the turkey strips that you are including in a pasta salad in the same water you will boil the pasta in. I do that in the Chicken Salad with Wagon Wheels (page 193), but I don't do it in the above Turkey Pasta Salad because the turkey requires a gentle hand. I find it easier to control the simmering with the smaller amount of water. However, if you really don't want to bother with two pots, you can always rationalize that you are saving energy by using only one.

If you do choose to use one pot, simmer the turkey first in the pasta water. Remove the cooked strips with a sieve. When the water returns to a boil, it will throw off some grayish scum that comes from the turkey. You can remove it if you wish, using a small strainer or a skimming spoon. If you leave it in, nothing terrible will happen to your salad. There might be bits of congealed turkey stuck to the pasta, but I don't think people will notice.

This dressing is fine with all pasta salads, except perhaps ones that contain seafood.

⅔ cup vegetable or olive oil
¼ cup white or red wine vinegar, or
    ⅓ cup lemon juice
2 teaspoons Dijon mustard
Salt and freshly ground black pepper

 Using a whisk or fork, combine the oil, vinegar, and lemon juice in a small bowl or jar. Season to taste with salt and pepper, and store, covered, in the refrigerator for up to 2 weeks.

VARIATIONS

Add any of the following to the dressing:
  1 tablespoon chopped capers
  1 tablespoon chopped pimientos
  1 teaspoon black or green olive paste
  1 teaspoon sun-dried tomato tapenade
  1 teaspoon dried herbs
  1 tablespoon minced fresh herbs
  1 tablespoon chopped imported olives
  1 teaspoon pesto

DRESSED TO PERFECTION

One pound of cooked pasta can take ½ to ¾ cup of a thin dressing and ¾ to 1 cup of a thicker dressing.

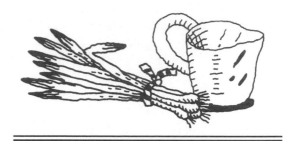

Blue Cheese Dressing

MAKES: *2 cups*
TIME: *10 minutes*

This dressing is especially suited to pasta salads that include vegetables, beans, or lentils. You can substitute other cheeses for the blue cheese. Parmesan, for example, would be delicious. This is also a great dressing for plain steamed vegetables such as broccoli, cauliflower, or asparagus.

4 scallions (green onions)
1⅓ cups vegetable oil
¼ cup white or red wine vinegar
1 cup crumbled blue cheese
Salt and freshly ground black pepper

1. Trim 3 inches off the scallion tops and cut the rest into thin slices.

2. Using a whisk or fork, combine the oil, vinegar, cheese, and scallions. Season to taste with salt and pepper, and store, covered, in the refrigerator for up to 1 week.

MIDDLE EASTERN ACCENT

If you are a lover of Middle Eastern food, you might want to try the following. Take a few spoonfuls of leftover baba ghanouj or hummus, blend it with fresh lemon juice and chopped fresh cilantro, mint, or parsley, and toss this dressing with cooked pasta mixed with steamed vegetables, beans, or poultry.

Anchovy Mayonnaise

MAKES: *about 2 cups*
TIME: *10 minutes*

This is one of the best dressings for pasta salads that contain vegetables, veal, chicken, or fish. And pasta salads aside, it is a wonderful dressing to serve with slices of cold roasted veal or lamb.

*1 cup (packed) fresh parsley or mint
    leaves
2 scallions (green onions)
1 can (2 ounces) anchovies, drained
½ teaspoon dried red pepper flakes
1 cup mayonnaise (regular or
    low-fat)
6 tablespoons lemon juice or tarragon
    vinegar
Salt*

1. Rinse the herbs and pat them dry. Trim and coarsely chop the scallions.

2. Combine all the ingredients except the salt in a blender or food processor, and process until smooth. Season to taste (carefully, because of the anchovies) with salt. Store, covered, in the refrigerator for up to 5 days.

VARIATIONS

Sour Cream Anchovy Dressing: Substitute ½ cup sour cream for ½ cup of the mayonnaise.

Anchovy Dressing (especially good for dieters): Substitute ½ cup low-fat mayonnaise plus ¼ cup vegetable oil for the total amount of mayonnaise. If you can stand a mouth-puckering dressing, increase the lemon juice or vinegar by 2 tablespoons.

Lean Anchovy Dressing Number 2: Substitute 1 cup plain nonfat yogurt for the mayonnaise and reduce the lemon juice or vinegar to ¼ cup.

Tart and Sweet Balsamic Dressing

MAKES: *2 cups*
TIME: *10 minutes*

Balsamic vinegar is sweet and mild, which means you can use more of it than you would a more astringent vinegar. This also implies that you can use less oil in your dressing—a definite plus for those of us watching our waists.

This dressing is lovely with vegetable, legume, and seafood pasta salads because it perks up the other more neutral-tasting ingredients.

I always like to make a basic dressing, like this one, in large quantities so it lasts the week. I can use it plain, or doctor it with a teaspoon or so of another spice, herb, or condiment.

1 cup olive oil
¾ cup balsamic vinegar
2 tablespoon Dijon mustard
6 cloves garlic, peeled
1 teaspoon dried red pepper flakes
Salt

Combine the oil, vinegar, mustard, garlic, and red pepper flakes in a blender or food processor and blend until smooth. Season to taste with salt, and store, covered, in the refrigerator for up to 2 weeks.

GARLIC PIECES

As much as I adore garlic, I prefer it in subtle doses. Sometimes I blend fresh garlic in a dressing, then strain out the garlic bits to produce a milder garlic flavor.

You can save the strained garlic; just add it to a plain vinaigrette or to some plain olive oil.

Citrus Dressing

MAKES: *about ¾ cup*
TIME: *15 minutes*

Although this is pleasing with poultry-and-pasta salads, it is even better with salads that contain seafood or vegetables. Note that you can't store this dressing for too long because it turns bitter within a couple of days.

⅓ cup vegetable or olive oil
⅓ cup lemon juice
3 tablespoons orange juice
½ teaspoon grated lemon zest
½ teaspoon grated orange zest
1 tablespoon minced fresh herbs, such
*   as mint, parsley, or cilantro*
*   (optional)*
Salt and freshly ground black pepper

Using a whisk or fork, combine the oils, juices, zests, and herbs in a small bowl. Season to taste with salt and pepper, and store, covered, in the refrigerator.

Rich and Creamy Dressing

MAKES: *2 cups*
TIME: *5 minutes*

I love this rich dressing, especially in pasta salads that also contain poultry or vegetables. To make a leaner version, use a low-fat mayonnaise and substitute low-fat yogurt for the sour cream.

1 cup sour cream
1 cup mayonnaise
½ cup ketchup
½ cup Dijon
*   mustard*
Salt

Combine the sour cream, mayonnaise, ketchup, and mustard in a blender or food processor, and blend until smooth. Season to taste with salt, and store, covered, in the refrigerator for up to 4 days.

Pasta from the Pantry

It is easy to pull together a quick pasta dinner with a frozen vegetable, a jar of prepared spaghetti sauce, or a can of tuna fish. Pasta is so versatile that it accommodates virtually any other ingredient, and a well-stocked pantry will always provide you with the makings of a meal.

The variety of pasta recipes you can dream up, based purely on what you have in your pantry, is truly astounding. Beginning with a basic spaghetti sauce made from pantry ingredients, you can add one, two, or three other ingredients, in myriad combinations, to endlessly vary your meals. Pasta and pantry ingredients can also be combined to create everything from hearty soups, salads, and vegetarian dinners to meals based on seafood or beans.

You can have fun improvising with pantry ingredients. You'll find that you can create a meal with a can of caponata or a jar of marinated artichokes. You'll discover that spaghetti, bread crumbs, and anchovies equal dinner. Pasta, salsa, and corn join forces for another tasty meal.

These recipes should not be reserved for times of panic. Turn to them when you want to use up leftover steamed vegetables or roasted meats. Think of them as beginnings to which you can add fresh ingredients. However you decide to use the recipes, you'll never be stuck for a dinner idea again, even when you're out of fresh food.

Almost Risotto

PASTA: *Tiny shapes*
MAKES: *4 servings*
TIME: *25 to 30 minutes*

Although this dish tastes like risotto, it's made with rice-shaped pasta, instead of rice. This pasta mix gets its creamy texture from the extra liquid, which turns into a sauce when you add the grated Parmesan. Dried porcini mushrooms, a typical risotto flavoring, complete the illusion.

I may be cheating a bit by including a fresh onion, but I do think of onions as a pantry ingredient.

I like this for dinner but it also makes a great side dish with poultry, meat, or beans. For dinner, if I have the ingredients in the house, I'll serve a cabbage salad, or a watercress and red pepper salad, or even, in season, a fennel and orange salad.

½ ounce dried mushrooms, preferably
  porcini
2 cups chicken or beef broth
¼ medium-size onion
2 tablespoons olive oil
1 cup orzo
Salt and freshly ground black pepper
¼ to ½ cup grated Parmesan cheese

1. In a medium-size saucepan, bring the dried mushrooms and chicken broth to a boil over high heat. Remove the saucepan from the heat and steep the mushrooms until they are soft enough to chop, 10 to 15 minutes.

2. Meanwhile, finely chop the onion.

3. When the mushrooms are tender, heat the olive oil in a medium-size saucepan over medium-high heat. Add the onions and sauté until they are golden and almost tender, 1 to 2 minutes. Add the pasta and sauté for a few seconds, just to coat it with the oil. Place a sieve over the saucepan, and strain the chicken broth through it, reserving the mushrooms. Bring the broth to a simmer, cover, and cook over low heat until the pasta is tender but there still is some liquid in the pot, about 10 minutes.

4. While this is cooking, mince the softened mushrooms and add them to the simmering orzo. When the "almost risotto" is done, remove the saucepan from the heat and season to taste with salt and pepper. Stir in the grated cheese, and serve immediately.

VARIATIONS

Almost Saffron Risotto: Instead of the mushrooms, steep ¼ teaspoon crumbled saffron threads in the broth. Add the saffron with the broth to the pasta in step 3.

Almost Curried Risotto: After you have sautéed the onion, stir in ½ teaspoon ground cumin or curry powder. Add the pasta and proceed with the recipe.

Almost Herbed Risotto: After you have added the chicken broth in step 3, add ½ to 1 teaspoon dried herbs, such as thyme or rosemary.

Artichoke Hearts and Walnuts over Linguine

PASTA: *Thin ribbons or strands*
MAKES: *4 servings*
TIME: *20 to 25 minutes*

I call this a "reversible" recipe because it works well whether it's served hot or chilled. Although the ingredients are simple pantry ones, the combination is sophisticated enough for serving to company.

Chop the artichokes and walnuts into very fine pieces so they will be caught by the strands of pasta as you twirl them around your fork.

A fruit salad of sliced oranges sprinkled with vanilla extract or with bananas would make a fitting end to this meal.

Salt
6 tablespoons olive oil
1 tablespoon black olive paste (olivada)
2 tablespoons lemon juice
2 jars (6 ounces each) marinated
    artichoke hearts
1 can (4 ounces) shelled walnuts
Freshly ground black pepper
1 pound linguine fine

1. Bring a large pot of salted water to a boil for the pasta.

2. While the water is heating, whisk together the olive oil, black olive paste, and lemon juice in a large mixing bowl. Drain the artichoke hearts, mince them, and add them to the bowl. Finely chop the walnuts, and add them. Toss the ingredients together and season to taste with pepper.

3. Cook the pasta in the boiling water until it is tender but still firm to the bite, about 8 minutes.

4. When the pasta is cooked, drain it and toss it with the artichoke mixture. Season to taste with salt and pepper, and serve immediately.

Note: If you plan to serve this at room temperature, rinse the hot pasta under cold water to stop the cooking. Drain, and pat dry. If you want to serve this chilled, you may want to add more lemon juice—but taste the pasta first.

You can serve this mixture with short pasta, such as fusilli. If you do, chop the artichokes and walnuts a little more coarsely—the short pasta will catch chunkier bits of ingredients.

Caponata Fusilli Salad

PASTA: *Medium-size fancy shapes or tubes*
MAKES: *4 to 6 servings*
TIME: *20 minutes*

I quickly tire of the powerfully sweet taste of eggplant caponata when it is served as an appetizer on crackers. But I never tire of this pantry pasta salad because the rich flavor is diluted by the pasta and dressing.

>   *Salt*
>   *1 pound fusilli or rotelle (wagon wheels), or mezzani or penne*
>   *2 jars or cans (7½ ounces each) eggplant caponata*
>   *¼ cup mayonnaise*
>   *¼ cup lemon juice*
>   *Freshly ground black pepper*

1. Bring a large pot of salted water to a boil. Add the pasta and cook until it is tender but still firm to the bite, about 10 minutes.

2. Meanwhile, finely chop the caponata; then transfer it to a mixing bowl. Whisk the mayonnaise and lemon juice into the caponata, and season to taste with pepper.

3. Drain the pasta and rinse it under cold water. Drain it again, pat it dry, and add it to the mixing bowl. Toss well, and season to taste with salt and pepper. Serve at room temperature, or chill for 1 hour and serve cold.

"Chilied" Black Beans and Penne

PASTA: *Medium-size tubes or fancy shapes*
MAKES: *4 servings*
TIME: *20 to 25 minutes*

Beans and pasta is as winning a combination as beans and rice. This pantry recipe is so easy and simple that it can be used as a blueprint for other bean-and-pasta combinations.

Follow this filling meal with a dessert of fresh fruit or ice cream.

Salt
½ pound (3 cups) penne, radiatore, or
　fusilli
2 onions, or 1 teaspoon garlic paste
¼ cup vegetable or olive oil
1 tablespoon chili powder
1½ teaspoons ground cumin
1 can (14 ounces) stewed or crushed
　tomatoes
2 cans (16 ounces each) black, red kidney,
　or pink beans, drained and rinsed
Freshly ground black pepper

1. Bring a large pot of salted water to a boil. Add the pasta and cook until it is tender but still firm to the bite, 8 to 10 minutes.

2. Meanwhile, peel and chop the onions.

3. Heat the oil in a medium-size saucepan over medium heat. Add the onions and cook, stirring occasionally, until they are tender and beginning to turn golden, about 5 minutes. (If you are using garlic paste, stir it into the hot oil and cook it for just 10 seconds.)

4. Stir in the chili powder and cumin. Then add the tomatoes; if you're using stewed tomatoes, break them up by mashing them against the side of the pot with a spoon. Bring to a simmer, and add the beans. Simmer over low heat, covered if you want a soupy mixture, uncovered if you want a thicker mixture, until the pasta is done. Season to taste with salt and pepper.

5. Drain the pasta and dish out each portion immediately, ladling the black bean sauce on top of each. Or return the pasta to the pot, off the heat, and add the sauce; then toss the two together.

Note: If you have any in the fridge, top the bean sauce with sour cream, plain yogurt, chopped jalapeños, green chiles, or shredded Cheddar cheese.

VARIATIONS

■ When you add the tomatoes in step 4, include 1 package (10 ounces) frozen vegetables, such as corn kernels or carrots (thawed); or add 1 to 1½ cups diced leftover cooked fresh vegetables.

■ For the ground chili and cumin, substitute any of the following seasoning combinations:
　1 teaspoon each of ground cardamom, ginger, cumin, and curry powder
　1 teaspoon each of dried thyme and tarragon
　1 teaspoon each of ground cumin, cinnamon, and cardamom
　2 teaspoons paprika and 1 teaspoon caraway seeds

Cannellini Sauce: Use cannellini (white kidney beans) and instead of the ground chili and cumin, season with 1 teaspoon dried rosemary leaves and 1 can (2 ounces) anchovies, drained and chopped.

Or season them with 2 tablespoons black olive paste or sun-dried tomato paste.

Chick-Pea Sauce: Use chick-peas, and for the ground chili and cumin substitute 1 tablespoon dried mint leaves and 1 teaspoon dried oregano.

Creamed Clams and Corn with Orzo

PASTA: *Small to medium-size shapes and ribbons*
MAKES: *6 servings*
TIME: *20 to 25 minutes*

Here's a sauce reminiscent of New England clam chowder. You could serve this over linguine, a more typical "bed" for clam sauce, but I prefer a small pasta like orzo because it absorbs the thin sauce better.

The only reason this recipe takes as long as it does is because it takes a few minutes to boil the water and cook the pasta. If you have leftover cooked noodles in the fridge, however, you can have dinner in 15 minutes—simply reheat the noodles right in the sauce.

By the way, this creamed clams and corn sauce is also terrific over baked potatoes, steamed broccoli, cauliflower, or carrots.

> *Salt*
> *1 pound orzo, tubetti, or linguine*
> *1 can (12 ounces) evaporated milk (whole, low-fat, or skim)*
> *1 package (10 ounces) frozen corn kernels, thawed*
> *1 large can (10½ ounces) or 2 small cans (6 ounces each) minced or chopped clams, drained*
> *⅛ to ¼ teaspoon cayenne pepper*
> *⅛ teaspoon ground nutmeg*
> *½ teaspoon garlic paste*
> *1 tablespoon butter (optional)*

1. Bring a large pot of salted water to a boil. Add the orzo and cook until it is tender but still firm to the bite, about 8 minutes.

2. Bring all the remaining ingredients, except the butter, to a simmer in a large saucepan over medium heat. Simmer until thickened slightly, 3 to 4 minutes. Season to taste with salt.

3. Drain the pasta, add it to the sauce, and stir in the butter. Serve immediately.

VARIATIONS

Super-rich Creamed Clams and Corn: Substitute 1 cup heavy cream for the evaporated milk, and blend in 2 tablespoons butter at the end.

Clams with Corn, Olive Oil, and Tomatoes: Instead of the milk, use ¼ cup olive oil and 1 can (14½ ounces) plum tomatoes, drained and chopped. Substitute ½ teaspoon oregano for the nutmeg. In addition you could blend in 1 teaspoon anchovy or black olive paste.

SECOND TIME AROUND

These leftovers taste best when turned into a soup: Mix 1 cup leftovers with 1½ cups liquid, such as stewed tomatoes, clam juice mixed with tomato juice, or vegetable juice.

Creole Chick-Peas and Pasta

PASTA: *Medium-size fancy tubes or shapes*
MAKES: *4 servings*
TIME: *25 minutes*

The first time I made this dish (dare I confess this, or will the food police hunt me down?), I actually used two different-shaped pastas in order to get rid of odds and ends in my cupboard. It worked out fine, as I knew it would, because the pasta cooks to an uncharacteristically soft stage. So remember this when you need to use up a collection of dried pasta. If creole flavors don't appeal to you, check out the variations.

This easy recipe can take on any gastronomic identity.

2 cans (14½ ounces each) stewed
    tomatoes, preferably "Cajun-style"
2 cups chicken broth or water
½ to 1 teaspoon garlic paste (optional)
1 package (10 ounces) frozen corn
    kernels, thawed
½ teaspoon dried thyme
¼ to ½ teaspoon cayenne pepper
1 bay leaf
1 can (16 or 19 ounces) chick-peas,
    drained
2 cups penne, fusilli, or rotelle
    (wagon wheels)

1. Combine the tomatoes and chicken broth in a large pot. Break up the tomatoes by mashing them against the side of the pot with a wooden spoon. Whisk the garlic paste into the tomatoes. Add the corn, thyme, cayenne, bay leaf, and chick-peas.

2. Bring the mixture to a boil over medium heat. Add the pasta, cover, and cook until the pasta is very soft, 12 to 15 minutes. Serve immediately in deep soup bowls.

VARIATIONS

■ Substitute fish broth for the chicken broth, and add 1 can (7 ounces) salmon or tuna fish, drained. Substitute tarragon for the thyme, if desired.

■ Use only 1 can of stewed tomatoes and increase the broth by 1 cup.

■ Substitute ½ cup dry white wine for either ½ cup of the broth or ½ cup of the tomatoes.

■ Substitute ¼ cup lemon juice for ¼ cup of the broth.

■ Substitute ¼ cup olive oil for ¼ cup of the broth or of the tomatoes.

■ Substitute 1 package (10 ounces) frozen petite peas or chopped spinach, thawed, for the corn.

■ Substitute 1 can white beans, or even 2 cups cooked lentils, for the chick-peas.

■ Substitute 1 package frozen petite peas or spinach, thawed, for the chick-peas.

Noodles with Rice, Japanese Style

PASTA: *Thin egg noodles*
MAKES: *2 main-course or 4 side-dish servings*
TIME: *25 minutes*

In this dish, the fine noodles dissolve into an irresistible creamy texture, somewhat like risotto. I especially like the tang of the vinegar against the smoothness of the noodles and rice.

This makes an interesting side dish for chicken and turkey, and it would be a great component of a vegetarian meal along with steamed broccoli and a carrot purée.

2 tablespoons sesame oil
2 tablespoons vegetable oil
2 cups fine egg noodles or vermicelli,
*   broken into 2-inch lengths*
½ cup long-grain white rice
2 cups chicken broth or water
¼ cup soy sauce, preferably "light"
¼ cup rice or white wine vinegar
1 teaspoon sugar
Salt and freshly ground black pepper

1. Heat the two oils in a medium-size saucepan over medium-high heat. Add the noodles and rice and cook, stirring continuously, until some of the noodles turn pale brown, about 1 minute.

2. Add the broth, soy sauce, vinegar, and sugar. Cover, bring to a simmer, and cook gently over low heat until the rice is tender and the mixture is creamy, about 10 minutes. Season to taste with salt and pepper, and serve immediately.

VARIATIONS

■ You can easily change the ethnic character of these noodles by altering the flavorings. For a Mediterranean accent, sauté the rice and noodles in vegetable oil only, and add some dried mint and curry powder or cumin. Substitute chicken broth for the soy sauce and vinegar; omit the sugar.

■ Play with the recipe by varying the liquid: try beef broth, vegetable broth, or combine the broth with a bit of fresh carrot juice or vegetable juice (to equal 2 cups). Experiment with spices and herbs according to your taste. If you keep the recipe plain, you could stir in a bit of grated cheese at the end.

■ If you have cooked chicken on hand, stir it in a couple of minutes before the rice is tender, to reheat it.

Pasta with Fried Peppers and Sardines

PASTA: *Medium-size fancy shapes or tubes*
MAKES: *4 to 6 servings*
TIME: *20 minutes*

A jar of sweet fried peppers and onions is a terrific pantry ingredient to have on hand, especially in the colder months of the year. I use this, as I do eggplant caponata, as a flavoring with other ingredients.

I usually serve this dish warm or at room temperature, but it is also good as a cold salad.

Salt
1 pound fusilli, rotelle (wagon wheels), or penne
2 jars (6 ounces each) fried sweet peppers with onions
2 cans (4 ounces each) smoked sardines, drained
1 teaspoon diced red pepper flakes
¼ cup lemon juice

1. Bring a large pot of salted water to a boil. Add the pasta and cook until it is tender but still firm to the bite, 8 to 10 minutes.

2. Meanwhile, drain the sweet peppers and chop them. Place them in a mixing bowl with the sardines, red pepper flakes, and lemon juice. Using a wooden spoon, mix until the sardines have broken up a bit.

3. Drain the pasta, rinse it under cold water, and pat it dry. Add it to the mixing bowl. Toss well and serve immediately. If you are going to serve it later, keep it, covered, at room temperature until serving time.

VARIATION

In step 3, add 1 package (10 ounces) frozen corn kernels, thawed.

Lazy Lentil Pasta Dinner

PASTA: *Small shapes*
MAKES: *4 to 5 servings*
TIME: *35 minutes*

This is the easiest, handiest recipe you can imagine—basically a blend of lentils and pasta, simmered in tomatoes and broth. It tastes great by itself and it also accommodates myriad seasonings. You can portion out each serving and let each diner season it to taste. Choose from the selection below.

1 can (14½ ounces) stewed tomatoes
3 cups chicken or beef broth
1 cup lentils
1 cup orzo or tubetti
Salt and freshly ground black pepper

1. Purée the stewed tomatoes in a blender or food processor. Transfer them to a medium-size saucepan, add the broth, and bring to a simmer over medium heat.

2. Add the lentils, cover, and simmer over low heat for 15 minutes. Add the pasta, cover, and simmer until the lentils and pasta are tender and all the liquid has evaporated, about 15 minutes. Season to taste with salt and pepper, and serve immediately—as is or with any of the seasonings that follow.

SEASONINGS

For each portion (about 1¼ cups), add:

- 2 teaspoons prepared pesto, black olive paste, or sun-dried tomato tapenade
- 1 tablespoon olive oil and 2 to 3 tablespoons grated Asiago, Parmesan, or sharp Cheddar cheese
- 1 tablespoon hot Indian pickle; serve with plain yogurt
- ¼ cup prepared eggplant caponata or sweet fried peppers with onions
- 2 tablespoons chopped fresh green chiles and 1 tablespoon plain yogurt

Linguine with Garlicky Clams

PASTA: *Thin ribbons or strands*
MAKES: *4 servings*
TIME: *20 to 30 minutes*

This classic tastes wonderful yet is remarkably easy and quick to prepare. I cannot imagine that it won't become a standard in your household. If you have some on hand, add the fresh parsley. It's not essential, but it does add color and zest.

Salt
¾ pound linguine fine, vermicelli,
    spaghettini, or fusilli lunghi
2 teaspoons garlic paste, or
    1 clove fresh garlic
2 cans (6½ ounces each) minced or
    chopped clams
½ cup (packed) fresh parsley leaves
    (optional)
⅓ cup olive oil
¼ cup dry white wine or chicken broth
½ teaspoon dried red pepper flakes, or
    ⅛ teaspoon cayenne pepper

1. Bring a large pot of salted water to a boil. Add the pasta and cook until it is tender but still firm to the bite, 8 to 10 minutes.

2. Meanwhile, if you are using fresh garlic, peel and mince it. Drain the clams. If you are using parsley, rinse, pat it dry, and mince it.

3. About 3 minutes before the pasta is done, heat the oil in a medium to large skillet over medium-high heat. Add the garlic and cook until you get a good whiff of its aroma, about 30 seconds.

4. Stir in the clams and cook until they are heated through, about 1 minute. Add the white wine and simmer until some has evaporated, about 1 minute. Stir in the red pep-

per flakes or cayenne, add ½ cup of the water in which the linguine is cooking (this will create a more fluid sauce), and remove the skillet from the heat.

5. Drain the pasta and return it to the pot, off the heat. Add the clam sauce, and the parsley if you are using it, and mix thoroughly. Serve immediately.

VARIATIONS

Linguine with Garlic, Clams, and Bacon: Instead of cooking the garlic and clams in the oil, mince 2 slices of bacon and cook it until the fat is rendered; then add the garlic and proceed with step 3.

Low-fat Red Clam Sauce: Instead of cooking the garlic in oil, bring 1 cup crushed tomatoes to a simmer. Whisk in the garlic, clams, and red pepper flakes or cayenne, and simmer until hot, about 1 minute (omit the pasta water).

Beans, Linguine, and Clam Sauce: Add 2 cups cooked fava beans or 1 package (10 ounces) frozen small lima beans, thawed.

Spaghetti with Creamy Spinach Sauce

PASTA: *Strands, ribbons, or medium-size fancy shapes*
MAKES: *4 servings*
TIME: *25 minutes*

You'll find this recipe even easier to make if you happen to have a stash of homemade white sauce in your freezer. The amount of chopped spinach you use depends on what texture you prefer. If you like a creamy sauce, use only one package; if you prefer a more coarsely textured dish, then use two.

Salt
¾ pound spaghetti, linguine, or fusilli
2 tablespoons butter or margarine
2 tablespoons all-purpose flour
2 cups milk or chicken broth
1 or 2 packages (10 ounces each) frozen chopped spinach, thawed
2 tablespoons grated Parmesan cheese, plus additional for serving (optional)
Freshly ground black pepper

1. Bring a large pot of salted water to a boil. Add the pasta and cook until it is tender but still firm to the bite, about 10 minutes.

2. Meanwhile, make a white sauce: Melt the butter in a small saucepan over medium heat. When it is bubbly, whisk in the flour and cook for a few seconds. Slowly add the milk, whisking all the while. When all the milk has been incorporated, simmer the mixture over low heat, whisking vigorously every now and then, until it has thickened and the raw flour taste has cooked out, about 2 minutes.

3. Using your hands, squeeze all of the moisture out of the spinach. Then add the spinach to the white sauce and simmer until it is hot, about 1 minute. Add the grated cheese, and remove the saucepan from the heat. Season to taste with salt and pepper.

4. Drain the pasta and divide it among four shallow bowls. Ladle some spinach sauce over each portion, and serve immediately. Pass the additional cheese on the side, if you like.

VARIATION

Creamed Spinach Sauce with Bacon: A bit of bacon makes an enormous difference in the flavor of this pantry supper. Cook ¼ pound of bacon until it is crisp. Discard the fat, crumble the bacon, and stir it into the spinach sauce or scatter it over the ladled-out sauce.

Pantry Lasagne

PASTA: *"Instant" lasagne squares*
MAKES: *4 to 6 servings*
TIME: *15 minutes preparation plus 30
minutes no-work cooking time*

Before you begin work on this recipe, please read what I have to say about precooked lasagne squares (page 74). I like having a box of them in the cupboard because they help me create a remarkably satisfying, albeit unusual, lasagne made entirely from pantry ingredients.

To guarantee the success of this dish, it is crucial that each lasagne square be entirely covered with sauce; if not, the pasta will turn dry and brittle.

> 5 or 6 sheets "instant" lasagne squares
> 1 package (10 ounces) frozen lima beans, thawed
> 1 jar (14 ounces) spaghetti sauce, or 2 cups Michèle's Tomato Sauce (page 245)
> 1 jar (6 to 7 ounces) roasted red peppers, fried peppers and onions, or eggplant caponata
> Salt and freshly ground black pepper

1. Preheat the oven to 400°F. Soak the lasagne squares in a bowl of hot tap water.

2. Coarsely chop the lima beans, and combine them with the spaghetti sauce in a mixing bowl. Chop the roasted peppers or other condiment, and mix them into the spaghetti sauce. Season to taste with salt and pepper.

3. Drain the softened lasagne squares and pat them dry. Spoon ½ cup of the sauce in the bottom of a 9-inch square baking dish, and top with a sheet of lasagne. Spread another ½ cup of the sauce over the lasagne sheet. Be sure to spread the sauce right to the edges. Repeat the layering, ending with a sheet of lasagne completely covered with sauce. Cover, and bake for 30 minutes. Let the lasagne set for 5 minutes before slicing and serving.

VARIATIONS

- If you happen to have some cheese in the house, it will make this pantry lasagne even more delicious. Sprinkle shreds of mozzarella, gratings of Parmesan, or spoonfuls of ricotta between the layers.
- Instead of the lima beans, add a can (16 or 19 ounces) of black beans, drained and chopped, to the spaghetti sauce. Season with 2 teaspoons ground cumin powder.
- Add ¼ cup minced fresh herbs, such as parsley, dill, or mint to the sauce.

Pantry Pasta "Potage"

PASTA: *Tiny shapes or cut thin strands*
MAKES: *6 servings*
TIME: *2 minutes*

This soup is light yet won't leave you hungry. And as you can see from the variations that follow the main recipe, it can be adapted in a number of satisfying ways.

If you have the ingredients in the house, you could serve this with a hearty sandwich, a green salad, or a fresh fruit dessert.

> 2 cans (14 ounces each) chicken broth, or
>   4 cups water
> 2 cans (14½ ounces each) stewed
>   tomatoes, either plain or "Italian-style"
> 1 package (10 ounces) frozen French-cut
>   green beans, preferably thawed
> 1 teaspoon dried marjoram
> ½ cup pastina (tiny pasta), orzo, or
>   anellini, or 2 cups cooked spaghettini
>   cut into 2-inch pieces
> Salt and freshly ground black pepper

1. Pour the chicken broth into a large saucepan. Strain the stewed tomatoes in a sieve set over the pan so that all the juices are added to the chicken broth. Chop up the tomatoes and add them to the broth as well.

2. Add the green beans and marjoram, cover, and bring to a boil over medium-high heat.

3. Reduce the heat to medium, add the pasta, cover, and cook until the pasta is tender but still firm to the bite, about 10 minutes (2 minutes for leftover pasta). Season to taste with salt and pepper, and serve immediately in deep soup bowls.

VARIATIONS

■ Substitute fish broth for the chicken broth, and add 1 can (7 ounces) salmon or tuna fish, drained.

■ Substitute ¼ cup lemon juice for ¼ cup of the broth.

■ Add 1 can (16 or 19 ounces) white beans or chick-peas, drained and rinsed.

■ Right before serving, stir in ½ cup grated sharp Cheddar or Parmesan cheese.

■ Season the finished soup with Tabasco sauce to taste.

Spaghetti with Lemon Bread Crumbs and Anchovy

PASTA: *Strands or stuffed shapes*
MAKES: *4 servings*
TIME: *20 minutes*

Here's a wonderful dish that takes little work, tastes terrific, and costs next to nothing. Why add bread crumbs to a pasta dish? For a nutty flavor and a slightly crisp contrast in texture. Try this and be amazed.

Salt
*1 pound spaghetti, spaghettini, vermicelli,
  or stuffed pasta*
¼ cup vegetable oil
2 tablespoons butter
1 to 1½ teaspoons anchovy paste
¼ cup dried bread crumbs
1 tablespoon lemon juice
Freshly ground black pepper

1. Bring a large pot of salted water to a boil. Add the pasta and cook until it is tender but still firm to the bite, 8 to 10 minutes.

2. About 3 minutes before the spaghetti is done, heat the oil and butter in a medium-size saucepan over medium heat. When the butter is bubbling, stir in the anchovy paste. Add the bread crumbs and cook, stirring with a wooden spoon, until they are lightly browned, 45 seconds to 1 minute. Watch carefully and adjust the heat if needed so the butter doesn't brown too quickly. Remove the skillet from the heat and stir in the lemon juice; season to taste with salt and pepper.

3. Drain the pasta and return it to the pot, off the heat. Toss the spaghetti with the bread crumb sauce, and serve immediately.

Rotelle with Tuna and Tomatoes

PASTA: *Tubes, twists, or fancy shapes*
MAKES: *4 servings*
TIME: *25 to 30 minutes*

With a couple of cans of tuna, a box of pasta, and a variety of pantry seasonings, you can develop innumerable tuna-and-pasta dinners. A word of caution: Don't cook the tuna in the sauce or it will taste odd; just warm it through.

On those nights when you wish to offer another course and you have fresh ingredients around, you could serve a green bean salad dressed with a mustard vinaigrette and chopped shallots.

Salt
¾ pound rotelle (wagon wheels), elbow
   macaroni, penne, or fusilli
2 cans (6 to 7 ounces each) tuna,
   preferably packed in water
1 teaspoon garlic paste, or
   1 clove fresh garlic
¼ cup olive oil
1 can (14½ ounces) crushed or
   stewed tomatoes
¼ to ½ teaspoon dried red pepper flakes

1. Bring a large pot of salted water to a boil.

2. While the water is heating, drain the tuna, transfer it to a bowl, and flake it with a fork. If you are using a clove of garlic, peel and mince it.

3. Add the pasta to the boiling water and cook until it is tender but still firm to the bite, 8 to 10 minutes.

4. Meanwhile, heat the olive oil in a medium-size skillet over medium heat. Add the garlic paste or minced garlic, and cook until you get a whiff of its aroma, about 10 seconds. Add the tomatoes and red pepper flakes, and bring to a simmer. Cook gently until heated through, 2 to 3 minutes. Add the tuna and simmer over low heat just to heat it through, about 1 minute.

5. Drain the pasta, divide it among four shallow bowls, and ladle some sauce on top of each one. Or return the pasta to the pot, off the heat, add the sauce, and toss until well mixed. Serve immediately.

VARIATIONS

■ In step 4, when you add the tomatoes, add also 1 can (2 ounces) anchovies, drained and chopped, or 2 teaspoons anchovy paste. Or add 2 tablespoons black olive paste, sun-dried tomato tapenade, or chopped capers.

■ Increase the olive oil to ⅓ cup. Omit the tomatoes and substitute 1 jar (7 ounces) roasted red pepper, minced, 2 tablespoons capers, minced, and 2 tablespoons black olive paste. In step 5, when you toss the pasta with the tuna sauce, add 2 to 3 tablespoons lemon juice as well.

ESPECIALLY GOOD FOR COMPANY

■ *The variation with roasted peppers is elegant and perfect for company when served over a beautifully colored pasta such as squid ink, saffron, or even spinach. For a perfect finish, top the sauce with ½ cup chopped fresh parsley.*

RICH AND CREAMY ROTELLE WITH TUNA: *Omit the olive oil. In step 4, whisk the garlic paste with ½ cup heavy cream in a large skillet over medium heat for 1 minute. Add the tomatoes, 1 package (10 ounces) frozen petite peas, thawed, and the tuna. Simmer until heated through, about 2 minutes. Season to taste with salt and freshly ground black pepper (omit the red pepper flakes). Serve with grated Parmesan or sharp Cheddar cheese.*

Red-Hot Smoked Clam Sauce over Spaghetti

PASTA: *Strands or ribbons*
MAKES: *4 servings*
TIME: *20 to 30 minutes*

Y ou'll be pleased to know that this clam sauce is as terrific spooned over baked fish as it is over pasta.

Salt
2 cans (3½ ounces each) smoked clams
¾ pound spaghetti or linguine
2 tablespoons olive oil
1 jar (14 ounces) spaghetti sauce
1 package (10 ounces) frozen corn kernels, thawed
¼ teaspoon cayenne pepper

1. Bring a large pot of salted water to a boil.

2. While the water is heating, finely chop the smoked clams.

3. Add the pasta to the boiling water and cook until it is tender but still firm to the bite, 8 to 10 minutes.

4. About 5 minutes before the pasta is done, heat the oil in a medium-size saucepan over medium-high heat. Add the clams and sauté for a few seconds. Add the spaghetti sauce, corn kernels, and cayenne, and simmer until the sauce is hot, about 2 minutes. Adjust the seasoning.

5. Drain the pasta and divide it among four shallow bowls. Spoon some clam sauce over each portion, and serve immediately.

VARIATIONS

■ For the smoked clams substitute smoked mussels, 1 can (10 ounces) minced clams, or 1 whole smoked chicken breast, skin removed, cut into fine dice.
■ In step 4, add ¼ cup red or white wine to the spaghetti sauce.
■ Stir in 1 teaspoon dried oregano when you add the spaghetti sauce.
■ In step 4, sauté 6 minced garlic cloves in the olive oil before you add the smoked clams.
■ Substitute 2 cups chopped freshly steamed carrots for the corn.
■ In step 4, after you add the clams and before adding the spaghetti sauce, stir in 1 package (10 ounces) washed, chopped fresh spinach.

Corn and Salsa over Twists

PASTA: *Medium-size fancy shapes*
MAKES: *4 servings*
TIME: *25 minutes*

If you enjoy your food spicy hot, then turn up the volume of the salsa or hot sauce here. If some family members prefer a milder sauce, just pass the Tabasco at the table.

> *Salt*
> *½ pound (3 cups) fusilli, rotelle (wagon wheels), or penne*
> *¼ cup vegetable oil*
> *½ teaspoon garlic paste (optional)*
> *½ teaspoon dried oregano*
> *1 can (4 ounces) chopped green chiles*
> *2 packages (10 ounces each) frozen corn kernels, thawed*
> *1 jar (4 ounces) sliced pimientos, drained*
> *¼ cup prepared salsa, or more to taste*
> *Tabasco sauce, or other hot sauce, to taste*

1. Bring a large pot of salted water to a boil. Add the pasta and cook until it is tender but still firm to the bite, 8 to 10 minutes.

2. Meanwhile, combine the vegetable oil, garlic paste, oregano, green chiles, corn, and pimientos in a medium-size saucepan. Bring the mixture to a simmer over medium-low heat, and keep it simmering, covered, until the pasta is done.

3. Drain the pasta and return it to the pot, off the heat. Add the corn sauce and the salsa, sprinkle with Tabasco, and mix the ingredients well. Serve immediately.

VARIATIONS

- If you have some on hand, top the pasta and sauce with ¼ to ½ cup sour cream or plain nonfat yogurt, ½ to ¾ cup grated sharp Cheddar cheese, or sliced jalapeño peppers.
- Either add as a topping or gently mix into the finished dish ¼ pound diced smoked ham, 1 peeled, pitted, and diced ripe avocado, or 2 seeded and diced tomatoes.

ESPECIALLY GOOD FOR CHILDREN

In step 2, heat half of the corn kernels with 2 tablespoons vegetable oil. In step 3, mix this simpler corn mix with half of the pasta, and add (if the kids like it) ¼ cup sour cream or grated Cheddar cheese.

For the adult portion, heat the remaining half of the corn in a small saucepan with the other sauce ingredients (adjust the amounts) and toss with half of the cooked pasta.

Perciatelli with a Sicilian Flavor

PASTA: *Strands*
MAKES: *4 to 6 servings*
TIME: *25 minutes*

....

The sweet and savory flavors here are inspired by a Sicilian pasta dish that includes sardines and raisins.

I like to serve this in summer because the only cooking required is sautéing the fennel seeds and boiling the pasta.

If ripe tomatoes are in season, then slice some, toss them with vinaigrette, and serve them alongside this scrumptious dish.

Salt
1 pound perciatelli, bucatini, or spaghetti
½ cup raisins
⅓ cup white wine
2 cans (3¾ ounces each) sardines packed
    in olive oil
1 can (2 ounces) anchovy fillets
Freshly ground black pepper
⅓ cup olive oil
1 teaspoon fennel seeds

1. Bring a large pot of salted water to a boil. Add the pasta and cook until it is tender but still firm to the bite, about 10 minutes.

2. Meanwhile, in a small mixing bowl, steep the raisins in the white wine. Drain the sardines, chop them, and place them in a large mixing bowl. Drain and finely chop the anchovies, and add them to the sardines.

3. When the pasta is almost done, chop the raisins and add them to the sardines and anchovies, along with the wine they were steeping in. Season to taste with salt and pepper.

4. Heat the olive oil in a small skillet over medium heat. Add the fennel seeds and sauté until you get a whiff of their aroma, 5 seconds. Add the oil and seeds to the mixing bowl.

5. Drain the pasta and add it to the mixing bowl. Toss well, and adjust the seasoning if necessary. Serve immediately, or cover, and hold at room temperature until serving time.

SECOND TIME AROUND

The leftovers of this dish might be dry, so moisten them with a lemony vinaigrette. Brighten the color with chopped fresh parsley and diced peeled, seeded cucumbers. Serve chilled or at room temperature.

Spinach Broth with Floating Stars

PASTA: *Tiny shapes*
MAKES: *4 servings*
TIME: *15 minutes*

Fifteen minutes is all you'll need to assemble this quick and flavorful meal. This is a great way, too, of recycling a cupful or so of leftover steamed vegetables—just substitute them for the spinach or add them to the broth along with the spinach.

Chinese five-spice powder is a combination of ground ginger, anise, fennel, cinnamon, cloves, and hot pepper. (I know, that's six spices—the name is more symbolic than factual!)

3 cans (14 ounces each) chicken broth, or
    6 cups frozen chicken broth, thawed
1 package (10 ounces) frozen chopped
    spinach, thawed
½ teaspoon ground ginger
½ teaspoon Chinese five-spice powder, or
    ⅛ teaspoon each of anise seed,
    cinnamon, ground cloves, and
    fennel seeds
¼ teaspoon dried red pepper
    flakes
¼ pound (¾ cup) tiny pasta, such as
    stelline, or 1 cup orzo
Salt

1. Pour the chicken broth into a large saucepan. Add the spinach, ginger, five-spice powder, and red pepper flakes. Bring to a simmer over medium heat.

2. Add the pasta, cover, and cook until it is soft, about 10 minutes. Season to taste with salt, and serve immediately in deep soup bowls.

VARIATIONS

■ Other spices also go well with this simple mix of spinach and pasta: mace, nutmeg, marjoram, mint, and oregano are a few examples.
■ Besides frozen spinach, you could try frozen carrots or lima beans.

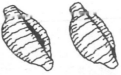

Succotash Pasta

PASTA: *Small to medium-size shapes*
MAKES: *6 servings*
TIME: *25 minutes*

There are as many ways to season this recipe as there are flavorings and condiments. You could make a big batch of this, portion it out, and let each person season to taste. See below for seasoning ideas.

Salt
1 pound orzo, shells, or gnocchi pasta
1 cup chicken or beef broth
1 package (10 ounces) frozen lima beans,
   thawed
1 package (10 ounces) frozen corn
   kernels, thawed
¼ cup olive oil, butter, or heavy cream
Freshly ground black pepper
Seasonings (suggestions follow)

1. Bring a large pot of salted water to a boil. Add the pasta and cool until it is tender but still firm to the bite, about 10 minutes.

2. Meanwhile, combine the broth, lima beans, and corn kernels in a medium-size saucepan. Heat this mixture over medium heat until simmering and heated through, 5 minutes.

3. Drain the pasta and return it to the pot, off the heat. Add the vegetable mixture and the olive oil, butter, or cream. Mix the ingredients together and season to taste with salt and pepper. Ladle out each portion, and season as suggested below.

SEASONINGS

For each portion (about 2 cups) add:

■ 2 teaspoons prepared pesto or black olive paste, or

■ 2 teaspoons sun-dried tomato "sauce" or tapenade and ¼ cup crumbled sheep's- or goat's-milk cheese, or

■ 1 teaspoon anchovy paste and 2 to 4 table-

spoons grated Asiago, Parmesan, or Pecorino Romano cheese, or

■ ½ cup eggplant caponata.

Summertime Pasta

PASTA: *Medium-size fancy shapes or tubes*
MAKES: *4 to 6 servings*
TIME: *25 minutes*

For this ideal summer recipe, you don't have to bother with anything more than boiling the pasta. Serve the dish either at room temperature or chilled, as you wish. It is a snap to make, it is delicious, and you can vary the type of canned fish.

Salt
½ pound rotelle (wagon wheels), fusilli, or
   penne
¼ cup olive oil
1 package (10 ounces) frozen corn,
   thawed
1 jar (6 or 7 ounces) roasted sweet red
   peppers or fried sweet peppers with
   onions
2 cans (7 ounces each) salmon or tuna,
   drained, or 1 can (15 ounces)
   mackerel, drained
½ teaspoon dried red pepper flakes
¼ cup mayonnaise (optional)

1. Bring a large pot of salted water to a boil. Add the pasta and cook until it is tender but still firm to the bite, about 10 minutes.

2. Meanwhile, in a large mixing bowl, combine the olive oil, corn, sweet peppers, fish, and red pepper flakes. Mix together with a wooden spoon until the fish is flaked and the ingredients are thoroughly combined.

3. Drain the pasta and add it to the mixing bowl. Toss well and serve immediately.

4. Or cover and refrigerate until serving time. Just before serving, stir in the mayonnaise (if using) and adjust the seasoning.

Tuna, Peas, and Pasta

PASTA: *Small or medium-size tubes or fancy shapes*
MAKES: *4 servings*
TIME: *25 to 30 minutes*

This is a variation of a pantry recipe I developed for my first Monday-to-Friday book. It was so good that I decided to include it here again. In the first version, I served this mixture with warm pasta—which you still can do—but here I cool the pasta first and serve the dinner at room temperature.

If time permits, steam a fresh green vegetable to go with the pasta salad.

Salt
¾ pound elbow macaroni, penne, ditali, or fusilli
⅓ cup olive oil
¼ cup lemon juice
2 tablespoons black olive paste or sundried tomato tapenade or paste
¼ to ½ teaspoon dried red pepper flakes
2 cans (6 to 7 ounces each) tuna, preferably packed in water
1 package (10 ounces) frozen petite peas, thawed

1. Bring a large pot of salted water to a boil. Add the pasta and cook until it is tender but still firm to the bite, 8 to 10 minutes.

2. Meanwhile, combine the olive oil and lemon juice in a mixing bowl, and whisk in the olive paste and red pepper flakes. Drain the tuna and add it to the mixing bowl. Pat the peas dry, add them to the mixing bowl, and combine all the ingredients thoroughly. Season to taste with salt.

3. Drain the pasta and rinse it under cold water to cool it. Drain it again, pat it dry, and combine it with the tuna mixture. Season to taste with salt, and serve.

VARIATIONS

■ Instead of the olive oil, mix the tuna with ⅓ to ½ cup mayonnaise and the lemon juice.
■ Instead of the black olive paste, season the salad with ¼ cup chopped roasted red peppers.

■ Omit the peas and combine the tuna and pasta with 1 jar (7 ounces) of roasted red peppers, drained and minced, 1 package (10 ounces) frozen corn kernels, thawed, and ½ cup mayonnaise.

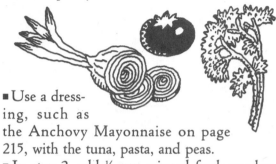

■ Use a dressing, such as the Anchovy Mayonnaise on page 215, with the tuna, pasta, and peas.

■ In step 2, add ¼ cup minced fresh parsley and either 2 ripe tomatoes, seeded and chopped, or 2 fresh red or green bell peppers, cored, seeded, and chopped.

JUICING LEMONS

If you ever have difficulty juicing fresh lemons or limes (especially limes), here's a tip: It helps if first you halve the fruit, then make a cross with the point of a sharp paring knife right on the white pith centered in the middle of each half. This will help break up the recalcitrant membranes so that the juice can flow more easily.

The Universal Pantry Pasta Sauce

PASTA: *Strands, ribbons, or medium-size shapes*
MAKES: *Enough for ¾ to 1 pound pasta, or 4 to 6 servings*
TIME: *10 minutes*

What makes this sauce "universal" are the tomatoes, the most ubiquitous of pasta companions, and the "universally" available pantry ingredients.

The sauce is essentially a blend of tomatoes and black olives, to which you can add any number of other ingredients to turn it into a main-course meal.

If you want cheese with this sauce, choose a hard grating variety such as Parmesan (see page 65 for other types of hard grating cheeses).

> ½ cup cured black olives, or 3 tablespoons black olive paste
> 1 can (14½ ounces) crushed tomatoes or "pasta-style chunky" stewed tomatoes
> 2 tablespoons red wine
> 2 tablespoons olive oil
> ½ teaspoon dried oregano
> Salt and freshly ground black pepper

1. Pit the olives and finely chop them.

2. Combine all the ingredients in a large

skillet and bring to a simmer over medium heat. Simmer until hot, about 5 minutes. Season to taste with salt and pepper.

FOR A MORE SUBSTANTIAL SAUCE . . .

Add any one or a combination of the following:

- 12 ounces minced clams, drained
- 1 package (10 ounces) frozen peas, lima beans, or carrots, thawed
- 1 jar (6 ounces) marinated artichoke hearts, drained and chopped.
- 1 can (16 or 19 ounces) black beans, drained and rinsed, or chick-peas, drained, rinsed, and roughly chopped
- 2 cups diced cooked poultry, meat, seafood, or vegetables, or 1 cup diced smoked ham or poultry, reheated

VARIATIONS

- Substitute another dried herb, such as sage, thyme, rosemary, or marjoram, for the oregano.
- Add ½ teaspoon dried red pepper flakes or ⅛ teaspoon Tabasco sauce.
- For the black olives, substitute 2 tablespoons chopped capers and 1 can (2 ounces) anchovy fillets, drained and chopped.
- Stir in 1 teaspoon garlic paste.
- Omit the red wine. When you add poultry, substitute chicken broth. When you add fish or clams, substitute clam juice.

Pasta Off-Center

Gathered in this chapter are recipes that are out of the pasta mainstream as well as out of the Monday-to-Friday genre. Some of the dishes you'll find here are on the sweet side, but not so much so that they fit only in the dessert category. Other recipes appear here because of some unusual feature, because of an unexpected combination of ingredients, or because they just don't fit anywhere else.

In addition you'll discover in "Pasta Off-Center" quite a few Sunday start-up recipes, which are too long to create during the week but are perfect for preparing on a weekend, when you have more time. These are the dishes that freeze well and become wonderful Monday-to-Friday time-savers during the workweek, when all you have to do is reheat them. I particularly recommend making the tomato sauce on page 245 because it is such a good starting point for so many pasta recipes.

Sunday's-Best Pasta Soup

PASTA: *Stuffed pasta or tiny shapes*
MAKES: *6 servings*
TIME: *20 minutes preparation plus 25 minutes no-work cooking time*

This hearty, meaty soup is a perfect Sunday afternoon recipe. Its uncomplicated taste lends itself to experimenting—it meshes well with any sort of pasta and is terrific when supplemented with rice, barley, lentils, or additional vegetables.

The base (minus the pasta) is perfect for freezing. When you don't have time to cook, pull some out of the freezer, bring it to a simmer, and add anything from meat ravioli to tiny tubettini. Voilà dinner!

1 onion
2 cloves garlic
2 carrots
2 ribs celery
¼ cup olive oil
8 cups beef broth
½ pound fresh mushrooms
1 pound boneless beef sirloin
1 teaspoon dried oregano
1 bay leaf
½ pound (2 cups) meat- or mushroom-stuffed pasta, or 1¼ cups orzo or tubettini
Salt and freshly ground black pepper

1. Peel the onion, garlic, and carrots. Finely chop them along with the celery—all together in a food processor, if you like.

2. Heat the olive oil in a large saucepan over medium-high heat. Add the chopped vegetables and stir to coat them with the oil. Reduce the heat, cover the pan, and cook until the vegetables are tender, about 5 minutes. If they start to stick to the bottom of the pan, add some of the beef broth.

3. While the vegetables are cooking, trim ¼ inch off the mushroom stems and cut the mushrooms into thin lengthwise slices. Remove all fat from the beef, and cut it into strips about ¼ inch wide, ½ inch thick, and 1 inch long.

4. Add the sliced mushrooms, beef strips, broth, oregano, and bay leaf to the saucepan. Cover and bring to a boil. Then reduce the heat to low and simmer gently until the beef is tender, 20 minutes.

5. Add the pasta to the soup, and simmer for 4 to 12 minutes, depending upon the type of pasta. Stir every now and then to make sure the pasta does not sink and stick to the bottom of the pot. Remove the bay leaf, and season to taste with salt and pepper.

Note: You can prepare the soup base up through step 4, then cool it to room temperature and store it in the freezer. When you are ready to serve it, just bring it back to a simmer and then add the pasta or other ingredients of your choice.

VARIATION

Right before serving, stir in ¼ cup minced fresh mint, dill, or parsley. Or stir in ½ cup grated Parmesan cheese.

Saffron Fish Chowder with Orzo

PASTA: *Tiny shapes*
MAKES: *6 servings*
TIME: *20 minutes preparation plus 25 minutes no-work cooking time*

This superbly flavored chowder is a delicious meal in itself as well as a wonderful base for soup. If you wish to make this as a soup base, omit the pasta and the fish. Store the base in the freezer to pull out on a rainy day and finish as you please.

The chowder takes just a bit longer to prepare than other recipes in this book, but it cooks mostly by itself and does not require lots of work. It is a fine main-course pasta soup to serve to guests.

> ½ pound fresh spinach
> 1 onion
> 2 cloves garlic
> ¼ cup olive oil
> 4 carrots
> 4 cups fish stock, or 2 cups clam juice mixed with 2 cups water
> ¼ cup white wine
> 2 cans (14½ ounces each) stewed tomatoes
> ¼ teaspoon crumbled saffron threads or ground paprika
> 1 pound sea scallops or skinless cod or monkfish fillets
> 1¼ cups orzo or tubettini
> Salt and freshly ground black pepper

1. Stem the spinach and place the leaves in a bowl of cold water; set it aside. Peel and finely chop the onion. Peel and mince the garlic.

2. Heat the olive oil in a large saucepan over medium-high heat. Add the onions and garlic and stir to coat them with the oil. Reduce the heat, cover, and cook until the onions are tender, about 5 minutes.

3. While the onions are cooking, peel and thinly slice the carrots. When the onions are tender, add the carrots to the saucepan along with the fish stock and white wine. Pour the stewed tomatoes into a strainer set over the

saucepan, adding the juices to the stock. Chop the stewed tomatoes and add them to the saucepan. Stir in the saffron. Bring to a boil over high heat, then reduce the heat and simmer, covered, until the carrots are completely tender, about 10 minutes.

4. Meanwhile, trim and discard the rubbery appendage from the scallops and cut the scallops in half or if they are large, into quarters. (If you are using fish fillets, remove any stray bones and cut the fish into 1-inch cubes.) Lift the spinach leaves from the water, shake off the remaining water, and cut them into shreds.

5. When the carrots are tender, add the pasta to the soup, cover, and cook until it is soft, about 7 minutes. Stir every now and then to keep the pasta from sticking to the bottom of the pan.

6. Add the scallops or fish to the soup and simmer, uncovered, until the scallops turn milky, 1 to 2 minutes. Add the spinach and simmer until it has just wilted, about 10 seconds. Season to taste with salt and pepper, and serve immediately.

Note: The broth can be made up through step 3 and then frozen.

Michèle's Tomato Sauce

PASTA: *Strands or ribbons*
MAKES: *About 2 quarts*
TIME: *30 minutes preparation plus 1½ hours no-work cooking time*

For many a Monday-to-Friday pasta recipe I rely on a good store-bought tomato-based spaghetti sauce. However, none of them appeals to me as much as my own version, a purée of tomatoes seasoned with onions and carrots. It has less body than some commercial sauces but a lot more flavor.

Every now and again during the cold winter months, I'll spend a lazy Sunday afternoon whipping up an extra batch of this tomato sauce so that later I can indulge in its mellow flavor on the spur of the moment. Other than a good dose of carrots to sweeten the sauce, there are few ingredients besides tomatoes. The flavor remains pure and simple, so I can add any number of other ingredients and seasonings for a particular recipe.

4 onions
1 pound carrots
¼ cup olive oil
¾ cup water
3 cloves garlic
2 cans (28 ounces each) plum tomatoes in tomato purée
Salt and freshly ground black pepper

1. Peel and chop the onions. Peel the carrots and cut them into ¼-inch-thick rounds.

2. Heat the olive oil in a large nonreactive saucepan over medium-high heat. Add the onions and carrots, and reduce the heat to low. Add ¼ cup of the water and the garlic cloves. Cover and cook gently until the vegetables are tender, about 15 minutes.

3. Stir in the tomatoes with the purée, using a wooden spoon to break up the tomatoes by mashing them against the sides of the saucepan. Add the remaining ½ cup of water, cover the pan, and simmer over low heat for 1 hour, stirring now and then.

4. Press the sauce through a sieve or a food mill and discard the solids. Season to taste with salt and pepper, and let cool to room temperature. Ladle the sauce into 1-cup freezer containers and freeze for up to a year (though it is too delicious to last that long).

VARIATIONS

■ Omit the carrots for a tarter and even more plainly flavored tomato sauce.
■ Season the sauce with 1 bay leaf, or 2 teaspoons dried thyme or oregano, or ½ cup (tightly packed) fresh basil leaves when you add the tomatoes.
■ Substitute 4 ribs celery, sliced, for half of the carrots.

SAUCE BY THE CHUNK

If you don't have enough 1-cup containers, there is another way you can freeze tomato (or any other sauce) to use as needed. Ladle the sauce into two 8-inch square baking pans. Freeze the pans of sauce until partially frozen, about 2 hours. Then, using a knife, cut the sauce into 4 pieces and insert a strip of waxed paper along the cuts. Freeze until solid, another 2 hours.

Turn the frozen sauce out of the pan. The chunks will break along the lines set by the waxed paper, giving you eight 1-cup chunks of frozen sauce which you can then save in small self-seal freezer bags.

Sunday's-Best Lasagne

PASTA: *Lasagne noodles*
MAKES: *4 to 6 servings*
TIME: *30 to 35 minutes preparation plus 1 hour no-work baking and standing time*

Once you understand the basics of creating lasagne, you can devise an infinite number of variations on the theme. I've named this one "Sunday's best" because it is ideal for making on a Sunday, or sometime during a weekend when you have time. If you are eager to create a lasagne during the week, turn to Instant Lasagne or Pantry Lasagne (see Index for both), both of which make use of precooked lasagne squares.

Classic accompaniments to all sorts of lasagne dishes are green salad and Italian bread. A plainly steamed fresh vegetable fits the bill, too.

> *Salt*
> *½ pound lasagne noodles (9 or 10 strips)*
> *½ pound lean ground beef*
> *4½ cups Michèle's Tomato Sauce (see*
>   *page 245) or 2 jars (14 ounces each)*
>   *spaghetti sauce*
> *Freshly ground black pepper*
> *1 container (15 ounces) part-skim ricotta*
>   *cheese*
> *1 egg*
> *½ cup grated Parmesan cheese*
> *½ pound mozzarella cheese*
> *Vegetable oil, for the baking dish*
> *1 tablespoon olive oil*

1. Preheat the oven to 375°F. Fill a large bowl with cold water and a few ice cubes, and set it aside. Bring a large pot of salted water to a boil for the pasta.

2. Add the lasagne noodles, a couple at a time, to the boiling water. When they have softened, stir them vigorously with a wooden spoon. Boil until slightly underdone, about 8 minutes. Drain the noodles, rinse them under cold water, and place them in the bowl of ice water; set it aside.

3. Crumble the beef into a medium-size skillet and sauté it over medium heat, stirring constantly to break up the clumps, until there are no more traces of pink, about 5 minutes. Using a slotted spoon, transfer the beef to a mixing bowl.

4. Stir the tomato sauce into the beef, and season to taste with salt and pepper. In another bowl, mix the ricotta, egg, and Parmesan together. Thinly slice the mozzarella.

5. Lightly oil a 9-inch square baking dish. Set a kitchen towel on a work surface. Lift the noodles out of the ice water and lay them in a single layer on the towel. Pat them dry. Cut them to fit the baking dish.

6. Spread a little meat sauce over the bottom of the baking dish. Arrange a single layer of noodles in the dish. Spread them with one third of the ricotta mixture, and top that with one third of the mozzarella. Cover with one fourth of the remaining sauce. Repeat the pasta, cheese, and sauce layers two more times, and end with a layer of noodles covered with the remaining sauce. Cover the

dish loosely with foil and bake until bubbling, 45 minutes to 1 hour. Remove the lasagne from the oven and let it stand for 15 minutes before cutting into it.

MINOR VARIATIONS

- Fold 2 to 3 tablespoons pesto (or any of the pesto variations, see Index) into the ricotta mixture.
- Fold 2 tablespoons black olive paste, or 1 jar (6 ounces) eggplant caponata, into the ricotta mixture.
- Fold ¼ cup minced fresh herbs, such as parsley or basil, into the ricotta mixture.

- Substitute 1 cup diced leftover roast pork, beef, turkey, or chicken for the ground beef.
- Sauté ½ pound sliced sweet or hot Italian sausage in 1 tablespoon oil for about 5 minutes, and substitute it for the ground beef.
- Substitute Italian Fontina for the mozzarella, or grated Asiago or Romano for the Parmesan cheese.

MAJOR VARIATIONS

Vegetarian Lasagne: Omit the meat. Instead, stir 1 can (16 or 19 ounces) chick-peas, drained and chopped, into the spaghetti sauce. Stir 1 package (10 ounces) frozen chopped spinach, thawed, into the ricotta mixture.

Three-Vegetable Lasagne: Omit the meat, mozzarella, and Parmesan. Sauté ¼ pound sliced mushrooms, 1 thinly sliced red or green bell pepper, and 4 thinly sliced carrots in olive oil until tender, about 10 minutes. Stir these vegetables into the spaghetti sauce along with ½ cup raisins.

Seafood Lasagne: Omit the meat, ricotta, and egg. Increase the amount of mozzarella to 1 pound. Drain and flake 2 cans (7 ounces each) tuna, and add it to the spaghetti sauce. (Or sauté ¾ pound diced shrimp, scallops, or monkfish fillet in 1 tablespoon olive oil until just cooked, 2 to 3 minutes, and stir this into the spaghetti sauce.)

Four-Cheese Lasagne: Omit the meat. Substitute Italian Fontina for the mozzarella. Add ¼ pound Gorgonzola cheese, crumbling it over the layers after you add the ricotta and Parmesan.

Pastitsio

PASTA: *Medium-size tubes*
MAKES: *2 dinners, 6 servings each*
TIME: *1 hour preparation plus 1¼ hours no-work baking and standing time*

This classic Greek dish is so delicious, it is really worth making—and you'll get two dinners out of a single effort. A hit with adults and kids, it is great for family meals as

6 tablespoons all-purpose flour
4 cups milk
Freshly ground black pepper
1 tablespoon vegetable oil
1 onion
4 cloves garlic
¼ cup olive oil
1½ pounds lean ground beef
1½ teaspoons dried oregano
1½ teaspoons ground cinnamon
2 jars (14 ounces each) spaghetti sauce
3 eggs
1 cup grated Pecorino Romano cheese

1. Preheat the oven to 350°F.

2. Bring a large pot of salted water to a boil. Add the pasta and cook until it is tender but still firm to the bite, about 10 minutes.

3. Meanwhile, make the white sauce: Melt the butter in a large nonreactive saucepan over medium heat. When it is bubbly, whisk in the flour and cook for about 1 minute,

when all the milk has been added, bring the mixture to a boil (this could take as long as 10 minutes). Whisk occasionally as the milk is heating so it does not scorch. When it reaches a boil, reduce the heat to low and simmer, still whisking, until the sauce is cooked through, 3 to 4 minutes. Season to taste with salt and pepper, and remove from the heat. Let the sauce cool while you prepare the meat sauce.

4. When the pasta is done, drain it and return it to the pot, off the heat. Toss it with the vegetable oil (this will keep it from sticking together).

5. Prepare the meat sauce: Peel and finely chop the onion and garlic (chop them together in a food processor if you like). Heat the olive oil in a medium-size skillet over medium heat. Add the onions and garlic, and sauté until they are sizzling, about 1 minute. Cover, and cook until the onions are tender, about 5 minutes. Crumble the beef into the

skillet and sauté, stirring constantly to break up the clumps, until there are no more traces of pink, about 5 minutes. Season with the oregano, cinnamon, and salt and pepper to taste. Transfer the meat sauce to a mixing bowl and add the spaghetti sauce to it.

6. Lightly beat the eggs with a whisk. Whisk the cooled white sauce to incorporate any skin that might have formed, and then add the eggs, whisking constantly so the remaining heat of the sauce does not curdle the eggs.

7. Set out two 9-inch square baking dishes. Spread 1 cup of the white sauce over the bottom of each dish. Then layer one fourth of the pasta, meat sauce, and cheese in each dish. Add some of the remaining white sauce. Repeat the layers, ending with about 1 cup of white sauce over the top of each. Bake the pastitsio for 1 hour; then remove it from the oven and let it stand for 15 minutes before cutting into it. (If you want to freeze one pastitsio for another day, do not bake it. Cover the dish with plastic wrap, then with foil, and freeze it. When you are ready to serve it, thaw it first, then bake as directed.)

Stuffed Manicotti

PASTA: *Large shapes for stuffing*
MAKES: *4 to 6 servings*
TIME: *25 minutes preparation plus 35 minutes no-work cooking time*

No book on pasta is worth its salt without a recipe for stuffed manicotti. Stuffing the shells takes some effort, so consider making a double batch and freezing one for a later date.

Salt
½ pound low-fat mozzarella cheese
1 container (15 ounces) ricotta cheese
*   (part-skim or whole-milk)*
1 egg
6 tablespoons grated Parmesan cheese
Freshly ground black pepper
14 manicotti shells (½ pound)
2 cups Michèle's Tomato Sauce
*   (see page 245) or 1 jar (14 to*
*   16 ounces) spaghetti sauce*

1. Preheat the oven to 350°F, and bring a large pot of salted water to a boil for the pasta.

2. While the water is heating, cut the mozzarella into fine dice. In a mixing bowl, com-

... over them. Scatter the remaining mozzarella and Parmesan on top.

5. Seal the baking dish with foil, and bake for 25 minutes. Then uncover the dish and bake for 10 minutes longer. Remove it from the oven and serve immediately.

VARIATIONS

■ Different cheeses: For half of the ricotta, substitute fresh chèvre cheese.

Substitute smoked mozzarella or Fontina for the mozzarella.

Herbed-Stuffed Manicotti: Add ¼ cup chopped fresh parsley or basil leaves to the riccota mixture.

Pesto-Stuffed Manicotti: Add 1 tablespoon prepared pesto, sun-dried tomato tapenade, or black olive paste to the ricotta mixture.

... hour, then uncover it and bake for another 30 minutes.

Super Deluxe Macaroni and Cheese

PASTA: *Small or medium-size tubes*
MAKES: *6 to 8 servings*
TIME: *35 minutes preparation plus 30 minutes no-work baking time*

This super-rich macaroni and cheese isn't designed for delicate eaters, nor for dieters. It's made the old-fashioned way, with a white sauce enriched with heavy cream and sharp Cheddar cheese. The sauce coats the tender macaroni and bakes under a topping of bread crumbs and butter.

You can make this with a whole pound of macaroni to feed more people, but the noodles will be dryer. You won't need more than a green salad served before or a fruit salad served afterward, to make the meal complete. For a version of macaroni and cheese you can make during the week, see New-Fashioned Macaroni and Cheese, page 80.

> *Salt*
> *½ pound sharp Cheddar cheese*
> *¾ pound elbow macaroni, elbow twists, or*
>   *penne*
> *8 tablespoons (1 stick) unsalted butter*
> *4 tablespoons all-purpose flour*
> *2 cups milk*
> *1 cup heavy cream*
> *Cayenne pepper*
> *⅓ cup bread crumbs*

1. Preheat the oven to 350°F.

2. Bring a large pot of salted water to a boil for the pasta. While the water is heating, grate the cheese with a rotary grater and set it aside.

3. Add the pasta to the boiling water and cook until it is barely tender, about 7 minutes. Drain, rinse under cold water, and drain again.

4. Melt 4 tablespoons of the butter in a nonreactive medium-size saucepan over medium heat. When it is bubbly, whisk in the flour and cook for a few seconds, just until it is combined. Whisk thoroughly so you gather all the flour into the butter. Slowly add the milk, whisking constantly so the flour paste absorbs the milk without creating lumps. When about half the milk has been added, you can add the rest at a faster rate, but continue to whisk constantly. Bring the mixture to a boil, whisking constantly but not frantically. When it reaches the boil, reduce the heat to low and simmer, still whisking occasionally, until the sauce is cooked through, 3 to 4 minutes. Remove the pan from the heat and add the grated cheese; whisk vigorously until the cheese has melted. Then whisk in the heavy cream, and season to taste with salt and cayenne.

5. In a large mixing bowl, combine the sauce with the drained macaroni. Transfer the mixture to a 13-x-9-inch baking dish, spreading it out evenly. Sprinkle the bread crumbs on top, and dot with the remaining 4 tablespoons butter. Bake until it is hot and bubbly, about 30 minutes. Let it stand for 5 minutes before serving.

VARIATIONS

Ham, Macaroni, and Cheese: Fold in ¼ pound diced smoked ham, or 2 ounces finely chopped prosciutto, when you combine the macaroni with the cheese sauce in step 5.

Sun-Dried Tomato Macaroni and Cheese: Fold in ¼ cup finely chopped sun-dried tomatoes when you combine the macaroni with the cheese sauce in step 5.

Vegetable Macaroni and Cheese: Fold in 1 cup diced cooked vegetables, such as carrots, when you combine the macaroni with the cheese sauce in step 5.

...mixed from a single effort.

The work is not difficult. Just boil... ble batch of pasta, chop th...

TIME AROUND

microwave.

Double-Smoked Eggplant and Pepper Gnocchi

PASTA: *Medium-size shapes or tubes*
MAKES: *2 meals, 4 servings each*
TIME: *1 hour*

I adore smoked eggplant, and here the smoky taste is echoed in the smoked mozzarella. Although this recipe requires too much work for a weeknight, it is worth the time over a weekend because you get two full

2 medium-size eggplants (about
    1 pound each)
Salt
1 can (14½ ounces) stewed tomatoes
½ pound smoked mozzarella cheese
¼ pound sheep's-milk cheese, such as
    Pecorino Romano, or a dry chèvre
6 cloves garlic
1 jar (8 to 12 ounces) roasted red peppers
1½ pounds gnocchi,
    medium-size shells, or penne
½ cup extra-virgin olive oil
Freshly ground black pepper, or
    1 teaspoon dried red pepper flakes

1. Using a fork, pierce the eggplants in a few places. Set the eggplants either directly in the flame of a gas burner or on an iron grill over a high flame. Watch them carefully. Turn the eggplants as each side becomes charred and blistered. It should take about 15 minutes for the skin to char all over and the flesh to soften.

2. When the eggplants are fully charred, remove them from the flame and let them cool until you can handle them without burning your fingers, 10 to 15 minutes.

3. While the eggplants are cooling, bring a large pot of salted water to a boil for the pasta. Take out two large mixing bowls. Drain and chop the stewed tomatoes, and add them to one of the bowls. Set both bowls aside.

4. Finely dice or shred the mozzarella, grate the Pecorino Romano, and peel and mince the garlic. Drain the roasted peppers and cut them into matchstick strips.

5. When the eggplants are cool, scrape off the blistered skin with a sharp knife and trim off the tops. Coarsely chop the flesh.

6. Add the pasta to the boiling water and cook until it is tender but still firm to the bite, about 8 minutes. Meanwhile, heat the oil in a large skillet over medium heat. Add the garlic and sauté until you get a whiff of

its aroma, about 10 seconds. Then add the pepper strips and the chopped eggplant. Cook, stirring occasionally, until the mixture is very hot, about 5 minutes. Season to taste with salt and black pepper or red pepper flakes.

7. Drain the pasta and divide it between the two large mixing bowls, one of which contains the tomatoes. Toss the pasta with the tomatoes, and set that bowl aside for the second recipe (you can deal with it after dinner). To the other bowl of pasta add half of the eggplant mixture and half of the mozzarella. Toss until thoroughly combined, season to taste with salt and pepper, and serve immediately.

BAKED DOUBLE-SMOKED EGGPLANT

To assemble the second dish, scatter half of the remaining eggplant mixture on the bottom of a 9-inch-square baking dish. Add half of the reserved pasta-tomato mixture, and sprinkle with half of the grated Pecorino Romano and half of the remaining mozzarella. Top with the remaining eggplant, pasta, and cheeses. Cover with plastic wrap and then aluminum foil; refrigerate for up to 2 days or freeze.

When you know which day you'll be serving the dish, leave time for it to thaw, if it is frozen. Preheat the oven to 375°F. Unwrap the baking dish and remove the plastic wrap. Replace the foil and bake for 30 minutes. Then uncover...

1. Bring a large pot of salted water to a boil for the pasta.

2. While the water is heating...

Caraway and Poppy Seed Orzo

PASTA: *Tiny shapes*
MAKES: *4 servings*
TIME: *20 to 25 minutes*

Here's a way to turn plain pasta into a tasty side dish for veal, poultry, or a plate of steamed vegetables.

Salt
½ pound (1¼ cups) orzo, stelline, or annelini, or 2 cups cooked pasta
2 tablespoons olive oil
¼ medium-size onion
1 teaspoon caraway seeds
1 tablespoon poppy seeds
Freshly ground black pepper

...way and poppy seeds and cook just to release their aroma, about 30 seconds. Add the pepper and remove the skillet from the heat.

5. Drain the pasta and return it to the pot, off the heat. Add the onion mixture and toss thoroughly to combine. Serve immediately.

VARIATIONS

■ Add ¼ cup minced fresh mint, dill, or parsley to the spices.
■ Just before serving, toss in ¼ cup crumbled feta, grated sharp Cheddar, or grated Parmesan cheese.

SECOND TIME AROUND

Add 1 cup frozen petite peas, thawed, some chicken broth, and a dash of minced pimientos. Simmer in a small saucepan until heated through.

Berry Sweet Pasta

PASTA: *Medium or wide ribbons
and small tubes*
MAKES: *4 servings*
TIME: *20 minutes*

A plateful of egg noodles tossed with pot cheese, sour cream, and a bit of sugar was a favorite dish my grandmother used to serve me. I found it soothing then and I still do now, as does my daughter. In this recipe I have added to the original some berries and a touch of cinnamon.

If this tastes too much like dessert to serve for dinner, precede it with something savory, such as a steamed vegetable, a salad, or a summer soup like chilled cucumber.

> *Salt*
> *¾ pound broad egg noodles or fettuccine,
>   or 2 cups elbow macaroni*
> *½ pound (1 cup) farmer's, pot, or cottage
>   cheese*
> *¼ cup skim or low-fat milk*
> *1 to 2 tablespoons sugar*
> *⅛ teaspoon ground cinnamon (optional)*
> *1 pint strawberries, blueberries, or
>   raspberries*

1. Bring a large pot of salted water to a boil. Add the pasta and cook until it is tender but still firm to the bite, 6 to 8 minutes.

2. Meanwhile, combine the cheese, milk, sugar, and cinnamon in a large mixing bowl, and stir to thoroughly mix. Rinse the berries and pat them dry. Stem the berries; then quarter them and set them aside.

3. Drain the pasta and add it to the cheese mixture. Toss well, and ladle out each portion. Top each portion with berries, and serve. (This is fine served warm or at room temperature, but I don't like it chilled.)

VARIATIONS

■ For a different cheese, try ricotta or mascarpone.
■ Instead of blending the cheese with milk, blend it with ¼ cup sour cream, plain yogurt, crème fraîche, or heavy cream.
■ Instead of topping the mixture with berries, top it with 1 cup chopped walnuts or pecans.

Fall Fruit Pastina

PASTA: *Tiny shapes*
MAKES: *2 servings*
TIME: *15 to 20 minutes*

This pudding is rich, creamy, and terrific enough to be a dessert during the week (the sour cream version) or a hearty breakfast (the yogurt version).

If you are going to serve this for dessert, serve it after a dinner that is especially easy to prepare—perhaps a "second time around" version of a recipe or a main-course salad. This dish is not hard to prepare, but it does take 20 minutes.

1 ripe

Hot Sweet Couscous

with

1. Peel and core the pear and apple, and cut them into ¼ inch dice.

2. Melt the butter in a small saucepan over medium heat. Add the diced fruits and sauté to soften them slightly, 2 to 3 minutes. Add the sugar, nutmeg, and apple juice.

3. Bring to a boil, add the pastina, and cook, covered, over low heat until the mixture is tender and creamy, about 5 minutes. (If you are using cooked pasta, cook for 1 minute to reheat it.) Stir every now and then—the mixture tends to sink and can scorch. (If you are using couscous, add it to the boiling fruit mixture, remove the saucepan from the heat, and let it stand until the couscous has absorbed the liquid and softened, about 10 minutes.) Serve immediately, with the sour cream or yogurt if you like.

doesn't adapt recipes to suit her children's tastes, one recipe prompted Susan's eldest daughter to say, "You know, Mom, the problem with

Michèle is that she's a little too . . . creative." And so I dedicate this delicious dessert to those who, unlike Susan's daughter, appreciate recipes that are "creative."

You may notice that I use less water than normal to plump the couscous here. This is because I want it dry and fluffy. What is so effective in this dish is the contrast between the heat of the sweet fluffy couscous and the chill of the fresh fruit. Pears would also contrast nicely with the couscous, but you would have to cut them up right before serving them to discourage browning.

This is quite filling, so precede this

dessert with a light main course such as a substantial salad or soup.

1 cup couscous
1 cup hot tap water
½ cup dried currants or raisins
1 tablespoon Madeira or port wine, or (for the kids) apple or orange juice
2 ripe plums
2 tablespoons unsalted butter
⅓ cup sliced, slivered, or chopped blanched almonds, or chopped unsalted shelled peanuts, pecans, or walnuts
2 tablespoons sugar
¼ teaspoon ground cinnamon

1. Place the couscous in a small bowl and cover it with the hot water; let it stand until the grains have swelled and are softened, about 15 minutes. In another small bowl, combine the currants and Madeira. Pit the plums, and cut the flesh into ½-inch cubes or thin slices.

2. Using your fingers, break up any clumps of couscous. Melt the butter in a large skillet over medium heat. Stir in the almonds and sauté until golden, about 2 minutes. Add the sugar and cinnamon, and sauté until the sugar dissolves and becomes syrupy, about 1 more minute.

3. Stir in the couscous and sauté until the ingredients are hot and well combined, 1 or 2 minutes. Remove the skillet from the heat,

fold in the chopped fresh fruit and the currants and Madeira. Serve immediately.

ALMOND TALK

"Blanched almonds" are skinned almonds. "Sliced almonds" are thin cross-sections of almonds with their skins on, and "slivered almonds" are lengthwise sections of blanched almonds.

Winter Spiced Apricot Pasta Custard

PASTA: *Thin egg noodles or strands*
MAKES: *8 servings*
TIME: *15 minutes preparation plus 50 minutes no-work cooking and cooling time*

This rich pasta dish is best on cold days—as a dessert, or if you have time to make it in advance, as a part of a fancy breakfast or brunch.

If you serve this as dessert, precede it with a very light meal, such as a salad or soup. Chilled sour cream or a dollop of vanilla ice cream goes very well with the spices and dried fruit.

Salt
½ *pound (2 cups) dried apricots*
1 *cup raisins*
½ *cup port wine or Madeira*
½ *pound very fine egg noodles or capellini
or vermicelli*

1. Preheat the oven to 350°F, and bring a large pot of salted water to a boil for the pasta.

2. While the water is heating, cut the apricots in half. Combine them with the raisins and the port in a small mixing bowl, and set aside.

3. Add the pasta to the boiling water and cook until it is just tender, 5 minutes.

4. Meanwhile, stir the sugar and spices together in a large mixing bowl. Whisk in the eggs.

5. Drain the pasta, rinse it under cold water

Walnut-Stuffed Cannelloni

PASTA: *"Instant" lasagne sheets, or lasagne noodles, shells, or cannelloni*

 MAKES: *4 to 6 servings*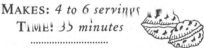
TIME: *35 minutes*

The idea for this dish was inspired by the Hungarian dessert called *palacsinta*, which is a crepe filled with either apricot jam or a sweetened walnut paste. Instead of making the crepes, here you use the "instant lasagne" sheets now available in supermarkets and specialty gourmet food stores.

Serve this curious but delicious pasta dessert after a speedy first course such as a light soup or a salad.

4 sheets "instant" lasagne squares,
   4 regular lasagne noodles, or
   8 cannelloni, manicotti, or jumbo shells
¼ cup unsalted butter
¼ pound (1 cup) shelled walnuts
½ cup raisins or dried currants
1 lemon, or 1 teaspoon grated lemon zest
2 tablespoons sugar, preferably
   "superfine"
½ cup heavy cream

1. Preheat the oven to 350°F. Soften the instant lasagne sheets in a bowl of hot tap water. (If you are using dry pasta, cook it in a large pot of salted boiling water until tender but still firm to the bite. Drain and pat dry.)

2. Meanwhile, melt the butter in a small skillet over low heat. Finely grind the walnuts in a food processor. If you are using raisins, chop them. In a mixing bowl, combine the walnuts, raisins, grated lemon zest, sugar, and melted butter.

3. Pour ¼ cup of the heavy cream into a 9-inch square baking dish. Remove the softened lasagne sheets from the water and pat them dry. Cut each one in half. Spoon some filling onto one end of each pasta rectangle and roll it up tightly. (Or spoon some filling in the cooked shells, manicotti, or cannelloni.) Place each rolled-up "cannelloni" seam side down in the baking dish. Pour the remaining ¼ cup cream over the top, cover, and bake until the pasta rolls are soft and the filling is hot, about 15 minutes. Serve immediately.

VARIATIONS

■ Substitute orange zest or 1 tablespoon unsweetened cocoa powder for the grated lemon zest.
■ Spread some apricot or raspberry jelly on the pasta sheet before you roll it around the filling; this will make the dessert sweeter.
■ Instead of the heavy cream, mix ¼ cup melted butter with ¼ cup bourbon, Cognac, dark rum, or port.

Pecan and Sour Cream Noodle Pudding

PASTA: *Medium or wide egg noodles*
MAKES: *6 to 8 servings*
TIME: *30 minutes preparation plus 30 minutes no-work baking time*

This is terrific as a dessert after a light supper of soup or salad. You'll find that some slices of a tart—sweet juicy fruit, such as fresh plums or pineapple, served alongside the warm pudding provide a lovely contrast to its creaminess.

This works equally well whether it's served hot, warm, or chilled. It is so rich-tasting that you'll have plenty of leftovers for a terrific breakfast the next morning. (Reheat it by the portion for about 30 ...

3. In a large bowl ...

... (1 pound) shelled
pecans or walnuts
3 eggs
1 teaspoon vanilla extract
¼ cup sugar, preferably brown
1 cup sour cream
1 cup raisins, preferably golden

1. Preheat the oven to 350°F. Bring a large pot of salted water to a boil. Add the noodles and cook until they are tender but still firm to the bite, about 5 minutes. Drain, and rinse under cold water until the noodles are thoroughly cool, about 1 minute. Drain again and set aside.

2. Meanwhile, melt the butter in a small skillet over low heat. When it has melted, pour enough of it into a 9-inch-square baking pan to grease it lightly. Finely chop the nuts.

Pecan and Cheese Noodle Pudding: Instead of the sour cream, use 1 cup cottage or part-skim ricotta cheese. For an outrageously luxurious effect, substitute 1 cup mascarpone cheese for the sour cream.

Low-Cholesterol Noodle Pudding: Omit the pecans and butter. Be sure to use a low-fat sour cream or cottage cheese. Instead of 3 eggs, toss the mix with 4 beaten egg whites. Bake until set, 30 to 40 minutes.

Savory Pecan Noodle Pudding: Turn this into a main course by omitting the sugar, vanilla, and raisins. Make the pudding with either sour cream or ricotta cheese. In step 3, toss the noodles with the beaten eggs and add 1 to 2 cups of chopped cooked vegetables, such as carrots or cabbage, along with 2 teaspoons caraway seeds or 1 tablespoon poppy seeds. Be sure to season with salt and pepper.

Index

VERMILLION PUBLIC LIBRARY
18 CHURCH STREET
VERMILLION, SD 57069